# BERIT GORDON

*Foreword by* Jennifer Serravallo

# THE JOYFUL TEACHER

## *Strategies for Becoming the Teacher Every Student Deserves*

**HEINEMANN**
Portsmouth, NH

**Heinemann**
361 Hanover Street
Portsmouth, NH 03801–3912
www.heinemann.com

*Offices and agents throughout the world*

The author and publisher wish to thank those who have generously given permission to reprint borrowed material:

Strategy 1.2: Adapted from "So You Think You're a Terrible Teacher: The Test" from *It Won't Be Easy: An Exceedingly Honest (and Slightly Unprofessional) Love Letter to Teaching* by Tom Rademacher. Copyright © 2017 by Tom Rademacher. Published by the University of Minnesota Press. Reprinted by permission of the publisher.

Cataloging-in-Publication Data is on file at the Library of Congress.
ISBN: 978-0-325-11829-1

*Editor*: Zoë Ryder White
*Production*: Victoria Merecki
*Cover and text designs*: Suzanne Heiser
*Author photo:* Kathryn Huang
*Typesetter*: Gina Poirier Design
*Manufacturing*: Steve Bernier

Printed in the United States of America on acid-free paper
1 2 3 4 5 6 7 8 9 10 CGB 25 24 23 22 21 20
March 2020 Printing

TO THE BRAVE AND PASSIONATE TEACHERS WHO OPEN UP THEIR CLASSROOMS, HEARTS, AND MINDS IN OUR WORK TOGETHER. YOU MAKE MY HEART SING!

# CONTENTS

## Staying Happy and Healthy in a Demanding Job 1

## Classroom Environment 28

# Management, Part 1: Routines and Rituals 52

# Management, Part 2: Relationship Building 86

# Independent Practice 112

# Formative Assessment and Feedback 144

# Planning Matters 172

# Teacher-Led Instruction 200

# Student Talk and Collaboration 228

# Summative Assessment and Grading 256

# (Coda): Keep Growing and Giving Back 285

# FOREWORD

Many years ago, I traveled to Japan with a couple hundred educators from the United States. Guests of the Japanese government, we were there to be immersed in Japanese culture and schools and to share what we learned once we returned home. I filled notebooks and took hundreds of photos, but when I close my eyes today to remember, what stands out most relates to what it is like to be a teacher in that country. A few details:

1. Any time I told someone "I'm a teacher" in Japan, the person I was speaking to would deeply bow (saikeirei ojigi) with gratitude and reverence.

2. New teachers in their first year(s) are considered apprentices, much like doctors start as residents. During this time, they are expected to hone their craft under the tutelage of an experienced educator.

3. Schools are designed to support teacher professional growth: every school featured a large common room where teachers gather, plan, reflect, and collaborate every day.

Since my trip to Japan, I've spent years traveling around the United States and Canada to visit classrooms and work with teachers, and I can't help but compare. Sometimes I'll discover that a principal reorganized the schedule to ensure a weekly professional learning community time. Some schools have mentor–mentee relationships set up, and newer-to-the-profession teachers feel supported by a colleague. Some districts fund teachers to attend workshops or state or national conferences. And still others have a full-time dedicated instructional coach, there to support all the teachers on staff. Although styles and methods vary from school to school or country to country, here's what I find to be universally true: the most joyful schools are ones where teachers are constantly learning, where teacher professionalism is respected, and where teacher expertise pays off with positive impacts on students.

Berit knows this. In *The Joyful Teacher*, her deep respect for teachers, teaching, and learning comes through on every page. She empowers each of us to set our own goals using helpful self-reflection checklists, and then guides us to chart a path to work toward them with strategies, activities, opportunities to learn alongside colleagues, and more. Berit strikes a perfect balance between choice and guidance, allowing each of us to grow into the best version of teacher we can be.

As I read each page, I found inspiration: how to stay happy and healthy in a demanding job, to help students be more independent and take ownership of their education, to refine formative and summative assessment practices so they align to my values, to improve student talk and collaboration, and more. But as inspirational as this book is, it's also incredibly practical.

*The Joyful Teacher* is filled with more than a hundred suggestions culled from research, theory, and practitioner-authored professional books. It's written in a get-right-to-the-point kind of way that is essential for a busy teacher. And despite the high number of practical suggestions, it's not at all overwhelming, and that's because Berit organizes these incredible ideas into ten chapters, each aligned to a goal, with ten ideas in each (plus a chapter about giving back with nine more suggestions), which helps us find what we need quickly. This is not a book you need to read cover to cover, but one you may find yourself dipping into and out of throughout your entire career.

Berit knows that we got into this profession because we love children, and we want to do our best job for them—to place them at the center of all we do in the classroom. Although *The Joyful Teacher* is designed to support *your* teaching practice, Berit grounds every suggestion in why it matters for children. Throughout the book, conscious attention is paid to making sure that all children feel a true sense of belonging and that our classrooms are places where they all want to be. Alongside each teaching suggestion, she describes the impacts to children's learning and practice that serve as proof that our teaching is getting stronger. This matters: unlike the Hollywood image of teacher as hero or entertainer, the masterful teacher is one who helps children belong in the classroom, find their passions and strengths, and grow. Although Berit shows us which are the consistent practices that are proven by research to "work," she empowers us to tap into our uniqueness as individuals, and honors that how it looks for each of us will be varied.

Although you may or may not have an official instructional coach, with this book you can coach yourself. Although your school building may not have been designed by an architect who saw to it that there was a physical meeting space for learning and growth, with this book you can be the architect of your own career and see to it that there is joy in the constant learning opportunities that this amazing profession affords.

—Jennifer Serravallo

# ACKNOWLEDGMENTS

This book wouldn't exist without the amazing teachers I get to work with and their bottomless energy, passion, and generosity.

Rosie Maurantonio offered a great deal of expert advice from a first-grade teacher's point of view, as well as wonderful examples from her classroom. Her thoughtful, smart perspective was invaluable throughout.

Other generous teachers shared ideas and images from their classrooms, including:

Stephen Caufield

Rebeccah Derks

Sarah Dutton

Frankie Faidley

Claire Friedland

Andrew Gordon

Sebastian Hill

Vanessa Jones

Glenny Lapaix

Lauren Martinez

Rosie Maurantonio

Karon McGovern

Jill Ramacciotti

James Robinson

Corie Robie

Sonya Squitieri

Robby Suarez

Abigail Turley

Alana Wenick

Your students are lucky to have you!

I'm grateful to Jen Serravallo for being a great friend and mentor, for writing the books that inspired this one, and for turning a canceled flight into a Hamilton night out.

To other teachers in my life who guide me in wise and wonderful ways: Stuart Bernstein, who gave me a great education in book publishing over just a couple of phone calls. Tricia Tunstall, who has been my daughter's piano teacher for over ten years and exemplifies everything I know about good teaching and kindness. And finally, to a favorite person—Ronnie Stern. You're a gift in my life and my family's life.

The many educators and authors whose books have graced my shelves and guided me in my own teaching, and whose ideas provided many gems throughout this book: thank you for your wisdom, for putting kids at the forefront, and for strategies that help teachers feel like and be experts.

The entire team at Heinemann was a joy to work with. Thank you to Catrina Marshall and Elizabeth Silvis for their smart, professional expertise. Victoria Merecki and Suzanne Heiser artfully shaped this work into the beautiful book it is now. I struck gold having Victoria's eyes on this book at a critical stage. Cindy Black's copy edits were invaluable—she did wonderful work. Zoë White is an editor extraordinaire: her careful reading, smart questions, and kind voice led me through the entire process. What a pleasure to do all this thinking and writing with her by my figurative side, or at least an email away!

Love and thanks to my smart, fun, and kind family members, including Frankie, Sara, Julia, Papa, Mom, Sam, Violet, Naomi, and Andrew. You helped with everything from title suggestions, images (Naomi's font-like handwriting was invaluable), classroom space, and lots of moral support. You are all my favorite teachers.

A special shout-out to Andrew. Your students are lucky to have you, and so am I.

# INTRODUCTION

I don't know if your training was different from mine, but I felt I was expected to know how to teach, from day one. If you're like me, you studied the theory, learned the pedagogy, spent a few months student teaching, then got your degree, and the ship sailed. Suddenly, we were in the high seas and expected to be crew, navigator, and all-around administrator of a classroom filled with kids. I can't count how many times I felt alone, incompetent, clueless and wanted to jump ship. The *joy* of teaching? All I wanted was to get over the *terror* of teaching.

I wish for more joy and less struggle in a profession where people put in such tremendous effort and do such essential work. What's the recipe, then, for getting to that joy and feeling of "I've got this"?

## Why do we need this book?

This book grew out of twenty-five years of experience as a teacher, then a teacher of teachers, whether through leading school-based professional learning, graduate school instruction, or teaching conferences. Time and again I meet teachers who need support as they are asked to do more and be more every year. They are asking for help, but they may not have mentors or instructional leadership; their schools may lack funding or resources. Many don't know where to turn.

Every teacher deserves to feel and be effective. And we know that students in high-impact teachers' classrooms learn far more than students in low-impact teachers' classrooms. And the feeling that we can have a great impact, together as teachers, is the most important goal for any school in terms of influencing student growth (Hattie 2012).

Expert teaching has a tremendous amount to do with attitude and expectations. When we feel empowered with tools of reflection and implementation, we are ready to make an impact. But so often that path to finding tools and feeling like an expert is unclear.

No one becomes a master teacher overnight, and there is no one-size-fits-all approach to improving. All learners benefit from taking it one goal at a time. We need help prioritizing what is most essential and working incrementally toward mastery.

And so, I wrote a handbook that you can use to improve skills on your own, focusing on self-reflection, goal setting, and practical strategies you can try right away. Think of it as continuing education without having to bring an expert to your school, sign up for a class, or attend a workshop (although I hope you get all these supports and then some!).

This book offers the hands-on guidance you need to continue on your way to being the high-impact teacher every student deserves. The expert teacher is already in you.

# Who is this book for?

**K–12 teachers from all content areas** can rely on this book as a practical guide to self-reflect, set professional learning goals, and find the tools you need to continually grow as a teacher. You are the primary audience, the reader every page was written for.

**Instructional coaches** can use this book to help identify goals and specific activities and strategies to help the teachers you support. Professional learning communities and department and grade teams will benefit from choosing goals and strategies to try out together.

**Administrators** can use this book to support teachers and set them up for success. You are tasked with balancing new initiatives and visions for change with what each of your teachers needs to grow. This book will help you with that balance so you and your teachers can cocreate goals that work for all. It will provide practical resources to help everyone meet those goals and thrive.

**Students** are not the audience for this book, but they are at the core of its creation. Every strategy is built around ways for teachers to help children and teens. Protecting, nourishing, and inspiring students is the end goal behind each and every strategy.

# What's different about this book? What's familiar?

Your bookshelves are likely filled with books on teaching: some dog-eared, and others mined for a few precious nuggets. This book aims to simplify your life with a collection of tried-and-true strategies and tips for improving instruction, all in one place.

Strategies are adapted from and inspired by current, research-backed, student-centered, and teacher-friendly books, blogs, and websites. If you're hungry to learn more after using a particular strategy, you'll have a reliable reference to continue exploring without having to wade through a Google search to get there.

There is no one-size-fits-all set of instructions here. You'll steer the ship in choosing goals and strategies that work for you and your students.

There is also no expert here telling you to teach their method. The expert is you. This warehouse of strategies is compiled from multiple voices, perspectives, and teaching styles, thereby allowing you to find your *own* voice.

Each strategy describes a specific step-by-step procedure to help build a thriving community of learners. Some elements of this book's structure may feel familiar to those of you who know and love Jennifer Serravallo's hugely popular *The Reading Strategies Book* (2015) and *The Writing Strategies Book* (2017). These phenomenal books organize specific strategies, broken down into step-by-step procedures, into a hierarchy of learning goals. This book gratefully borrows from that useful structure to provide strategies for teachers' growth, also organized into a progression of goals. The aim is to provide a structure to help you reflect on your own professional development needs, set a goal, and access a host of practical strategies that will help you meet that goal. After all, if differentiation is what matters for kids, then teachers need individualized strategies, too!

# How do I use this book?

This book will not require a start-to-finish read. Rather, it offers a collection of ideas you can dip into as needed. Although you may jump from chapter to chapter, the goals and strategies are organized in a progression that will set you up for the most success and highest impact. To get started, look at the progression of teaching goals that form the organizing structure for the book's chapters. The goals—and chapters—are ordered so that each focus area builds on the ones before it. The research and rationale for organizing goals in this order can be found in each chapter's introduction.

## Progression of Teaching Goals

1. Staying Happy and Healthy in a Demanding Job
2. Classroom Environment
3. Management, Part 1: Routines and Rituals
4. Management, Part 2: Relationship Building
5. Independent Practice
6. Formative Assessment and Feedback
7. Planning Matters
8. Teacher-Led Instruction
9. Student Talk and Collaboration
10. Summative Assessment and Grading
11. (Coda): Keep Growing and Giving Back

All of these areas of teaching are essential—none more important or sophisticated than another. But they are ordered in such a way that addressing the topmost sets you up for greater success when working on what comes below it on the list, and so on and so on. The first chapter helps you to grow and protect your own happiness (and sanity) as a teacher. We need to prioritize the ability to thrive as people and professionals! The second chapter will help you create an organized and student-friendly environment to support all the work to come. Then, you'll take on management, first through routines and rituals (Chapter 3), and next through relationship building (Chapter 4). When routines are in place and when students know we care, they are ready to learn! Chapter 5 will offer strategies that grow and support students' independence. After students are taking on learning and "doing" with ease, you'll have greater success looking at another essential goal: checking for understanding and providing feedback (Chapter 6). Each of the goals up to this point supports long-term and day-to-day planning (Chapter 7), as well as how you deliver teacher-led instruction (Chapter 8). With your own talk and teaching solidly in place, you can focus on strengthening student talk and collaboration (Chapter 9)—helping students grow thinking through rich conversation and group work. As a near finish, it will be time to focus on summative assessments (Chapter 10)—both the student work that all our units build toward and how to grade those works in a way that is fair and productive and doesn't exhaust you in the process. Last but not least, Chapter 11, a coda of sorts, offers quick, practical ways to keep feeding your teaching souls and giving back to your teaching communities. Hopefully our teaching careers encompass decades of learning and growing, and cycling through these chapters is one way to help ensure that lifelong process.

So, although you might pop into chapters and pull out the strategy for what you need in the here and now, you'll nurture your long-term professional growth by starting with the first chapter/goal's checklist that you answer "sometimes" or "not yet" on several components of the self-assessment. Here's how to start:

1. Use the goal checklists, starting with the first goal in the progression—Staying Happy and Healthy in a Demanding Job—to help you find the goal that's right for you. Start with that first checklist, whether you are a veteran teacher or a newbie. You may find that before all else, you need to concentrate on finding more happiness in your job. Or, you might know already that you want to work on management, so you'll try the checklists for Chapters 3 and 4 and choose one of those goals to start. As you work through the checklists and find your own entry point, remember that there is no "right" place to start, no goal that is more sophisticated or more important than any other. They all matter. (See hein.pub/JoyfulTeacher [click on Companion Resources] for the complete collection of checklists.)

   See the following checklist for Chapter 2, "Classroom Environment." This chapter offers strategies that help you work toward the goal of creating an organized, welcoming, user-friendly environment for you and for students.

# What do you notice?

| | Yes | Sometimes | Not yet |
|---|---|---|---|
| Walking into my classroom, it's clear what I value most as a teacher. | ☐ | ☐ | ☐ |
| Students and I can find things easily and put them back where they belong. | ☐ | ☐ | ☐ |
| Students and I regularly look at and refer to what's displayed on the classroom walls. | ☐ | ☐ | ☐ |
| My classroom resources and materials reflect a rich diversity, equal to that of the rich diversity of my students and the world. | ☐ | ☐ | ☐ |
| I would want to be a student in my classroom. | ☐ | ☐ | ☐ |

2. If you answer "Sometimes" or "Not yet" for some of the checklist questions, it's a good idea to stick with this chapter and try out the strategies until you feel like you've met the goal.

3. Once you've determined which goal you'll start with, you'll look at the list of strategies in that chapter and choose one to try. The strategies toward the beginning of the chapter are apt to be easier to implement and work up progressively toward more complex methods. Start with some of the early ones if you're feeling particularly overwhelmed in that area.

## Chapter 2 Strategies

4. Once you've chosen a strategy, begin with the first section: "Try This," which offers step-by-step instructions for how to try it out. There is often a little explanation for why and how the strategy works, as well as a detailed how-to section so you can give it a go. See an excerpt below.

**Try This**

Look at your wall space, including bulletin boards in the hallways, and make a rough estimate: What percentage of the walls are student created? If it's less than 80 percent, decide which teacher-created walls can be cleared to make room for student-created displays.

Crowded wall spaces can create visual and mental clutter for many students—the opposite of what we want. Take down the things that were purchased or teacher created. Toss or recycle visuals that do not serve as "silent teachers," providing useful reminders or how-tos. If a visual is not regularly referred to by you and students, ditch it.

5. Read on for indicators that this is indeed a strategy that will help you, in the section "How do I know if this idea will help?"

**How do I know if this idea will help?**

- Many bulletin boards and wall displays are teacher created or purchased.
- Displays have been up for more than one unit.
- Students do not regularly look at, refer to, and use classroom wall displays.
- You spend prep periods and free time designing and creating bulletin boards on your own.

6. The next section provides a set of indicators you can refer to as you're implementing the strategy that will help you determine whether or not it's helping.

**How do I know if this idea is working?**

- The majority of classroom wall space is student created.
- Students regularly look at and refer to wall displays.
- Wall displays rotate regularly (at least every marking period).

7. Use grade-level modifications to help you make the strategy work best for you and your students. The essentials of good teaching are universal, but child development is not. What makes one strategy sing in an eleventh-grade classroom needs to be modified to work with a group of six-year-olds. Check the grade-band suggestions, which keep those developmental needs in mind, as well as the different teaching lives of those who teach multiple sections of class periods versus those who are with one group of students across the bulk of the day. When appropriate, there are also adaptations for newer/more experienced teachers.

**Adapt for K–5**

- Remember to keep wall space physically accessible by keeping student-created displays free of bulky furniture underneath, providing step stools, and lowering the height range.

| | |
|---|---|
| **Adapt for 6–8** | • Coming into and leaving class can be a choppy transition in buildings where students travel a distance. Allowing a minute or two on each end for students to add to and check out the wall displays can serve as a useful buffer time. |
| **Adapt for 9–12** | • Don't assume that older students aren't interested in what's on the wall or don't care about having their work publicly displayed. Just check out any teen bedroom, sticker-laden laptop case, locker wall, or Instagram feed to see their fondness for rocking an image. Bare classrooms can feel sterile, so include them in the process of filling up at least half of the blank wall space. |

8.  Whenever possible, enlist a friend or two. Use the "How to try this with others" section so you don't go it alone. Real change and impact takes place with others, not in isolation. Plus, it will be more fun.

| | |
|---|---|
| **How to try this with others** | • Do a shared classroom wall inventory, visiting one another's rooms and assessing wall space together. Help a teammate clear wall space.<br><br>• Visit one another's classrooms and look at the walls from a student's perspective. Which rooms are most inviting? Visually calming? Interesting to look at? Why? Set short- and long-term goals together for how you will boost the look of your classroom walls. |

*Want to know more about this strategy and others like it?*

**Check out:** Hertz, Christine, and Kristine Mraz. 2018. *Kids First from Day One: A Teacher's Guide to Today's Classroom.*

9.  Each strategy explanation gives you everything you need right on the page. But teachers are go-getters, and certain strategies are going to make you hungry for more. See the section, "Want to know more about this strategy and others like it?" for references that will help you explore similar strategies (see sample at left). I wish that you'll read these nods to other professional authors no matter what, as I include each citation with gratitude for offering up smart, tried-and-true ideas.

10. Try as many strategies as you want or can before you feel like you can go back to the self-assessment checklist and answer "yes" more often.

Choose another goal from the progression when you're ready, but don't fret over checking each one off. All in due time. You've got a lifetime of teaching and growing, and you'll get there.

11. Pat yourself on the back. You'll never do enough of that. Do it again.

Keep unearthing your inner expert bit by bit. Celebrate every effort and achievement along the way.

Here we go!

# Staying Happy and Healthy in a Demanding Job

## Why is our health and happiness so important?

As teachers, we put students' needs first. But your needs matter, too. And for most of us, those needs are not being met. Ninety-three percent of teachers experience high stress levels on a regular basis. Despite being stressed out all the time, studies show we have few or no coping skills to deal with the flood of constant mental pressure (Walker 2018). Is it any wonder that 40 percent of teachers leave the profession within five years (NEA 2005)?

I've had my own moments of wondering if I could show up at school the next day, or if I'd ever get through a day without feeling like a failure. Many of us experience fluctuating levels of emotional turmoil.

We love our students and we care deeply about our jobs. *And* we are stressed, exhausted, and overwhelmed.

There is another way. We can decide to choose mental and physical health as our first professional goal. If we don't take care of ourselves, we won't have a chance to get better at all of the other stuff, and we won't have the time, patience, or energy to teach well.

Our students deserve rested and sane adults in their lives. They will experience our best teaching selves, and they'll see models of healthy ways to be in the world. We are the adults in the room. Let's increase the odds that students, too, will find ways to survive and thrive in demanding circumstances.

## Is this the goal for me?

- Do you respond "yes" and "sometimes" for most statements? Consider moving to the next chapter. You've got this!
- Do you have a mix of "yes," "sometimes," and "not yet" answers? This might be the goal for you.

## What do you notice?

| | Yes | Sometimes | Not yet |
|---|:---:|:---:|:---:|
| I'm generally content to go to work each day. | ☐ | ☐ | ☐ |
| When people ask me what I do, I tell them the positive things about teaching. | ☐ | ☐ | ☐ |
| I have some tough days, but overall, the good in my job outweighs the bad. | ☐ | ☐ | ☐ |
| I approach problems in my job and try to solve them. | ☐ | ☐ | ☐ |
| In five years, I foresee myself teaching. | ☐ | ☐ | ☐ |
| Students, not summer vacations, are the best thing about my job. | ☐ | ☐ | ☐ |

# 1.1 Set the Bar Where You Can Jump It

**Try This**
How many days do you leave school patting yourself on the back for a job well done, noting questions thoughtfully answered, emergencies dealt with, multitasking accomplished, students listened to?

Now, how many days do you head home beating yourself up for what you didn't do? If your second number outweighs the first (by a *lot*, right?) it's time to set a new bar.

Choose a bar that you aim to reach each day and make it one that you can *step* over. For example: "I will show students that I care." Aim for meaningful goals that reflect what you truly value—not "I will make all my copies during my prep." Make it count.

You may be new to teaching, dealing with a personal crisis or health issue, caring for a young child or a sick parent, or straddling a lot of new roles in school this year. Be kind to yourself! Strive to do great things—but know that you won't get there by comparing yourself to the mythical teacher who does it all. That teacher doesn't exist, and keeping your bar set at a fantasy level won't help you.

Write your achievable teaching bar goal on a sticky note. Stick it on your steering wheel, metro card, or notebook. Put it someplace you will see it frequently. When you see it, practice taking note of one or two things you did that got you to that bar. Then switch gears and let the rest go. Save your energy for problem-solving when you're fresh, not at the end of a long day.

When you get home, tell your cats, partner, plants, kids—whomever you go home to—what you did well today. You'll feel awkward and boastful. Good. Do it again. Remind yourself to stick with the positive.

When you're ready, set a new bar. You can use this book to do so!

**How do I know if this idea will help?**

- You can easily list what you didn't accomplish on any given day, but you can't list what you *did* accomplish.
- You feel guilty when you do something other than schoolwork.
- You have a new challenge in life that's taking a lot of your energy and strength.

**How do I know if this idea is working?**

- You can readily articulate what you did well on most days.
- You feel proud of your teaching, and you have set reasonable goals to keep growing.
- When you consider the level of kindness you afford to your students, you see that you are giving the same level of kindness to yourself.
- You may see yourself being more forgiving of others around you—administrators, tricky students, caregivers—as you see they are also doing the best they can.

I will find strengths in every student. ♡ ♡ ♡

I care that every student knows they are capable of great things.

I can always learn more about being a better teacher.

Keeping your core belief short and sweet, and putting it where you see it on the regular, means you're more likely to catch yourself feeling like "I've got this."

**How to try this with others**

- Create and share your bar statements. Make sure everyone has set an achievable goal that is aligned to their values. Check in after a week or so of working toward that new bar. Revise statements as needed together.

- Set a weeklong or monthlong goal on your own or with your grade-level team. Take notes on how you have worked toward it.

- Create a goal-oriented bulletin board in your faculty room/office. With the staff goal on top, teachers can post anecdotes about how they are working toward that goal.

*Want to know more about this strategy and others like it?*

**Check out:** Goldsmith, Marshall, and Mark Reiter. 2010. *Mojo: How to Get It, How to Keep It, How to Get It Back When You Lose It.*

Allison, Jay, and Dan Gediman. 2007. *This I Believe: The Personal Philosophies of Remarkable Men and Women.*

# 1.2 Take the "Good Enough" Test

When I worked at a school on Eighteenth Street in Manhattan, there were days that I could keep it together on my walk home only until I got to the corner of Twenty-Third. There, I'd amass a ball of snot-filled tissues, lamenting my mistakes. I wish I could tell my past self that *I would make it*, and that even though I was making mistakes, that I was doing more good than bad. And that this ratio is enough to keep going.

If you have cried on your way home from school, or just gotten stuck on that endless "I'm a rotten teacher" loop, try taking this test, adapted from a longer (and funnier) one by Tom Rademacher in his book, *It Won't Be Easy* (2017):

Check all that apply:

- [ ] I care about teaching.
- [ ] I care about students.
- [ ] I try to do right by my students.
- [ ] When I make mistakes, I spend some time figuring out how I could do better next time.
- [ ] I apologize for my mistakes.
- [ ] I make it a mantra: do no harm.
- [ ] When I do harm, I work to repair it.
- [ ] I try to think about school through a student's eyes.
- [ ] I try to make things relevant.

Look at your answers. The truth is that if you checked one and two, you're good to go. The rest will come in due time, as your checklist becomes more sophisticated and personalized over your teaching career. But caring about teaching and students will always be the essential litmus test for any teacher.

As Rademacher says, "Do you care? You'll be fine. Do you care a lot? You'll probably be great." Remember that teaching is brutally difficult to "get right" and that no one ever really does. We just need to take care of ourselves enough to keep working at getting better. Look for your own sweet spot combo of being kind to yourself and kind to your students. Everything else will come.

| **How do I know if this idea will help?** | • You feel like a failure. |
| | • You're questioning your choice of being a teacher. |
| | • You look at other teachers and feel like you don't stack up. |

| **How do I know if this idea is working?** | • When you have bad days, you are able to reflect and move on. You don't let those moments define you. |
| | • You compare yourself to others less. Who has the time? |
| | • You keep turning your energy back to the students and sometimes let the rest be white noise. |

| **How to try this with others** | • Be on the lookout for a colleague who's having a bad day. Give them this test without telling them the catch. Remind them that they only need the first two and they're good to go. |
| | • Make it a catchphrase with your teaching buddies. Tough day? Mention (and playfully remind them), "But you still care!" and give them a hug. |

*Want to know more about this strategy and others like it?*

**Check out:** Rademacher, Tom, and Dave Eggers. 2017. *It Won't Be Easy: An Exceedingly Honest (and Slightly Unprofessional) Love Letter to Teaching.*

# 1.3 Establish Core Beliefs

Why did you first decide to go into teaching? What do you care about most in terms of impacting students' lives? What is it about your own favorite teachers that you most admire?

If that feels fuzzy, try this brief writing exercise:

## Finish the sentences

- If I could have a lasting impact on students, it would be to . . .
- What is most important to me that students are able to do/know/understand is . . .
- The reason I'm a teacher is because I want to . . .
- The most important role of a teacher is to . . .

Circle what stands out as representative of your beliefs, and make a list. The list may distill into one core belief, or you may have several. Think of these written beliefs as your guiding principles. Keep them visible so you can reflect and revise when needed.

Now, make sure your actions back up those beliefs. When you're asked to do something extra at school that does not align with your beliefs, think long and hard before taking it on. One of my favorite tools is to say, "Let me think about it." Wait a day. If you still feel it doesn't align, then just say no. Politely, of course.

If your time is currently filled with activities that do not support these beliefs, consider eliminating them. Then consider what activity *would* support your core beliefs. If you want most to establish a relationship with every student, could you devote one lunch period a week to inviting rotating groups to your class to eat with you? If you value making learning an authentic real-world experience, can you organize a field trip into the community? If you want every student to feel like a scientist, can you organize or participate in a science club?

| I Believe | So I Will . . . |
|---|---|
|  |  |
|  |  |
|  |  |

- Your flexible time is filled with responsibilities not aligned to your core beliefs.
- When you ask yourself, "Why do I teach?" you don't have a ready answer.

- Your calendar has newly freed-up spaces, and what's there reflects what you value most.
- You can readily and with clarity finish the sentence, "I teach because . . ."
- You don't feel guilty saying no to extra responsibilities.
- You feel confident in taking on responsibilities that you care about.
- You feel a renewed energy for your job.

| I Believe | So I will... |
|---|---|
| I can always learn more about being a better teacher | Visit a colleague's classroom during my prep at least once a month |
| | Find two Edchats on Twitter to follow |
| | Read Zaretta Hammond's Culturally Responsive Teaching and The Brain over winter break |

- It's likely you've done some of this work in your teacher-education program by writing a philosophy statement or something similar. How has your list of core beliefs shifted now that you have your own classroom? Reread your preservice philosophy statement to refresh those beautiful ideals that got you into teaching.
- Say no to as much as you can, especially long-term responsibilities. Resist the temptation to volunteer for extras until after your first year. Save the bulk of your time and energy for planning and being in your classroom.

- Think back to the reasons you first entered teaching and channel those first impulses—they were authentic, life changing, and meaningful. They may serve to reenergize you.
- Expect that your reasons for teaching and your core beliefs have evolved a great deal. You have been exposed to new information, new research, and new experiences that shape who you are and what you care about. Make sure your beliefs continue to revolve around students.
- If yours is the first car out of the parking lot, or you don't frequently see your students outside of class, find one school-related activity that aligns to your core beliefs. See if it energizes you or depletes you.

- Sitting together with your weekly calendars, do the core beliefs writing exercise mentioned in the "Try This" section. Offer suggestions so colleagues' beliefs are precise and easy to declare with certainty.

  - Try to distill your list into one overriding, core belief. Circle it. Share it out.

  - Go through your calendars and star the activities that align to your core beliefs. Underline those that do not.

  - Share out and discuss which underlined activities could be delegated, eliminated, or minimized.

  - Brainstorm ways to spend flexible time in ways that directly align to your beliefs. Discuss if there are ways to share such time together, for instance, co-planning a field trip or running a club together.

- With a colleague, choose a goal together, asking yourselves:

  - What is our goal, and why have we selected it?

  - What books might we read on this topic?

  - Whose classroom might we visit to see this in action?

  - What ways will we see evidence of this growth/work in our instruction?

  - How might we share what we have learned with colleagues?

*Want to know more about this strategy and others like it?*

**Check out:** Keene, Ellin Oliver, and Matt Glover. 2015. *The Teacher You Want to Be: Essays About Children, Learning, and Teaching.*

# 1.4 Find the Positive; Be the Positive

**Try This**

Get to know other teachers who like their job. Positive feelings are contagious, and happy colleagues' enthusiasm will spur you to do your job well and with gusto. When you have the chance to collaborate, to sit with someone in the teachers' room, or to meet someone outside of school, choose those who spend more time talking about what they enjoy than what's wrong. Do the same for others.

**How do I know if this idea will help?**

- If someone asks you about your job, you start by listing what's wrong with it.
- You find yourself talking frequently about the deficits of your school, students, community, resources, or the teaching professional in general.

**How do I know if this idea is working?**

- You start to speak positively about your students and school even when you don't need to: with your partner, your family, your friends outside of work.
- Your students take note of your "up" mood, or tease you about your enthusiasm (trust me, they love it!).
- You volunteer for certain tasks or committees as your investment in the school community grows.
- You help an overwhelmed colleague by problem-solving, not just commiserating.

Although there are plenty of imperfect aspects to any teaching life, focusing on what's great will keep you going.

| Pros | Cons |
|---|---|
| * Students! | * Not earning enough $ |
| * Work w/ great people | |
| | * Stay late every day & still not caught up |
| * Never boring | |
| * I love learning new ways to teach math! | * Grading |
| | * Can't go to the bathroom until 3rd period |

- Having a sunshiny personality is not a prerequisite for teaching young people. Be true to yourself in finding the good, as even very young students can sniff out false cheer. Remember how perceptive our students are about the way we talk and carry ourselves. Show every child you are happy they are there, whatever your style is.

**Adapt for
6–8**

- Your collaborative work is often departmentalized, so keep a keen eye out for those in your department who speak highly of their students and their job. Sit next to them at lunch, or invite them for coffee. Remember, too, that positive vibes exist everywhere. The most important thing is to be part of conversations with those who enjoy their job, whether within your department or not.

- Also, although students may start to gravitate toward a sarcastic sense of humor during these years, they still thrive on the attitudes of genuinely positive adults. Laugh at their jokes when appropriate, and don't be afraid to be the earnest, noncynical adult in contrast.

**Adapt for
9–12**

- Sometimes the happiest colleagues are those who don't hang out much in the teachers' room or linger after professional learning community meetings. They're too busy engaging! Finding them might mean getting out of the staff room and onto the playing fields, helping out at extracurricular activities, or poking your head into classrooms during other teachers' prep periods.

- Also, high school students' lives are emotionally fraught as they look to their upcoming independence. Don't mistake teens' craving for autonomy as no longer needing adult role models. They still desperately want to feel cared for and noticed. Remember what a bad rap teens get in our society. They are used to adults giving up on them or stereotyping them as rude, lazy, uninformed. Work hard to avoid negative generalizations.

- Having adults as role models who genuinely like coming to class, who speak openly about caring for kids, and who don't complain about their jobs can be life changing.

**How to try this
with others**

- If a meeting becomes overrun by negative comments, try stopping and listing out what's bothering people. Circle items within teachers' control. Leave things like public policy, pay scales, and parental roles to the side for the time being. What remains on the list will likely focus on instruction, which will help shift the conversation back to how we can best help students.

- If you are part of a group who enjoys teaching and students, invite a discouraged colleague to join you during lunch or meetings. Let them know your group works to keep it positive as a way to energize yourselves and problem-solve.

- Start a positivity chain. Put an anonymous note in a colleague's mailbox complimenting them on some specific aspect of their work, and ask them to pay it forward with a compliment to someone else.

- Get on edchats on Twitter, which can be a great problem-solving community, especially if you seek out the positive. For a schedule of all the various educator chats going on, check out: https://sites.google.com/site/twittereducationchats /education-chat-calendar.

- Turn negative conversations toward proactive discussion by saying, "I know how rough that can be. What have you tried to . . . ?" or, "Something I've found helpful is . . ." Make it clear you are there to problem-solve.

- Suggest a protocol at staff meetings, department meetings, or PLCs to have teachers begin with a small moment of success.

*Want to know more about this strategy and others like it?*

**Check out:** Gonzalez, Jennifer. 2019. "Find Your Marigold: The One Essential Rule for New Teachers." *Cult of Pedagogy.* www.cultofpedagogy.com/marigolds/.

# 1.5 Schedule Self-Care and Track What Gets in the Way

We know that no student can learn without first feeling safe, calm, fed, and rested. But don't just apply this to your students. No teacher can teach without feeling safe, calm, fed, and rested. Model making your own emotional and physical health a priority.

Get out your weekly planning calendar. Fill in nonnegotiables (apart from instructional time) such as staff meetings, parent-teacher conferences, doctor's appointments, and paying taxes. Do *not* yet include your book club, fantasy football league, or non-essential meetings.

Fill in regular appointments for moving your body, food shopping and meal prep, and, yes, bedtimes that set you up for eight hours a night. Then schedule adequate blocks of time to plan, grade, organize materials, and anything else that gets you ready to have a productive day in the classroom. Now, if there are blank spaces left, go back and judiciously add activities that fit around those nonnegotiables.

At the end of the week, reflect—how did it go? Before planning the next week, tweak it. Maybe you can walk around the track at lunch, get groceries delivered to your home, or start a carpool for your kids' soccer practices. If you find you need to make more painful cuts, be brave. Send out an email that you will no longer host the block party (no excuse or reason given). Channel that unapologetic "just-say-no" self. Try your week again.

Still struggling to fit in self-care? Consider that the average person spends 2.8 hours a day watching television and five hours on our phones. Install an app that tracks your phone usage. Cancel your social media accounts. Cancel Netflix. Block YouTube. Give away your TV. Brag about how much time you have and how well you sleep. Inspire me to do the same.

**How do I know if this idea will help?**

- At multiple times throughout the day, you feel overwhelmed, stressed, anxious, or tired.
- You spend a lot of time driving around after work taking care of things.
- Your gym membership is active, but you haven't been there in months.

- Your calendar shows regular appointments for exercise and self-care.

- You are able to eat healthily most days, including bringing a nourishing lunch to work.

- You say no to extras without guilt.

- You treat a dance class or going to bed at 9 p.m. as protectively as you would any other scheduled event.

*Want to know more about this strategy and others like it?*

**Check out:** Goldsmith, Marshall, and Mark Reiter. 2010. *Mojo: How to Get It, How to Keep It, How to Get It Back When You Lose It.*

Lucas, Lisa J. 2017. *Practicing Presence: Tools for the Overwhelmed Teacher.*

| Week of | | | | |
|---|---|---|---|---|
| Monday | Tuesday | Wednesday | Thursday | Friday |
| Walk w/ Dana @ lunch<br><br>Staff meeting 3-4 pm<br><br>* PREP LUNCHES *<br><br>Lights out!! 10 pm | Organize desk & planning materials 3-3:45<br><br>Zumba @4:30 | Walk w/ Dana @ lunch<br><br>Homework Club 3-4 | Arrive @ 7am & reorganize library shelves<br><br>Yoga @ 5pm<br><br>Book Club @7 | Transfer images of student projects to class website 3-4<br><br>Potluck @ Charlene's |

This teacher revamped her calendar. It now includes school stuff, a sane bedtime, regular exercise, and getting together with friends.

## 1.6 Find Your People with Buddies, Mentors, and Study Partners

**Try This**

Teaching can be isolating. Most of the people surrounding us are students, not potential support systems. The odds of our success, however, go up the moment we enlist other adults in our teaching lives. Don't go it alone.

Invite colleagues to serve as buddies, mentors, and study partners. It's possible you'll find the unicorn who does all of these things at once, but it's more likely you'll seek out and enlist different people to serve different roles.

Find and enlist (and by enlist I mean invite with a cup of coffee):

- **A buddy.** This is someone with whom to carpool, attend school functions, eat lunch, get coffee, and so on. Teaching can take up so much time, and it's nice when social life sometimes overlaps with work life. Plus, we all need allies in the hard work we do. This is the person you can let your guard down around, who knows your birthday and what you like in your coffee, and who points out you are wearing one blue shoe and one black one.

- **A mentor.** You might have a mentor or coach designated for you. If so, work to make that relationship helpful by protecting the time, preparing for it with questions and artifacts, and following up on suggestions. Remember that everyone has something to offer us, even if their style is different from ours. If the fit isn't great, or the mentorship feels more evaluative than energizing, see if you can change it or find an unofficial mentor. In fact, find another anyway! Varied mentorship is important. It's likely you'll have many over the span of a healthy teaching career.

- **A study partner.** Your study partner may also be a buddy or mentor, but it's not necessary to be best friends or to aspire to be like this person as a teacher. Your study partner will commit to trying things out with you, communicating with you honestly about what's working and what's not in their (and your) practice, co-planning toward a common goal (even if not in the same curriculum), debriefing after a conference, or goal setting using this book or other professional resources.

**How do I know if this idea will help?**

- You eat by yourself in your room or stick to your classroom in general for preps and after-school planning.

- You don't see colleagues outside of school hours.

- You don't have others' personal cell phone or email contact info.

- You rely solely on blogs, Twitter, books, and other remote resources to help you plan and figure things out.

- You regularly touch base or meet with at least three different people in your building whom you are not mandated to meet with.

- You find yourself saving up questions, challenges, success stories, and/or resources to share with specific people at work.

- When you face a problem, you don't panic. You know you have avenues for help next door or down the hall.

- For more experienced teachers, you know this is working if you are doing something different this year than last, as a result of a conversation or work with a colleague or mentor/mentee from the previous year.

- When someone new comes to work at your school, you think about what you can offer them in terms of support.

Sonya and Glenny meet up regularly to think about teaching and professional texts that inspire them. This time with a colleague or mentor can feed our teaching selves.

**Adapt for newer teachers**

- Give yourself some time to get to know the people in your building. The best teachers might not be immediately obvious. Keep an eye out, listen, and observe.

- Fellow newbies can be a lifeline of support, but they can also be just as overwhelmed as you. Make sure to also seek those who are a stage or two ahead of you.

- Find someone you can trust. Take time to find teachers who refrain from gossip and build up colleagues.

- Take the initiative—seasoned colleagues may be perfectly happy to get to know you. Take the risk of asking for help, admitting you need help, and/or simply inviting someone to eat lunch with you.

- Spend time with colleagues by helping them out with something. You might not strike up a friendship with everyone, but you will get a reputation as an open and helpful colleague.

Adapt for more experienced teachers

- Seek out colleagues who continually push your thinking.

- Our lives may be jam-packed with family responsibilities, after-school roles, and/or second jobs. Nurturing relationships takes work, and it may be some of those school relationships have lapsed. Prioritize them so you keep thriving.

- Pay it forward. We all stand on the shoulders of many before us who offered a hug, a hand, or help. Newer teachers need you. They need your open door, your offer to watch their class while they run to the bathroom, your tips for making the copier work, your invite to eat lunch, and, when they're ready, your professional expertise and personal wisdom. And, who knows, they may just have a new tip up their sleeve to share, too!

Rikki, Alexis, and Tim eat lunch together every day. As new(ish) teachers, this daily companionship is a lifesaver.

*Want to know more about this strategy and others like it?*

**Check out:** Rami, Meenoo. 2014. *Thrive: 5 Ways to (Re) Invigorate Your Teaching.*

# 1.7 The Pomodoro Technique and Other Time Management Tips

Try This

The to-do list in teaching is never-ending. As you read this book, in fact, your attention is likely pulled by everything that you're not getting to. Try to chunk tasks into manageable pieces and increase your focus and productivity, using the Pomodoro technique. This technique is based on the amount of times our brains are best suited for focusing and then for taking restorative breaks.

- First, choose the task. It doesn't matter if it's a big thing or a little thing. It can be a stack of grading, lesson prep, organizing your desk, or cleaning your bathroom.
- Set your timer for twenty-five minutes. Dive into the task and stick with it until the timer goes off.
- Take a break, setting the timer for five minutes. Stretch, get a drink, or just space out.
- Return to that task or start another, again setting the timer for twenty-five minutes.
- Repeat the cycle of working and then taking a break until the fourth time. The fourth time, set the timer for a longer break, such as a half hour. Let your brain and body recharge.
- Use the breaks to reflect on (and celebrate) what you got done, to decide next steps, and to ensure you don't burn out.

Vary this strategy depending on the time you have. Divide a shorter time frame into fifths. For example: You have fifteen minutes. Spend twelve of them on a task and three on a break. If you find your attention span increasing, adjust the work time (and possibly break time) for longer stretches.

No need to be wed to the timer—this is just a framework to help you feel productive. If you can't focus another second, just stop the timer and take a break. Or, do you feel like you're really making progress? Let the timer go off and wait to break until you're spent or done with the task.

If you're a person who likes to use tech tools, try one of these apps to help you:

- **Marinara Timer** (Web)
- **Tomighty** (Windows and Mac)
- **Pomodorable** (OS X)
- **Focus Booster** (Android)
- **Focus Keeper** (iOS)

**How do I know if this idea will help?**

- The sense of being overwhelmed by all the things "to do" makes you feel stuck.
- You don't know how to best use your prep time.
- After a prep or staying late at school to catch up, you feel like nothing much got done.

**How do I know if this idea is working?**

- You are able to complete one or two "Pomodoros" before getting distracted or losing focus.
- You have a feeling of accomplishment after a prep period or work time.
- You can look at a task and mentally budget how much time you'll need to complete it.
- You feel more determined to get big projects done because you know you can accomplish them across smaller chunks of time.
- You get more accomplished during your preps.

| To Do | Time | Done? |
|---|---|---|
| * Pay bills | 10 – 10:30 | ☑ |
| * Follow up IEP meeting | 10:30 – 10:40 | ☑ |
| * Post projects on class website | 10:45 – 11:00 | ☑ |
| * Lesson Plans | 11:30 – 1:20 w/ breaks | ☐ |

Track what you get done in your timed bursts of work, such as this teacher's weekend work time. You're likely to feel productive with all that you have accomplished.

*Want to know more about this strategy and others like it?*

**Check out:** Cirillo, Franscesco. "Do More and Have Fun with Time Management." francescocirillo.com/pages /pomodoro-technique.

If you tried this and you're ready for more ways to use your time well, consider:

- **Answer emails once a day.** You might read them at any point in the day (although doing that less often is also a smart switch), but choose a set time in which to reply, such as early morning. This helps your time management, and it also decreases the number of unnecessary emails you receive. Replying quickly and consistently can enable questions that might be answered on their own, or emotional replies that tend to simmer down and even fade out completely if left alone for a day. Consider letting others know when you will check and respond to emails so there is no panic when they don't hear from you immediately.

- **Turn off alerts.** Everyone will be OK if they can't get you right away. People (your kids, your partner, your colleagues, your administrators) will all manage until they can find you in person or until you check your phone because you decided to.

- **Reflect on your best time of day to get it done.** I can get more done from 6–7 a.m. before my kids are awake than I can for three hours in the evening. Now, I don't even try to get things done at night, knowing I'll be better off going to sleep and setting the alarm for earlier in the a.m. Others find staying at school in the afternoons and not bringing work home is how they accomplish the most. Find your time and protect it.

- **Create a to-do list.** If you don't love timing, try looking at the scope of your week and creating a to-do list on Todoist (a task managing app) or just on paper. One teacher keeps a "to-do list" book with headings of the days of the week. For certain tasks that are completed weekly, you'll be able to look for patterns and plan which tasks to focus on which days.

- Take a PLC or prep period to tackle some tasks, setting the timer, working quietly, and using the breaks to chat or grab a cup of coffee together.

# 1.8 Make a Happy File

Try This

- Let images and words boost you. Practice keeping note of the successes and stockpiling them for the not-so-great days.

- Designate a folder or box as your happy file. Splurge on a nice one that you actually like to look at.

- Go through your sticky notes, cards, papers, emails, and texts to gather (or print) anything that includes kind words for your teaching.

- If you haven't been saving these joy-inducing artifacts, it's time to start. Even if you are the most minimalist, Marie Kondo–style teacher, start to hold onto things that inspire pride in your teaching self.

- If you have artifacts that won't keep or fit in a file (homemade cookies, flowers, gifts), take a picture. Print it out and jot a note on it saying who gave it to you and why.

- If you get a warm fuzzy with no tangible object to hold onto (a tooth-baring smile from a shy kid, a pat on the back from the principal, a grateful phone call from a parent), take a minute to write it down. Now put that note into the file. This is not time wasted! You'll be glad you did so later on.

- Jot down the things your students say that make you laugh. Rosie jotted down the time a kindergarten student asked her where her bed was, shocked that Rosie didn't live at school. Berit wrote down the time her seventh grader asked how old Berit was, then let out an anguished sigh. "You mean I'm still going to be getting zits when I'm twenty-four?" Revisiting these will remind you of the incredibly unique and tender perspectives of young people and why we are there to help them.

- Teachers (especially of younger children) often receive drawings and cards. If you don't have physical space to hold onto them all, take a picture for your digital files.

How do I know if this idea will help?

- You are quick to catalog what's not happening in your teaching. Seeing what's working is harder for you.

- In any feedback that includes both positive comments and suggestions, you glom onto the suggestions or criticism and forget what was praised.

- You tend to give credit for successes to others or attribute good moments in your teaching life to luck.

| How do I know if this idea is working? | • You have a file and get excited to add new artifacts.<br>• Your file is growing.<br>• You are energized to replicate moments of success by doing *more* of what inspired the happy file artifacts. |
|---|---|

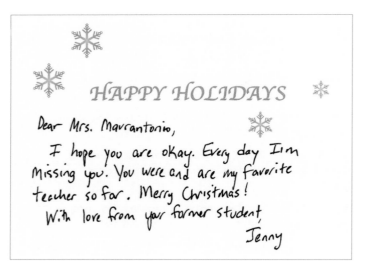

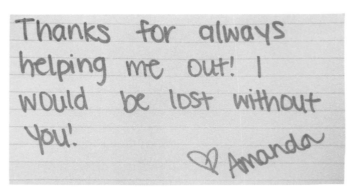

| Adapt for newer teachers | • Each day during your first year of teaching, write down *one* thing that went well on that day. Fold up the paper and put it in a jar. By the end of the year, you will realize that you did a whole lot of things right! This is also a great activity for kids. Invite them to do it with you! |
|---|---|
| How to try this with others | • In a staff meeting, create one starter artifact for the colleague sitting next to you. Everyone uses an index card to jot down one positive thing they've seen, overheard, or noticed their colleague doing.<br>• After giving everyone some time to generate these files, consider a share-out or celebration. Ask teachers to bring a favorite artifact to share. Listen to colleagues brag on themselves by reading letters from students, sharing a happy moment, relaying a small success. Make sure everyone has one thing to share, and cheer each other on! |

*Want to know more about this strategy and others like it?*

**Check out:** Lucas, Lisa J. 2017. *Practicing Presence: Tools for the Overwhelmed Teacher.*

# 1.9 Banish Gossip

**Try This**

For one day, keep track of conversations with other teachers and staff members. Create a simple negative/positive T-chart on a piece of paper and carry it around with you. If conversations involve a complaint or criticism, check the "negative" or gossip column. If they don't, check the productive or "positive" column.

What's your ratio? Typically, about 65 percent of people's interactions lean toward gossip or negative talk (Goldsmith and Reiter 2010, 161–62). That means well more than half our interactions are totally unproductive. Gossipy interactions might feel good in the instant, but they won't help you, your school, your students, or your coworkers. Plus, it turns out that complaining actually rewires our brain to be depressed (DailyHealthPost 2019).

Work toward shifting that ratio so more of your interactions involve sharing information, noting the positive in others (including administrators and students), problem-solving, or asking questions.

When interactions veer toward gossip, don't agree or add to it. Even smiling and nodding can be tacit endorsement. If the talk is simply harmless negativity, you might not respond to it at all. You might instead ask others about their work, their goals, or what is going well.

Or, be braver. Take a deep breath and say, "This conversation makes me uncomfortable. I'd rather talk about something that doesn't involve criticizing others." Or, try this: "It sounds like X person isn't doing so well (or isn't part of the group here). What could we do to help them?"

Try to start interactions off so they steer toward positive. Note when you begin interactions by complaining (so easy to do!) and shift gears.

Of course, if what you hear moves beyond gossip and into truly harmful talk (for example, negative talk about students or their families, racist or homophobic comments, comments that could be considered sexual harassment) do not remain silent. In these situations, be an upstander. Speak up for what is right.

**How do I know if this idea will help?**

- You find yourself frequently bonding with others by complaining.
- You can easily list what's wrong with your school, coworkers, students, and so on, but you can't easily list what's great.
- You can't recall the last time you problem-solved with a colleague in a way that felt productive.
- You can't remember the last time you complimented someone outside of their presence.

- You can review your last few interactions and think of positive conversations.
- You are noticing good things about your school, coworkers, and students more often.
- You frequently discuss positive aspects of your school community with others.
- You never let a truly harmful comment slide. You stand up.

## Want to know more about this strategy and others like it?

**Check out:** Goldsmith, Marshall, and Mark Reiter. 2010. *Mojo: How to Get It, How to Keep It, How to Get It Back When You Lose It.*

Lucas, Lisa J. 2017. *Practicing Presence: Tools for the Overwhelmed Teacher.*

| Who I spoke to | Positive Interactions | Negative Interactions |
|---|---|---|
| Special Ed teacher | ✓ | |
| Breakfast monitor | ✓ | |
| Para | | ✓ |
| Special Ed teacher, student, counselor | ✓ | |
| Special Ed teacher, para | | ✓ (me venting) |
| Para | | ✓ |
| Para | ✓ | |
| ESL teacher | ✓ | |
| Team meeting | ✓ | ✓ |
| Dual teacher | ✓ | |
| Para | | ✓ |
| Para | | ✓ (me venting) |
| Teacher | | ✓ |
| Principal | ✓ | |
| Teacher | ✓ | |
| Secretary | ✓ | |
| Teacher | | ✓ |
| Teacher | ✓ | |
| Sub | ✓ | |
| Janitor | ✓ | |
| Para | ✓ | |
| Para | ✓ | |
| Para | ✓ | |
| Para | | ✓ |
| Bus driver | | ✓ |
| | | |
| | | |

- Tell others about your goal to banish gossip and to shift the ratio of productive interactions. This lets others know why you're responding less to negative chat, and it encourages them to change the subject to productive talk.
- Enlist others to try this with you. Track the productive versus negative interactions for a day, and check in with each other at the end of the day. Set goals for how much you'll try to reduce that number the next day, and check in again.
- Discuss with a colleague: What parts of the day or week are you most tempted to rely on gossip and complaining? Seek each other out at those times, or send one another a GIF or text as a reminder to stay positive.
- Let students know what you are trying. Enlist them to join you. Give them conversational moves, sentence starters, and phrases that they can use for easy reference.

# 1.10 Give Wait Time for New Initiatives

**Try This**

Change can feel daunting. Especially, sometimes, the large-scale change of new initiatives. The next time an initiative is announced, try this:

1.  Listen. Hear the whole thing out.
2.  Ask genuine questions.
3.  Stop there for *at least twenty-four hours*.
4.  Once you've had a good night's sleep, revisit the initiative.
5.  Consider it from the school's point of view: How might this help kids? The school? You? Think through how the new initiative might actually help.
6.  Try it. Make sure you aren't letting your doubts unconsciously sabotage the effort. Present this change to your kids with a positive (or at least neutral) tone, and follow all the steps. This matters. Your genuine attempt will give you time to react more diplomatically, and it will increase the legitimacy of your concerns if you need to push back. Your concerns will be rooted in what actually happened when you tried.

**How do I know if this idea will help?**

*   Concerns (OK, complaints) about new initiatives are voiced immediately upon hearing about them or, of even greater concern, when administrators aren't present.
*   You have new administrators: there *will* be change, and they need your support.
*   There are naysayers to almost any change, even changes that are likely to help students.
*   Concerns regarding change are rooted more in how they impact teachers than in how they impact students.
*   There haven't been many successful or long-term changes to your school culture, department, or curriculum in the last few years.
*   Conversely, if there are *many* initiatives coming down the pike, this strategy is still helpful. It will give everyone the time needed to reflect and respond.

**How do I know if this idea is working?**

*   Your blood pressure doesn't spike during staff meetings when new initiatives are announced. You know you have time to think them through.
*   You make a plan for trying things.
*   Some changes that you thought would be disasters actually worked.
*   Administrators or change agents in your school listen to voiced concerns, because they know they are coming from a place of trying and reflecting.

- Students are at the forefront of any discussion around change.
- Teachers' sanity and job satisfaction are treated as essential factors in any change.

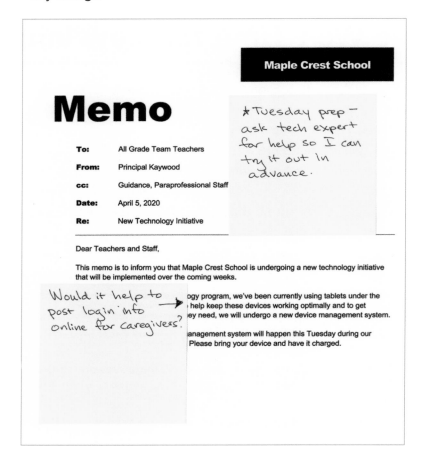

**Adapt for newer teachers**

- Even without years of experience, you have every right to participate in this conversation. You have your education and your own experience as a student to help you know what makes sense and what doesn't. And now you will also have the wait time and the fact you've made a legitimate go of things to support your feedback.
- If you waited, tried this change, and it didn't work, *ask for help*. Your administrator and colleagues would rather find ways to help you than have you nod and pretend things are great when they're not.
- Listen first. Talk later.

**Adapt for more experienced teachers**

- You've earned the right to be hesitant about anything that promises a magic fix. But remember that your colleagues, especially newer ones, are looking to you to set the tone.
- If you have seen this same work fail in the past, approach your administrators. Let them know what happened so they might use that knowledge to prevent a repeat demise. And assure this administrator that you will still do the next step.
- Give it a *genuine* try.

- Commit to holding off discussing a change until you (and your colleagues) take twenty-four hours to reflect on it.

- Share out potential upsides. It may be that a colleague will benefit from this approach, or that their students will. Likewise, share ways you think students might benefit that others haven't articulated.

- Study this initiative with your team and make a plan for implementation. Sometimes panic can ensue before we think through what the change will really look like.

- After giving it a try, reflect together. What worked? What didn't? Do you have evidence such as student growth, or lack of it, to back that up?

- If there is evidence that this approach or initiative did not benefit students, or that the benefit came at a great cost in terms of time and effort, decide together how you will share that information with administrators. Document the lack of growth or the time it took. Designate a respected teacher to voice the concerns. Be ready to offer suggestions and to listen to administrators' point of view.

# Classroom Environment

## What is classroom environment, and why is it important?

Our classroom environment is the first thing students experience. It sets the tone for everything that follows. What's in our space and how we organize it reveals what we value, and it has a profound impact on learning.

A well-designed space immediately tells students they are safe, welcomed, and valued. Brain science tells us that a sense of safety is imperative for any learning or growth or occur (Willis 2014). Once a safe space is established, our classrooms also need to say to every child, "This is your home. You belong here." If we cannot manage that, we can't expect students to engage.

Environment is not just about decorating but about laying the groundwork for real learning. Images on the wall of successful women and people of color impact students' sense that they all belong and that they are expected to achieve. Arranging furniture for student independence has a direct impact on behavior (Cheryan et al. 2014). This chapter is not about making a room beautiful but about making it supportive and functional for you and your students.

Beyond the nonnegotiable of a safe space, we need to think about comfort. If our students are uncomfortable, they will not be able to focus and learn. Make a middle school classroom feel just a bit like a well-worn café, and you're likely to see some happy tween learners.

Many of our schools were designed to fit a work world that was very different from the world our students live in. Rows of desks facing a teacher and blackboard are no longer relevant to the flexible and collaborative spaces, tables, and quiet areas of today's offices.

Let's see how to design intentional learning spaces that become homes for each and every student who comes through our door.

## Is this the goal for me?

- Do you answer "yes" and "sometimes" for most statements? Consider moving to the next chapter. You've got this!

- Do you have a mix of "yes," "sometimes," and "not yet" answers? This might be the goal for you.

- Do you answer "not yet" for most statements? Go back and try the checklist from the previous chapter. You're likely to enjoy greater success and see quicker results by focusing there.

## What do you notice?

| | Yes | Sometimes | Not yet |
|---|---|---|---|
| Walking into my classroom, it's clear what I value most as a teacher. | ☐ | ☐ | ☐ |
| Students and I can find things easily and put them back where they belong. | ☐ | ☐ | ☐ |
| Students and I regularly look at and refer to what's displayed on the classroom walls. | ☐ | ☐ | ☐ |
| My classroom resources and materials reflect a rich diversity, equal to that of the rich diversity of my students and the world. | ☐ | ☐ | ☐ |
| I would want to be a student in my classroom. | ☐ | ☐ | ☐ |

# 2.1 Be the Student: Look at Your Room Through a Student's Eyes

Try This

Students should be at the forefront of any design efforts. Delete Pinterest, put away the glue gun, and stop paying for bulletin board borders. These well-intentioned efforts may not be the things students need, want, or enjoy.

Instead, *be* the student. Take a notebook and pen and walk into your room imagining you are one of your students. Make it someone specific and someone unlike you. (Maybe they are a very different size or personality, or they have a disability you do not.) Jot down what you notice.

1. As you walk in, what makes the room feel welcoming or uninviting? Where are you drawn to go? Are you allowed to go there? What about the lighting, temperature, or space makes you want or not want to enter?

2. Do you know where to go?

3. What do you do with your things? Do you have an accessible space to store your belongings? Does it feel safe to put them there? Is it clean?

4. Sit down in your spot. If you can, sit there for the amount of time a lesson would usually be. If there are fifteen minutes of listening before students can move, make yourself sit there for fifteen minutes at a minimum.

   a. Who or what's in your sightline: The board? The teacher? Other students? What is not?

   b. Who or what can you hear the most easily? Who or what can't you hear?

   c. How do you feel mentally: Engaged? Or, are you restless or tempted to get out your phone?

   d. Are you physically comfortable? If not, can you adjust your seat or desk? Can you move to different parts of the room?

   e. Is anything pulling at your attention?

5. Imagine you have to go to the bathroom, are hungry, or are thirsty. What can you do? Are you able to meet your basic needs without feeling embarrassed, unsafe, or uncomfortable?

6. What do you see on the walls? Is it interesting or helpful? Is it cluttered or distracting?

7. Imagine you need something to write with, to charge your phone/laptop, a piece of paper, a tissue, a calculator. Do you know how to get these things? Are they available?

8. Try this as more than one student. Sit where they sit. Try to "be" them at different points in the day—after or before lunch, first or last part of the day, when a friend is absent, if you forgot your homework. How does that change things?

Look over your notes. What jumps out at you that was uncomfortable, distracting, unsafe, unclean, or unwelcoming?

Start with *one thing* that you can change.

Let students know when you have changed it and why. Tell students you have other changes you are going to work on as well. Ask them for help if appropriate. You can also let them know you'll be asking for their input as a follow-up step to making the classroom a better fit for you all (Strategy 2.3, "Ask Students What Serves or Distracts Them").

| **How do I know if this idea will help?** | • You spend time telling students where to go/sit/get materials, to pay attention, to listen, to stop doing X. |
| | • Students complain about sitting in certain parts of the room or beg to sit in others. |
| | • The bulk of your classroom design energy has been for your own supplies, materials, and desk area. |
| | • You don't know what students think of the classroom design. |

*Want to know more about this strategy and others like it?*

**Check out:** Hertz, Christine, and Kristine Mraz. 2018. *Kids First from Day One: A Teacher's Guide to Today's Classroom.*

| **How do I know if this idea is working?** | • You enjoy entering your classroom. |
| | • Your students comment on liking your classroom more. |
| | • Students are excited over changes or new spaces. |

| Entering room: | |
|---|---|
| Where are you drawn to- what's inviting? | Tables with lots of space to work and clean surfaces. Wonder wall - markers at the ready |
| What's least inviting? | Fixed desks - uncomfortable. Tiny & cramped. Teacher desk makes far corner feel off-limits |
| Do you know where to go and when? | Nametags on tables helpful unclear when to use tech or reading nooks |
| What do you do with your things? | Hooks don't have enough space for bag & winter coat |
| During class: | |
| Who and what can/can't you see? | Can see teacher, tablemates but not other students behind me Hard to see smartboard - more tables closer? |
| What can you hear? Is it distracting or helpful? | Can hear teacher but hard to hear other tables Seeing nurse's office if door open is distracting. Cover window? |
| How do you feel physically and mentally? | Great at tables Uncomfortable at desks and very cramped at tech station |
| Can you move if you need to - where? | Feels good to stand up and go to water fountain! Am I letting them move enough? |

After studying the classroom through the eyes of her students, this teacher has new ideas for how to improve the space.

| **How to try this with others** | • Be a student in a colleague's room, and then switch around and have them do the same for you. Offer feedback according to what you notice in their room, as we may unintentionally have blinders in our own spaces that are hard to avoid. |

# 2.2 Stop Decorating and Turn Classroom Walls over to Students

**Try This**

Look at your wall space, including bulletin boards in the hallways, and make a rough estimate: What percentage of the walls are student created? If it's less than 80 percent, decide which teacher-created walls can be cleared to make room for student-created displays.

Crowded wall spaces can create visual and mental clutter for many students—the opposite of what we want. Take down the things that were purchased or teacher created. Toss or recycle visuals that do not serve as "silent teachers," providing useful reminders or how-tos. If a visual is not regularly referred to by you and students, ditch it.

Frame spaces on bulletin boards and leave the space inside the frame empty, so students know these spaces are theirs to fill. You might choose one label in advance, such as "Works in Progress" or "Shout-Out Wall," but leave the rest to be decided upon by students as time goes on.

Tell students the classroom is a shared space in which they are not guests but the most important residents. Help them choose work for displays, and designate times when they can post it. Show them student-created wall space in other classrooms or from images online, and let them brainstorm possibilities on their own. Some I've seen recently: "Words That Intrigue Us," "Time Line of Our Project," "Lines We Love," "Hopes and Dreams for the Year," "All About Us," and "Our Goals."

Embrace visual resting spaces and blank walls. Know they will be filled with student creations when it's time!

| **How do I know if this idea will help?** | • Many bulletin boards and wall displays are teacher created or purchased.<br><br>• Displays have been up for more than one unit.<br><br>• Students do not regularly look at, refer to, and use classroom wall displays.<br><br>• You spend prep periods and free time designing and creating bulletin boards on your own. |
|---|---|
| **How do I know if this idea is working?** | • The majority of classroom wall space is student created.<br><br>• Students regularly look at and refer to wall displays.<br><br>• Wall displays rotate regularly (at least every marking period). |
| **Adapt for K–5** | • Remember to keep wall space physically accessible by keeping student-created displays free of bulky furniture underneath, providing step stools, and lowering the height range.<br><br>• Create and protect space for temporary displays such as block creations, art work, sculptures, and other 3-D work from choice time or centers.<br><br>• If parent volunteers are available, enlist them to help, but clarify that their role will not be in decorating or arranging but assisting students to do so.<br><br>• Keep the rotation of student-created wall space as frequent as possible. The more often it changes with fresh material, the more often students will seek out these spaces. |
| **Adapt for 6–8** | • Coming into and leaving class can be a choppy transition in buildings where students travel a distance. Allowing a minute or two on each end for students to add to and check out the wall displays can serve as a useful buffer time.<br><br>• Incorporate the wall displays into your teaching as much as possible, or they risk becoming wallpaper. Take time to check out what students are posting, and include those in your lessons or handouts or even as images on your class website when appropriate. |
| **Adapt for 9–12** | • Don't assume that older students aren't interested in what's on the walls or don't care about having their work publicly displayed. Just check out any teen bedroom, sticker-laden laptop case, locker wall, or Instagram feed to see their fondness for rocking an image. Bare classrooms can feel sterile, so include them in the process of filling up at least half of the blank wall space.<br><br>• If you share a classroom, consult with that colleague(s) in advance to determine what space you each will use. Consider sharing spaces for bulletins such as "Words That Intrigue Us" or "Our Goals." |
| **How to try this with others** | • Do a shared classroom wall inventory, visiting one another's rooms and assessing wall space together. Help a teammate clear wall space.<br><br>• Visit one another's classrooms and look at the walls from a student's perspective. Which rooms are most inviting? Visually calming? Interesting to look at? Why? Set short- and long-term goals together for how you will boost the look of your classroom walls. |

*Want to know more about this strategy and others like it?*

**Check out:** Hertz, Christine, and Kristine Mraz. 2018. *Kids First from Day One: A Teacher's Guide to Today's Classroom.*

# 2.3 Ask Students What Serves or Distracts Them

Try This

Ask students, "What in this room is helping you, and what is getting in the way?" Have a quick discussion or use an online survey or polling app. Take stock of what students say. No one will have more meaningful suggestions for how to create the best kind of classroom environment than they do!

You might hand out sticky notes for students to place on items that are a distraction or that they don't use. See how many of those items you can fit into the trunk of your car to take to a donation center. Or, have students put sticky notes on their favorite parts of the room or the things they look at and use the most. Protect those and think about how you can build on them.

It is important to not only open yourself up to student feedback but to do something about it.

Look for patterns to maximize your efforts. *One* response that a student isn't a fan of the seating chart doesn't mean you must abandon it (although you could tweak it). Multiple requests to have seating choices, such as a group of six desks, a group of two or four, a long table of twelve, and a few desks on their own, means it's worth a try. Moving chairs doesn't require a big financial or time investment, and it's a huge gesture toward supporting students to choose what works best for them.

You can ask for suggestions if you're not sure how to answer students' needs, and you don't need to head straight to the store to make it happen. You can do a ton with what is there. Arranging chairs in a new formation, allowing individuals or pairs to work in the hallway, or clearing off shelves and tables to provide collaborative spaces are all free and doable.

The important thing is to solicit student input. Even if you can't accommodate everything, students will be honored that you're asking their opinion. Asking for their input clarifies that the room is a shared space and that students' role in it is essential. And keep asking. Robert Dillon, coauthor of *The Space*, noted in his calendar to ask students for feedback every two weeks, a reminder to me of how important it is to treat our space as a living, adaptable component of our instruction (Hare and Dillon 2016).

| | |
|---|---|
| **How do I know if this idea will help?** | • Students have never been asked what they like or don't like about the classroom. |
| | • You have had the same classroom design for a long time. |
| | • You aren't sure what students think of the classroom space. |
| | • Things you thought would go over well with students haven't always resulted in positive change. |
| **How do I know if this idea is working?** | • You hear students' ideas about what is working and not working. Some of these suggestions and comments surprise you. |
| | • You've made changes according to students' feedback, and you let them know what you've changed and why. |
| | • Students offer feedback spontaneously, letting you know what they're using or not using, knowing you'll listen. |
| | • You see students using the space in more productive ways. |
| **How to try this with others** | • Collect feedback from students and then join colleagues to look at it together. What suggestions can they envision that you may not be able to see? Commit to each shifting one thing and reporting back on the impact. Remind one another to keep asking for student feedback, knowing that our classrooms will never be "done." |

*Want to know more about this strategy and others like it?*

**Check out:** Hare, Rebecca Louise, and Dr. Robert Dillon. 2016. *The Space: A Guide for Educators.*

# 2.4 Document the Walls: Who Is Represented? Who Isn't?

**Try This**

- Think about the students who come into your room on a regular basis, and list how they identify in terms of race, gender, culture, family background, language, nationality, disabilities, and more. For example, the start of an extensive list might look like this:

    - Somali, Hmong, Filipino, adopted, American born with immigrant parents, American born with American-born parents, Tagalog speaking, Spanish speaking, English language learner, native English speaker, wheelchair user, has an intellectual disability, nondisabled, transgender, cisgender, single-parent family, same-sex parents, multigenerational family . . .

    - If you do not know certain information, such as whether you have adopted students, queer students, or students with undocumented family members, work on the assumption that you do or you will.

    - If your group is somewhat homogenous, then compose your list with groups from the global community. Even if your class is not particularly diverse, the world certainly is. Use this list to get them participating in that world as open, informed citizens.

- Perform a slow, methodical walk around your classroom, focusing on books and materials. For each visible image and resource, place a tally mark next to any group represented therein.

- At the end, look over the list. Which groups are represented? Which are not? Which groups have many tally marks, and which have few? Does this match the percentage of similarly identifying students who come into the room?

- Prioritize acquiring resources for nonrepresented groups, and then the groups with limited representation, especially if those groups are well represented in terms of numbers of students.

- Find texts, resources, visuals, and more that you can purchase, and ask your administration for help.

    - Put resources on classroom wish lists.

    - Register on adoptaclassroom.org and donorschoose.org for resources.

    - Check out diversebooks.org, leeandlow.com (multicultural children's book publisher), and tolerance.org, and search "diverse books" on nerdybookclub. wordpress.com.

- Let your students know when resources are added and that you are consciously trying to reflect and celebrate all the groups of people in the school community. Invite them to suggest other resources, to make or donate visuals or images, and to alert you if they see gaps in representation.

- Resources and visuals reflect one group more than others.
- You can walk into your room with a student in mind and not see them reflected on the walls or texts.
- In your class or school, groups with historical privilege (white, cisgender, English speaking, nondisabled) participate more than others or perform at academically higher levels than others.
- Your own identity represents historical privilege. If you are white, cisgender, straight, Christian, neurotypical; if your first language is English; and/or if you were born in the United States, you are duty bound to take a hard look for gaps in representation. If you don't see any, take another look. Privilege can obscure our perception. That doesn't mean we are excused from doing the hard work.

**Want to know more about this strategy and others like it?**

**Check out:** Earick, Mary E. 2009. *Racially Equitable Teaching: Beyond the Whiteness of Professional Development for Early Childhood Educators.*

**How do I know if this idea is working?**

- Students comment on and notice what's on the walls and what books are offered.
- Minoritized groups participate as often as groups with majority representation.
- Your classroom resources reflect a rich diversity of groups.

| Who is looking to see themselves in my classroom? | How many texts, images, authors, resources represent that group? |
|---|---|
| Latinx – Colombian | ++++ |
| Costa Rican | I |
| Guatemalan – incl. Mayan | O |
| Adopted | I |
| Neurodivergent | III |
| Grandparents are guardians | O |
| African American | ++++ II |
| Same sex parents | I |
| Wheelchair | III |
| Mandarin-speaking | I |

**How to try this with others**

- Respectfully share less obvious information as appropriate.
- Do a classroom inventory with grade-team members together, visiting each classroom as a group and comparing notes. Delegate resource finding among yourselves.

# 2.5 Share Responsibility for the Room with Jobs

**Try This**

Do you find yourself spending lots of time tidying up your room? Are you stooping to pick up wrappers under desks or checking that all laptops are connected to chargers? Creating authentic classroom jobs will instill a shared sense of responsibility for the classroom space and routines.

You can create these roles, or better yet, have students think through what needs doing. Generate an evolving list of tasks. If boots and jackets can't fit in cubbies, ask students for ideas. Then, give someone the job of hanging bulky outerwear on added hooks or of collecting boots and moving them to the supply closet.

Whether you teach first or eleventh grade, many tasks can be turned over to students.

You can assign jobs, choose students randomly, or ask for volunteers. If you opt for volunteers, however, think through how you will help the room feel like a wholly shared investment. Can nonvolunteers be tasked to take part when jobs rotate?

You may want to rotate frequently at the beginning of the year, so everyone understands each job's responsibilities. Then, the longer students have jobs, the better and more automatic they will be at them.

Set students up for successful job completion. Invest time early on to teach students how to do each job correctly, what to do if a job holder is absent, how to ask for help, and so on. Allow for partners to sign up for jobs together or for students to relinquish a job that isn't working for them.

It can be hard to not fix or do jobs that were forgotten or ignored. If the laptops are not replaced correctly and they don't get charged, leave them uncharged if you can possibly stand it. Long term, it will be more important for everyone to learn that this job is essential for a working classroom than it is for them to start the I-Search the next morning. If lines of ants crawl across the floor from granola bar wrapper to soda can, let students see them. Feign surprise and bafflement: "Oh no! How did that happen? What can we do?" Truly turn over responsibility for your shared space to students, including experiencing the consequences for not taking care of it correctly. If you have to nag students to do the job, you might as well be doing it yourself. Let a little failure, discomfort, or frustration be its own teacher whenever possible.

**How do I know if this idea will help?**

- You stay in the room late or arrive early to tidy up, organize, and so on.
- You tell yourself it is easier to just do it yourself.
- You are working harder than the students.
- The custodial staff has to do more than they should in your room.
- You spend a fair amount of class time doing things like passing or collecting supplies.

- Students remind each other to do their jobs.

- Students notice when something is not done, such as a pile of books shelved incorrectly.

- You spend less time on procedural tasks, such as passing out or collecting materials.

- You notice students more because your attention is less compromised.

### Ms. K's 7C Classroom Jobs

| Attendance | GABE |
|---|---|
| Materials | ALYSSA |
| Recycling | CHLOE |
| Smart Board Guru | XAVIER |
| Paper Returner | JOSIAH |
| Board Cleaner | SYDNEY |
| Desk Straightener | JORDAN |
| Greeter | HANNAH |
| Supply Collector | IMANI |

- For K–5, no job is too big or too small. Whether a child is assigned to be "custodian" (cleaning up the floor at the end of the day) or "cubby monitor" (calling kids to cubbies to pack up), they love the responsibility.

- Change the jobs no more than once every two weeks, so kids don't get bored but you don't have to manage too much rotation.

- Some 6–12 teachers have students apply for jobs by explaining in writing why they are suited for those jobs and their qualifications, and then students stick with those jobs for a month or more. This becomes especially powerful during persuasive writing units!

- Give official-sounding titles for jobs and avoid cutesy ones if you want teens to opt in. Instead of "library helper," use "librarian." Instead of "paper passer," try "teacher assistant" or "materials manager."

- Add jobs that suit their interests and talents. Designate a classroom photographer to document what your class is doing. Assign another "website builder" and have them upload and design images on the class website.

*Want to know more about this strategy and others like it?*

**Check out:** Emdin, Christopher. 2016. *For White Folks Who Teach in the Hood . . . and the Rest of Y'all Too: Reality Pedagogy and Urban Education.*

Rapp, Whitney H. 2014. *Universal Design for Learning in Action: 100 Ways to Teach All Learners.*

- Meet with colleagues. Share your job charts and expectations. Discuss which help and which create more work for you. What shifts might build a greater sense of student responsibility and involvement? If someone is having great success in shifting the balance of classroom duties to students, visit their room to see it in action.

# 2.6 Remove Obstacles for One and All: Room Design and Tools That Support Everyone

Try This

Protecting and supporting kids who have disabilities or who are learning English benefits all students. Every student is going to need support at different times—when they face personally challenging content, when they're tired, when their parents go through a divorce, when they've been out sick for two weeks, and on and on. When support tools are used by those other than students getting Tier 3 support, we level the playing field and destigmatize difference.

Just as lever door knobs, jumbo light switches, and ramp entrances work for any person regardless of mobility or physical needs, think through design switches for your classroom that allow everyone to succeed. Encourage students to see such tools as resources for everyone. Provide access to these tools, and allow students to choose what works for them.

Classroom environment tools that help one and all:

- Provide fidget tools, such as beaded balls; Koosh balls; plastic bottles filled with water, food coloring, and oil; stress balls; water tubes; smooth rocks; ribbons; bendable straws; mini-Slinkies; fidget spinners; and Unifix cubes.

- Provide various seating options, such as beanbags, rocking chairs, sofas, reading pillows, carpet squares, folding camping chairs. Provide clipboards or lap desks for written work.

- Use tennis balls to soundproof the bottoms of chair legs to avoid screeching noises.

- Tape cardboard or 8 × 14 manila folders together to create study carrels to help eliminate visual distractions and overstimulation.

- Make the lighting friendly. Fluorescent bulbs, especially if they flicker, can be a major distraction. Replace fluorescent bulbs with LED or incandescent bulbs. Add lamps, take advantage of natural light if possible, use upward-projecting light versus downward-projecting light, or string white holiday lights and night lights to create a soothing effect.

- Use desktop cheat sheets. Use packing tape to attach an index card, sticky note, or cardstock to the desk with essential information and visual reminders. Students can create and attach these themselves, too. Include vocabulary words, equivalency charts, personal reminders—whatever it is that students "need to know."

- Create tabletop charts. Convert large posters and anchor charts into 8.5 × 11 or smaller pages that can be placed on students' desks or tables.

| How do I know if this idea will help? |
|---|

- Students have a hard time paying attention, sitting still, staying at their desks, or focusing on their work.
- When you ask students if the light or seating bothers them, they say yes.
- There are already unavoidable sensory distractions such as noisy hallways, announcements on the loudspeaker, construction or movement outside the windows, or harsh lighting that can't be turned off.

| How do I know if this idea is working? |
|---|

- Students seek out your room in between classes, at lunch, and other times.
- Students are excited about the seating choices, fidget options, and so on.
- You notice an uptick in attention spans or focus, or a downtick in disruptive behavior.
- You feel good when you walk into your classroom.

*Want to know more about this strategy and others like it?*

**Check out:** Kluth, Paula, and Sheila Danaher. 2010. *From Tutor Scripts to Talking Sticks: 100 Ways to Differentiate Instruction in K–12 Inclusive Classrooms.*

Tabletop charts and seating options are examples of supports that work for *everyone.*

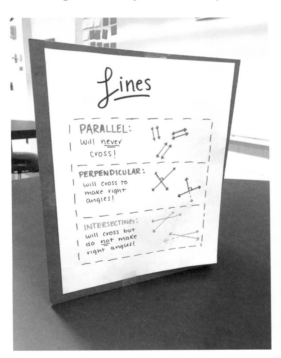

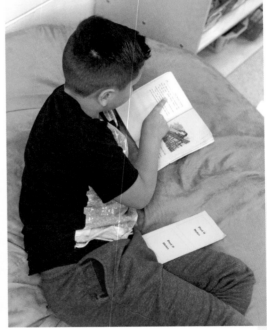

| How to try this with others |
|---|

- Walk through a colleague's rooms. Help them see potential gaps or distractions that might be invisible to them through repeated exposure. Ask them to do the same for you.
- Enlist the special education staff to do walk-throughs of classrooms, pointing out potential distractions and challenges and offering suggestions for new tools or designs that would help all students.

# 2.7 KonMari Your Classroom

**Try This**

Borrow from the popular organizing consultant, Marie Kondo, and declutter your room. Start with one area or category (cubbies, cabinets, paper piles, your desk, or the classroom library). If the space is used by students, decide if you will involve them. Pull everything from that category and pile it onto the floor or a table. Hold each thing and ask yourself (or have students ask): "Is it useful? Is it worth holding onto? Is it helping us learn?" If so, put it in a holding spot. If not, recycle, trash, or donate.

Organize! Find permanent homes for the kept objects. Group like objects together. Scan and file papers digitally. When possible, store things vertically so that they don't disappear in a pile.

KonMari spaces used by students *with* students. You might enlist them to pull the entire collection of books off the classroom library shelves onto the floor, for example, and to put sticky notes on books they're interested in reading or enjoyed reading. Books with sticky notes go back on the shelves. For those without, ask yourself, "Is this worth holding onto?" If so, consider how you will introduce that text and try to spark interest in it. Recycle or donate what's left. Have students help reshelve the keepers, noting if new baskets or labels are needed.

**How do I know if this idea will help?**

- You have to put things away because students do not know where things go or materials are often messy.
- You or students have trouble finding things.
- There is more than one filing cabinet of papers in your room.
- You have full boxes, bins, or drawers, and you're not sure what's in them.
- Shelves and cabinets are completely filled. There is little or no space to add new materials.

**How do I know if this idea is working?**

- Students independently access materials and put them away in the right place.
- You and students can find things easily.
- There are open spaces on shelves and in cabinets.
- Your desk has newly cleared spaces that stay clear.

These students are helping to organize the classroom library.

- There is no teacher desk. It's happened! Many teachers have discovered they prefer storing their materials in a file cabinet and sharing a table/work space with students when needed.

**Adapt for K–5**

- Resist the urge to do this on your own, even though involving students may make it messier and less efficient in the short term. You might share a popular video of first graders in Japan cleaning their classroom, where it is typical for schools not to have custodial staff. In the long term, students' collective ownership of the classroom space will benefit everyone.

**Adapt for 6–8**

- Students' organization skills are often challenged in middle school. They often have lockers for the first time, and they need to travel with the right materials from room to room—things get lost in the process. Start with backpacks, lockers, or desks to show them the impact of streamlining and organizing one's space. Take before-and-after pictures to mark progress and to serve as a reminder when things get messy again.

- Encourage students to try this at home for their work spaces or bedrooms, and check in on results. You might share your organizational work in class with caregivers to inspire their support.

**Adapt for 9–12**

- Remember that in a very short time, students will be responsible for organizing their lives, their dorm rooms, their work spaces at a new job, their calendars and to-do lists, and so on. Creating and maintaining a user-friendly space is as essential for teens as any other content-related skill.

- If you absolutely can't take time to do it in the classroom (yet), take 10–15 minutes to tackle backpacks.

- Encourage students to try this with their bedrooms, lockers, cars, or at home. Poll them for feedback and results.

- KonMari the staff room together. Enjoy an eating space free of broken mugs, old ketchup packets, and expired yogurts. Ask everyone who uses the space to share in the project as a way to ensure maintenance.

- Devote an afternoon or prep period to helping a colleague KonMari one part of their room.

- Ask a group of colleagues to all work on one part of their rooms on the same afternoon, then visit one another's spaces to admire.

- Bring custodial staff well-deserved thank-you gifts if they are helping cart away boxes and bags of old papers and ~~junk~~ treasures.

*Want to know more about this strategy and others like it?*

**Check out:** Schwartz, Sarah. 2019. "Marie Kondo in the Classroom: How Teachers Are Tidying Up." *Education Week—Teaching Now.*

Kondo, Marie. 2016. *The Life-Changing Magic of Tidying Up: The Japanese Art of Decluttering and Organizing.*

# 2.8 Whose Room Is It? Personalize the Space

**Try This**

I recently took my son to a birthday party where each child's place setting was a paper plate with a drawing of that child and their name, done by the birthday boy in advance. A small and lovely gesture by a pint-size host, and one with great impact—every child asked to bring theirs home! They ate off napkins instead.

Our classrooms can reflect the same personalization for our students so they feel welcomed, honored, and reminded that they are an integral part of this space.

Make your room reflect your kids by personalizing a few select spaces and resources in advance and then asking students to personalize other aspects.

Options include:

- **"Student in the Spotlight"** on the classroom door or on the board. Post a photo taken during the first week of school along with a blurb describing something that student accomplished academically, socially, or otherwise. These can be seemingly small things such as sharing materials or mastering a new concept. Rotate it weekly.

- **"Problem of the Week"** on a bulletin board along with sticky notes and pencils for students to post solutions. Problems can relate to content (a complex word problem using fractions) or to the class (what to do with nonrecyclable trash from snacks or how to get class started right away).

- **Mailboxes** where students can leave each other notes or other "mail." Students of all ages still love getting a hand-written note.

- **Chalk paint walls** that students can adorn with "graffiti," hashtags, drawings, their names, and more. Clean and start over on a regular basis so it keeps feeling fresh and noticeable.

- **An "All About Us" bulletin board** with photos from home, drawings, or quotes. Again, modify the postings regularly to keep it interesting. Don't forget to add your own.

- **A garden "shelf"** with a few packs of seeds and other planting materials at the beginning of the year. Students are responsible for watering and plant care.

- **A Bitmoji or paper figure cut out of each student.** Use these endlessly: align them next to student jobs, post next to student work on the bulletin board, use for groupings, as a seating chart, to call on students, to show who is present/absent, and so on.

- There is no clear imprint by the students who use this space, such as student names, handwriting, or artwork.
- Your handwriting is more present on resources and walls than students'.
- Students rarely look at or add to what's on the walls.

- What's up on the walls matches the students who enter the room.
- Every student can see their work, handwriting, or image at least once on the walls.
- Your desk is not center stage. Students' spaces are the focal points.

## Want to know more about this strategy and others like it?

**Check out:** Emdin, Christopher. 2016. *For White Folks Who Teach in the Hood . . . and the Rest of Y'all Too: Reality Pedagogy and Urban Education.*

Smith, Dominique, Douglas Fisher, and Nancy Frey. 2015. *Better Than Carrots or Sticks: Restorative Practices for Positive Classroom Management.*

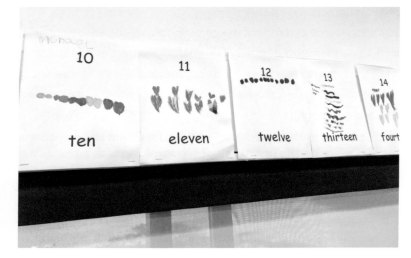

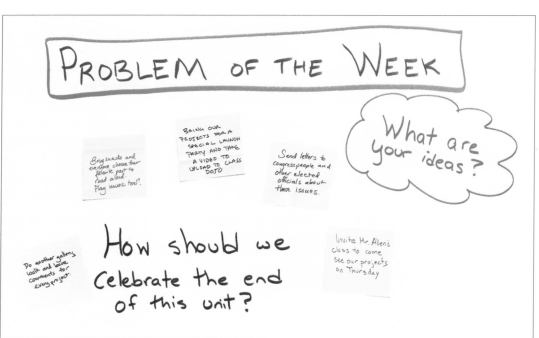

# 2.9 Organize Your Library

**Try This**

There are many systems and ideas out there for organizing your classroom library, and you can easily spend a few weeks researching all of them and then another few weeks making this space beautiful and functional. It's easy to feel overwhelmed! But making the library inviting, accessible, organized, and supportive for every reader in your room can be the difference between non-readers and readers leaving your room at the end of the year. Plan to set aside sufficient time to making it work, and reassure yourself that it doesn't have to all be in a day, week, or even a year. Building and maintaining a strong library will be an ongoing part of your teaching.

After a few weeks of getting to know your students as readers and choosing a system, it's time to organize. Create a clearly designated space for shelves and displays. Have your boxes or shelves of diverse books (diverse in terms of genre, level, and representation of a broad range of characters, authors, and settings) ready to go. (Use Lee & Low Book's Classroom Library Questionnaire [Educator Resources 2017] to help you assess and aim for an appropriately diverse range of books.) Make sure you have adequate shelves and bins/baskets before you start. If resources allow, invest in durable, heavy-weight plastic bins. Have a way to label books (stickers to write on or permanent markers) ready as well.

Enlist the help of a colleague, parent volunteer, and/or your students. Arrange books—cover out—in inviting bins and baskets by category and/or genre. Give away books that do not fit your class (because of level, topic, etc.). Place bins on shelves that are at your students' eye level whenever possible. Reserve the tops of shelves for displays, using stands to stably position books cover out.

Establish a checkout system for books or a way for you to keep track of what titles are with which students. Designate "book shopping" times.

Expect to spend time at the beginning and throughout the year teaching students how the library is organized, how to find books, how to take care of the books, and how to return them.

Send students home with books! It will be tempting to keep those preciously organized books in the confines of your room at all times. But that is not how robust readers are made. They need access to books (notice plural!) at all times. Give them (even older students) a big ziplock bag to store their books, celebrate those who remember their books the first day they bring them home, and reinforce this as needed.

**How do I know if this idea will help?**

- Students take a long time to choose books or can't easily find what they're looking for.
- You have taken on the role of finding books for students.
- The library is not a clearly defined or well-used space.
- Books aren't going home, or reading isn't happening at high volumes.

- Students "see" themselves in the library (their interests, levels of readability, and so on are reflected in the books that are included and in the organization system).
- Students can find books easily and get right to reading.
- Students check out books regularly that they want to and can read. Those books come back to the library when they are done reading.

This first-grade library has some books leveled in baskets, and every reader has lots of choice books in their book bin.

These first-graders also choose from book baskets organized by topic and genre, not just by level.

This fourth-grade classroom has almost all of the books arranged in bins based on author, topic, series, or cleverly titled student-driven topics. All of the books are leveled, but when a child goes to choose a book, their first thought is, "Who am I as a reader?" Then, once they've found a bin they are interested in exploring, they can check which are at the right level of readability.

This high school classroom library has higher shelves so students see titles at their eye level, and it's packed with current, high-interest, and diverse titles that teens want to read. Other high school classroom libraries might be grouped in labeled baskets. Some students curate these baskets with such labels as "Grab Your Bathing Suit, These Books Are Deep" and "Books Older Than Your Grandparents, aka Classics."

**How to try this with others**

- Have library organizing parties—groups of teachers can go room by room leveling and organizing books together. You'll start to get to know books—who wrote them, what level they are, and what topics to organize them into.
- Take a tour of other classroom libraries in your building on a learning walk with your colleagues. Reflect on what's working and what you might try in your own classroom.

# 2.10 Flexible Spaces for Creating and Collaborating

**Try This**

Flexible seating is a trend for a reason, but before investing in a bunch of beanbags, café tables, and a sofa, think carefully about your overall purpose. We want students to have a variety of spaces to work collaboratively, to work on their own, and to have some choice. So even beyond flexible seating, it's helpful to think in terms of flexible *spaces*—spaces that can adapt and be reconfigured easily and quickly by students. Students who can move are more engaged and are more open to learning. Create spaces for meeting areas for the whole class, small groups, and partnerships and for quiet work.

Sketch out what these different configurations could look like. If purchasing furniture, instead of going for variety, it's helpful to look for just one or two types of modular seating and one or two types of work surfaces—this actually increases the ways students can intersect, change postures, and create collaboratively and independently as the seating can fit together with multiple other pieces instead of needing to exist in isolation.

Keep it simple. No need to blow the budget—work with affordable, easy to replace, and durable materials when possible. Floor tiles, carpet squares, or cushions are easy to store to the side and easy for students to maneuver into work spaces of their choice. Milk crates are stackable and versatile. Putting casters on tables, desks, or chairs means students can move them as needed.

Even simpler: use desks you already have. Put twelve desks in a large group with two rows of six desks facing one another. Form a couple of groups of three to four desks for smaller groups. Then, place the rest of the desks in spaced-out corners or nooks for quiet work. You just created flexible spaces without spending a dime or more than fifteen minutes of sweat equity.

Grants, generous parent-teacher organizations, and sites like adoptaclassroom.org can help write the checks, so to speak, for luxurious new arrangements. But it's likely you'll have limited time, energy, and resources to redesign. If a neighbor is getting rid of a picnic table or a restaurant has a booth to offer, that might work too! The point is to provide options for a variety of work needs, easily managed by students so they feel ownership of the space.

**How do I know if this idea will help?**

- Seating arrangements are fixed. Students sit and work in the same space almost all of the time.
- Every student sits in the same kind of position, such as desks in groups of four.
- Students refer to the space as "your" room, not "our" room.
- Keeping students focused and on task at various parts of the lesson or day feels challenging.

- Students can choose where and how to sit during various parts of the period or day.

- Students use spaces according to what they need to do—single desks to work on their own, groups of desks to collaborate, and so on.

- There are fewer disruptions and less need for you to get students back on task.

Any seating spot can be a work space with a clipboard available as a writing surface.

**Adapt for K–5**

- Young students will enjoy helping create rules for various seating. For instance, if you have ball chairs, they might suggest that keeping one's feet on the floor will prevent others from being distracted by big bounces. A visual reminder next to that kind of seating will help remind students of what is expected in each spot.

- Plan on at least one lesson explaining each separate seating option, plus how and when to use it.

**Adapt for 6–8**

- Make desk arrangements easy to reconfigure for next class, especially if you share a room. Provide verbal and visual instructions, practice each step, and save time before the bell rings so you're not stuck doing this.

- Many middle school students are attracted to adultlike spaces. Your students will love café tables, comfy window seats, sofas, and so on. That said, many middle schools rip off the Band-Aid from the homey styles of elementary school, so any gesture toward nontraditional seating can go a long way.

Here's a classroom nook that any middle school student would love to sit in and read, plus there's a great reminder of how to use the space right on the wall.

**Adapt for 9–12**

- If you're near any college campus, take a tour or pop into some classrooms. Take note of the work spaces in hallways and public areas. You'll tend to see large tables surrounded by movable chairs versus stationary desks, cozy nooks in hallways with arm chairs, café tables, and private carrels. Or, check out any modern work space. Again, flexibility and variety are taking the place of traditional rows of cubicles. Even taking a look at a website like WeWork (which offers popular work spaces across the globe) will reveal stools, sofas, benches, tables, and private nooks all in one room. Use these to inspire your classroom setup. Know that teens crave and will respond to spaces they can manipulate as needed.

**How to try this with others**

- Visit one another's classroom to both generate and offer ideas. It is hard to see our own space with objective eyes—we are in it too much to "see" it clearly. Ideally you'll even stay to move furniture around together, then do the same in your room another day. It will go much faster and you'll have more fun.

*Want to know more about this strategy and others like it?*

**Check out:** Hare, Rebecca Louise, and Dr. Robert Dillon. 2016. *The Space: A Guide for Educators.*

Dillon, Robert W. 2016. *Redesigning Learning Spaces.*

# Management, Part 1 *Routines and Rituals*

## What is "management" in terms of routines and rituals, and why is it important?

If you find yourself frequently directing and redirecting your students, your teaching energy will be sapped, no matter how thoughtfully designed your classroom. If you've tried behavior charts, rewards, consequences, or calls home, these tactics may have worked for a bit, but it's likely that behavior soon started unraveling all over again. This chapter proposes an entirely different way to think about "classroom management." Rather than controlling students, we want classrooms where everyone has a voice and everyone thrives. In fact, although this chapter is titled with the commonly used term *management*, it is actually what this chapter helps us avoid. By putting routines and structures in place, students will feel safe, included, and independent, and our energy can be put toward teaching and learning.

You won't find strategies about rewards, punishments, or behavior charts here. Rewards and punishments are based on power and compliance. They can work to keep order, to an extent, but no one will have much fun, students won't thrive, you'll be exhausted trying to enforce them, and, most importantly, you won't help students grow as empowered and thoughtful citizens.

## What does the research say?

Rewards may work in the short term, but they tend to fail in the long term. Rewards don't build self-esteem, independence, or decision-making skills, and they ultimately lead to low motivation. We're in the business of building future citizens, and we all know these lifelong skills and competencies matter far more than getting a task done quickly.

Punishments are even more damaging. Punishments tend to lead to increased aggression and lack of cooperation. In the long term, punishments lead to students feeling less control over their lives and decreased self-esteem and confidence (Kohn 2018). Our students' emotional health and futures deserve better. We need to become aware of and work to address microaggressions—comments or actions that subtly express prejudice. We need to get away from a controlling system that damages kids instead of empowering them.

School suspension rates in this country reveal a system that mimics the prison system. Both penalize black, disabled, and male students more than any other (Hoffman 2012). Even preschools are suspending students of color at alarming rates (Malik 2017). Regardless of age and place, suspension rates affect already marginalized groups—such as students of color—the most. Not only do authoritarian, punitive systems not work, but more importantly, they are grossly unjust.

We're going to do better. We're going to look at ways that support our students to cultivate empathy, make smart choices, and build safe and healthy communities.

## What can happen as a result of the strategies in this chapter?

In this chapter, you will find strategies that teach students ways to treat themselves and others in healthy and empathic ways, that create consistent and predictable routines that make students feel safe and help them to take risks, that support students in independently taking on the learning, and that foster vibrant and caring communities, long term.

If that sounds like a la-la land, believe that it can happen. What will help, in this chapter more than any others, is to try these strategies with others. If you can come together as a grade team or department, or even better, as a building, to create consistent routines and practices, there's a huge payoff: a kind and responsible school. Let's join forces to build a school culture we all want to be in.

## Is this the goal for me?

- Do you answer "yes" and "sometimes" for most statements? Consider moving to the next chapter. You've got this!

- Do you have a mix of "yes," "sometimes," and "not yet" answers? This might be the goal for you.

- Do you answer "not yet" for most statements? Go back and try the checklists from the previous chapters. You're likely to enjoy greater success and see quicker results by focusing there.

## What do you notice?

| | Yes | Sometimes | Not yet |
|---|---|---|---|
| Students need few reminders of what to do, how to do it, and when to do it across various parts of the day/class. | ☐ | ☐ | ☐ |
| I spend an appropriate (minimal) amount of time redirecting students who are off task. | ☐ | ☐ | ☐ |
| Students can explain to a newcomer, a substitute, or a guest what to expect for different parts of the class. | ☐ | ☐ | ☐ |
| I reflect on and check for microaggressions by me and among students regularly, working toward an equitable environment for all. | ☐ | ☐ | ☐ |
| There are regular routines that cultivate community and empathy and few that instill hierarchy and power. | ☐ | ☐ | ☐ |

# 3.1 Cocreate Classroom Norms, Not Rules

We can start off the year with a set of rules, or we can begin by generating norms with our students. That seemingly small difference sends a profound message to students about the kind of classroom community we want to build and the role they play in it. Since they might seem similar, but in fact differ, let's look at rules versus norms:

| Classroom Rules | Classroom Norms |
| --- | --- |
| Teacher generated | Class generated |
| Imposed by teacher | Agreed to and upheld by everyone |
| Explained on the first day | Developed early on then revisited and revised across the year |
| Affect the rule breaker | Affect everyone |
| Designed to control students and instill compliance | Designed to influence students and cultivate respect for all |

Cocreating norms rather than presenting rules helps us shift to a cooperative, rather than top-down, classroom. And we don't have to sacrifice an orderly system to get there. Here's how:

1. Start with a classroom discussion about rules and fairness, especially if students are more accustomed to hearing a set of rules given by the teacher. You might ask one or two of the following: "What is a rule? When and who do rules help? When and who do rules hurt? When is it difficult to follow a rule? What could you do if a rule is hurtful? What kinds of rules do we want for our classroom so it is a place we all thrive?"

2. Have pairs or small groups of students name the qualities of the kind of classroom they want to be a part of. Model one or two if they need help getting started.

3. Bring the class together and share out, listing those qualities. Work together to combine certain qualities and categories. It works best when sets of norms contain no more than five.

4. Generate a list of concrete behaviors and actions that go with each quality. For example, *respect* might look like saying each other's names correctly, letting people finish their thoughts without interrupting, and no put-downs. Help the class come to consensus.

5. Ask what steps students would like to use if class members do not act according to the norms. Write those, too.

6. Decide how students will officially agree to the norms. Writing their name on the chart? Signing a contract? Sharing it with caregivers? Inviting in another class or an administrator and presenting the norms to them?

This list of norms won't cover every possible scenario. When you see the need for norms in more specific situations, such as when there is a substitute, go through the same process and create additional, more tailored sets of norms. Some possible areas:

- partner or group work
- free or choice time
- dealing with sensitive or confidential topics
- when there is a substitute
- when you feel confused or frustrated
- use of technology/cell phones.

Norms will need to be agreed to and then revisited at appropriate times, and with regularity. For example, before group work, review the norms for working together. At the end, ask the students to reflect on them. Do the norms need adjustments?

**How do I know if this idea will help?**
- Few students follow or refer to the existing set of classroom rules.
- It is difficult and/or exhausting to enforce your classroom rules.
- Rules are frequently broken, regardless of consequences.
- You spend a lot of time enforcing and reminding students about classroom rules.

**How do I know if this idea is working?**
- Students refer to a posted set of classroom norms.
- You hear students reminding one another of norms and appropriate behaviors.
- You revisit norms on a regular basis, and students are part of the discussion.
- Your norms are revised across the year.

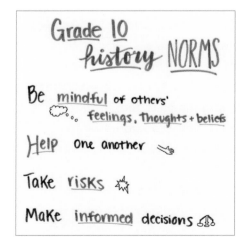

Grade 10 history NORMS

Be mindful of others' feelings, thoughts + beliefs

Help one another

Take risks

Make informed decisions

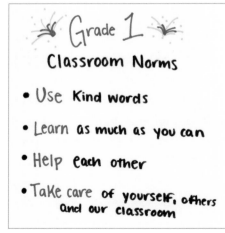

Grade 1

Classroom Norms

- Use kind words
- Learn as much as you can
- Help each other
- Take care of yourself, others and our classroom

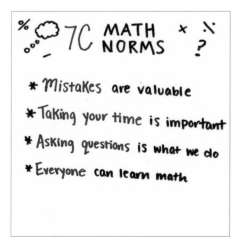

7C MATH NORMS

* Mistakes are valuable
* Taking your time is important
* Asking questions is what we do
* Everyone can learn math

| | |
|---|---|
| **Adapt for K–2** | • Young students are all about fairness. They can absolutely take part in these discussions—but keep the language user-friendly. Start small. Space the conversations out—don't try to have them all in one session.<br><br>• You may need to help extract overall qualities based on children's contributions to the conversation. You might provide a starter list of terms—*respectful, kind, fair*, and so on.<br><br>• Ask students to name what abstract norms look like. What do we do and say to be kind? Write those examples in a chart. Use visual reminders as often as possible. |
| **Adapt for 3–6** | • Start by having a whole-class discussion about rules, using the questions in the "Try This" section. Ask them, too, what kind of classroom do they want to be a part of? What does it look like? What qualities will they live by? Condense the qualities into about four or five overall. You might end up with something like: fair, kind, respectful, and hardworking.<br><br>• Put a sticky note with one of these qualities at each table or group. Then, ask each group to generate specific actions or behaviors for that quality. What does *respectful* look like? Have them write on chart paper or sticky notes. After five or so minutes, have groups rotate. They can add stars or smiley faces to the actions they agree with as well as adding more of their own.<br><br>• Use these lists and sticky notes to create a class document that can be revisited throughout the year. |
| **Adapt for 7–12** | • Involve students in discussions about compliance versus justice.<br><br>• Ask questions to prime their thinking before establishing norms. This is time well spent, even if you feel anxious to dive into curriculum!<br><br>• What is a rule?<br>   ◦ Should you follow rules? Why or why not?<br>   ◦ What if rules treat you or others unfairly? Should you follow them?<br>   ◦ What makes it safe to follow or not follow a rule that treats you or others unfairly? What makes it not safe?<br>   ◦ What can you do if you get into trouble for not following a rule that you believe treats you or other people unfairly?<br>   ◦ How are we going to use rules in our classroom? What rules should we use? What should we do if rules stop working?<br><br>• Acknowledge that those with privilege in our society might be able to exercise noncompliance with rules more easily than those without privilege. Get them thinking about rules and what we do when rules hurt other people. |
| **How to try this with others** | • Before launching into classroom norms, try the process with a professional learning community or at a staff meeting. As you do so, take notes on what feels doable and whether any steps might need to be added or deleted for your group of students. Reflect afterward: How did it go? If a part was hard for you all as adults, how will you scaffold it further for students? |

*Want to know more about this strategy and others like it?*

**Check out:** Shalaby, Carla. 2017. *Troublemakers: Lessons in Freedom from Young Children at School.*

Hertz, Christine, and Kristine Mraz. 2018. *Kids First from Day One: A Teacher's Guide to Today's Classroom.*

# 3.2 Teach Basic Routines, Even Ones Students "Should" Know

**Try This**

End the frustration of having to reexplain class procedures. Show students in specific steps exactly what you expect. Let them practice, and while they do so, coach in until they complete those moves and behaviors smoothly and without reminders.

First, take a day to pay attention to the very first moment things derail. Was it when students entered the room? When you asked them to pass in homework? When you started to teach the lesson? Jot down the first time things felt chaotic or a task took longer than it should.

Start here. This will be the basic procedure you will teach tomorrow. If these moments of going off the tracks tend to happen all at once, choose the one that is easiest for students to learn and that will have the most impact. Set them up for a quick success! For example, unpacking bags, sharpening a pencil, transitioning to a new activity, and handing in homework are high-yield procedures because all students are affected if they're not done smoothly, and they're fairly easy to improve.

Before teaching the procedure, try it yourself. Jot down exactly what you did in a series of concrete moves. Remember to consider what students will do when they've finished the task and the fact that they won't all finish at the same time. If you're asking yourself, "Why do I have to teach this? Any X grader knows how to enter a room!" take a deep breath. Students who have challenges are not being jerks. They need us.

Put yourself in the mindset of a few students with varied learning styles. Try the process again, considering any potential obstacles for those students. Jot down adjustments or variations that would help those students succeed. Make those the steps for everyone, not just for students with specific needs. For instance, if a student with grip issues has a hard time sharpening a pencil with a manual pencil sharpener, invest in an electric sharpener for everyone. Or, if a few students are too shy to find a replacement turn-and-talk partner when theirs is absent, add a new step: before talking to their partner, every student looks around and makes sure everyone has someone to talk to. Have them invite in a third or create a new pair if anyone is without.

Create a visual reminder of those steps on an anchor chart. Explain to students that you will all practice the process so it can become second nature. Model it, narrating the steps on the visual as you do so. As students practice, coach in. Practice it again if needed. Later, when students try it as part of the class, notice and praise what's working. Remind them of any steps they still need to work on. Keep practicing and providing feedback each day until the process becomes habitual.

- When it's time to (line up, work with a partner, hand in homework, etc.) students need reminders and coaching.
- You find yourself running out of time and not getting to everything on your instructional plan due to student behavior.
- Students regularly cause disruptions during routine tasks.

- You finish lessons without running out of time.
- Key procedures and behaviors happen without your reminders.
- Students remind one another of key behaviors and procedures.
- You see students referring to the visual reminder at appropriate times.
- Your instructional time is spent teaching skills beyond behavior and routines.

---

Unpacking Checklist:

- Take down your **chair**.

- Put **lunch and snack** (if you have one) in cubby.

- Put away **Blue Homework Folder**.

- Put your **book** in your **book box**.

- Put away your **backpack**.

- Put **notes** in the blue bin.

- Make your **lunch** choice.

- Read a **book** at your desk.

---

### *Starting a Book*

1. Select a *new book*.
2. *"Check Out"* your new book via the iPad/computer.
3. Get a *new bookmark*.
4. Fill out the bookmark.
5. Write the title of your book in your "Independent Reading Notebook."
6. Begin reading.

** If your book is falling apart, please place it in the book hospital so surgery can be performed. The book will return after it has fully recuperated.

---

## Working With Your Partner:

1. Read

2. Think

3. Talk

4. Write

| | |
|---|---|
| **Adapt for K–5** | • Ahead of time, on a separate sentence strip, write each step in the process you're teaching. With your class, talk through the steps, discussing why they are in that particular order. Then, mix up the sentence strips and have students help you put them in the correct order. Finally, have everyone try the process on their own. |
| | • Make anchor charts and visual reminders that are heavy on images, low on text. |
| | • For review, have one student walk through the procedure while you narrate it aloud. |
| | • Use a song to narrate the procedure. Replace the lyrics of any well-known song, such as "Row, Row, Row Your Boat" with a few key words that will remind students of the steps. |
| | • Introduce one behavior at a time, and practice it each day until it feels like a habit. |
| **Adapt for 6–12** | • Don't bypass teaching a behavior because students "should" know how to do it by now. Just teach into it, without judgment or shaming. If you can make it playful, with a wink in your eye and a lightness to your voice, you'll work wonders in melting resistance. |
| | • Think of the behavioral moves and procedures that will be especially important when navigating college and jobs. Handing things in, asking for help, listening to others, helping a classmate, and managing time are life skills worth addressing in class. |
| **How to try this with others** | • Create a list of class procedures that you all feel students need support with. Decide as a group how you will make expectations as consistent as possible and when you will teach into them. If you all see the same group of students, you might delegate the explicit teaching of various routines so time is not wasted. |

*Want to know more about this strategy and others like it?*

**Check out:** Anderson, Mike. 2015. The *First Six Weeks of School.*

Rapp, Whitney H. 2014. *Universal Design for Learning in Action: 100 Ways to Teach All Learners.*

# 3.3 Beginnings That Welcome and Set the Tone

Try This

Reflect back on your last few class periods (grades 6–12) or days (grades K–5):

- How did class time start?

- Did the beginning of class welcome students in and set the tone?

- Were students calm and content, or even joyous? (Yes, I said joyous. It's possible—read on!)

The first few minutes of class matter. If we leave the beginning moments up to chance, we risk losing students at the get-go. Be intentional in creating a replicable routine, one that will set a welcoming tone.

Your beginning routine might be as simple as looking each student in the eye and saying, "I'm glad you're here," before diving into the lesson. This is a small but significant move. But ideally there is more of a "soft start." Soft starts are just that—they soften the transition into the room by allowing a few minutes of a gentle activity, such as quiet reading, sharing of personal updates, games, and more. Which of the following routines speaks to you? What room would you want to enter most? Keep your routine as consistent as possible. Students have enough unpredictability and chaos in their lives. Let coming into your class be a comforting and known entity.

## Routines for beginning

- **Soft starts.** In his book, *The Curious Classroom,* Harvey "Smokey" Daniels (2017) uses the term *soft starts* to describe time in which students choose a quiet activity of interest to pursue on their own or in pairs. Soft starts set the stage for curious minds, and they allow students to independently gear up and ease into class. Sara Ahmed (Daniels and Ahmed 2015) has her students leave their shoes at the door—a symbolic and beloved routine for entering her room.

- **Fuel for Thought Fridays.** Post an inspirational or thought-provoking quote. Students can bring in their own, too. Let students write and talk about the quote, and/or do a "whip around" where students quickly share their thinking aloud to the group, moving around the room one by one.

- **Say a word.** Ask students to share one word with a partner or group about how they are feeling right then. It can relate to classroom work or it can simply be an emotional status check. Later, you might invite students to share the word with the class. Don't be surprised if at first the words are generalized basics such as *good*, *fine*, and *tired*. Model using more specific words—for example, *optimistic*, *frustrated*, or *serene*.

- **Write a status check.** You might ask students in grades 3–12 to take a few minutes to write the "status of their minds." As they jot down everything that is going on for them right then, students are often able to let go of stresses before transitioning to the work at hand.

- **Independent reading.** The amount of time students put eyes to print across their day is a solid predictor of their overall academic success. Ask them to get out their independent reading book or provide a choice of texts related to your content area. Set aside five to ten minutes at the beginning of class for students to quietly read.

- **Get them moving.** This is not just for the little people. Lead students (and eventually ask students to lead) stretches, jumping jacks, yoga or dance moves.

- **Share good news.** Students can share (with the class or with a partner) something that's going well in their lives.

- **Book buzz.** Model sharing a book that you loved. It can be related to class content or not—the point is simply to encourage the habit of reading and offering title suggestions. Say a bit about the book and what kind of reader might enjoy it, but don't give away the ending! After you've modeled several times, you might have students try. Have the students keep a running list of books they want to check out.

- **Meditation.** The value of stillness, breathing, and quieting one's mind is undisputed. And most kids get very little of that mental quiet. Lead students in a brief meditation. There are many apps and videos that can offer support.

- **Play a part of a podcast related to your content area.** There are so many podcasts out there—explore the range and find one appropriate for and interesting to your students. Decide each day if you can play just a minute or if you have more time.

- **Google Form polls or Plickers.** Provide a quick set of warm-up questions that connect to that day's learning. If you have a Smart Board, project the form results.

- **Person of the day.** This can rotate all year long with a variety of information shared by and about the student.

- **Morning meeting.** Gather the class at a rug or in a circle of desks, if possible, and do a greeting, play a game, review yesterday's learning, introduce today's learning, go over any "business" items, and/or have some Q and A time.

**How do I know if this idea will help?**

- Students wait for you to signal that class is starting.

- There is no regular routine for the start of class, or perhaps the routine is that kids come in and you start teaching, but this is rarely smooth or seamless.

- You feel frantic to get things ready at the beginning of class.

- There are lots of questions and stories for you right when kids walk in, and you're usually unable to address them all.

- When students enter, they come in without a smile. They may just move to a spot to sit without any pep in their step.

- Students know what is coming at the beginning and end of class.
- You don't rush to talk over students as they enter. They have something to do that they can handle on their own.
- Students enter with a smile or an eager look to you or a friend.
- You are able to meet students at the door.
- If you were to come into class a minute late, your students are doing what they're supposed to do. You're not worried.

3/8 Quickwrite
Can you fill most of your paper in 5 minutes?
"Whatever you are, be a good one."
- Abraham Lincoln

**Adapt for K–5**

- Create visual reminders for what students need to do upon entering the room.
- Aim for total independence. Keep practicing morning routines until students can complete them on their own, and resist the urge to step in and rescue.
- Students often enter wanting to tell you a story or detail. Let them know that time will be provided and remind them of the "need-tos" that should happen first, such as hanging up their backpack. Then, protect that time to hear their stories after procedures are completed.
- Try morning tubs with math manipulatives, MagnaTiles, Story Cubes, Interlox, Lego, playing cards, puzzles, stencils, magnetic letters, marbles, play dough, dice, dominoes, beads instead of morning work. Play is learning! Plus, when the first activity is play based, you tend to run into much less dawdling over backpacks and lunch selections. Make sure tubs can be stored in an accessible area so students can retrieve and put away tubs on their own.
- Once students are using the eight or ten minutes or so of morning routine independently, use this time to read with a student, model social interactions with groups, follow up with anyone who needs emotional or learning support, and more.

- Greet them at the door whenever possible. Older students still need and deserve this powerful recognition. You will gain valuable information as you observe how they carry themselves and who they walk in with—if anyone.

- Protect routines that bring everyone together and cement a sense of community. Investing in routines to get to know one another and checking the emotional pulse of the room is time well spent and will ensure greater gains in the curriculum overall. Don't shortchange community to race through curriculum.

- A middle or high school art class will likely need more start time built in than a math class. Consider what procedural time you will need to allow supply distribution and work setup.

- Students often arrive at staggered times depending on your bell transitions, how far they are traveling, and the culture of lateness in your building. Creating a starting routine separate from the day's learning provides a buffer that saves you from having to play catch-up with latecomers.

- Sometimes, let them choose, let them be, and listen. Consider a buffer minute or two during which students can socialize, sit with their thoughts, or organize their materials. If you can manage it, listen in. Take part. And let them know that when time is up, socializing is done.

How to try this
with others

- Visit the classrooms of other teachers who feel confident about their classroom start routines.

- At a staff meeting, have everyone quickly share out their start routines. List them. Circle back and ask people to share in more detail routines that are new to others.

- Some schools create soft start beginnings to the school day, playing fun music in the halls and allowing a dance party to start then and there! Discuss what a soft start might look like for the day, not just for individual classes.

## Want to know more about this strategy and others like it?

**Check out:** Anderson, Mike. 2015. *The First Six Weeks of School.*

Daniels, Harvey, and Sara K. Ahmed. 2015. *Upstanders: How to Engage Middle School Hearts and Minds with Inquiry.*

# 3.4 Endings That Provide Purposeful Closure and Reinforce Learning

**Try This**

Reflect back on your last few class periods (grades 6–12) or days (grades K–5):

- How did your day or class end?
- Did the ending provide an opportunity to ask questions or reflect on and reinforce the day's learning?

Decide what new or adjusted routine you want to create for the ending of your class period or day. As with beginning routines, choose something that you can easily replicate day after day, that feels time appropriate, and that has a concrete structure, such as a class meeting. Take sufficient time to introduce the new routine. Explain what your role will be and what students' roles will be. Practice with them, and offer feedback on what they did well. Adjust the routine as needed, but keep it as consistent as possible. Students have enough unpredictability and chaos in their lives. Let leaving your class be a comforting and known entity.

Routines for ending class include the following:

- As students work in class, or as you're reviewing their work later, keep an eye out for particularly striking answers, phrases, or passages. Take a picture or cut and paste a passage into a new document. For math and science, this might mean artfully solved problems or out-of-the-box thinking. For art, you might take pictures of entire pieces or close-ups of details that stand out. At the end of class, simply project one passage or snapshot. You may choose not to explain why it is being highlighted; let students determine the wow factor for themselves and carry that inspiration with them as they go (Gallagher and Kittle 2018).

- If you assign homework on a regular basis, save the last five minutes or so to let students get started. This can increase the chances of it being completed later on, and it also allows unforeseen questions to come up while you're there to help as opposed to later on when students are more likely to give up.

- Have students use SurveyMonkey, a scrap of paper, or a sticky note to rate themselves on a scale of 1 to 10 on their learning, participation, or understanding that day. They might provide a sentence or two explaining their rating. Or, they could write what they need to better understand the material. You can use that information for follow-up as needed. Asking them to include names will help you follow up with specific students.

- The minute paper or exit ticket: Ask students to answer one of the following (or other questions) on sticky notes or on a Google Form: What surprised you? What was the most important thing you learned today? What questions do you have? Use their answers to follow up with students or the whole class the next day.

- After a test, ask students to write down how they prepared in a few sentences. Make a slide-by-slide comparison with overall scores to help students understand the science of learning and what helpful study habits look like.

- My favorite mistake. You collect mistakes and display them anonymously, praising the effort and the learning taking place. Students can also share their mistakes. Celebrate errors and imperfect work as part of the learning process.

- Shout-outs. Time for the teacher and students to publicly praise one another. These are quick, specific acknowledgments for moments and gestures both big and small.

- Do not let students leave if there are food wrappers or other trash on desks or on the floor. Students need to be citizens of the world, and that includes picking up their own trash and not leaving it for you or a custodian. One teacher I work with introduces custodians, food service staff, and crossing guards to his students. He makes sure students refer to and address these essential staff members by their full names. Students will be more likely to pick up a soda can or gum wrapper, greet the crossing guard with respect, and thank the lunch aide when they see these people as respected adults and known entities. An added bonus is that your room will look neater at the end of the day!

**How do I know if this idea will help?**

- Class ends because the bell rings.

- Students begin packing their bags or cleaning up before you signal for these things to happen.

- You have students lingering with last-minute questions or comments after others have left or as you need to move on to the next thing.

- You feel rushed to explain last-minute details such as homework or other reminders as students leave class.

**How do I know if this idea is working?**

- Students fall into step at end of class—they know what is coming.

- You don't rush to talk over students as they leave class.

- You are able to say goodbye to them.

Check out these beautiful words! {

collected all of it! A sudden thought hit me. Wasn4 it a bit odd to have money in a fountian?
"Do you think it's weird to have coins in a fountian?" I asked my sis. She shrugged. But as soon as I splashed myself with water, the thought washed away. After me and my sis cooled off, we started collecting the money.
I saw my Mom walk over with a questioning look on her face. She looked at us, then back to us with all the money in our hands. She

Rebecca
1. Today I learned:
the three different types of rock and how they vary

2. My question:
what is the difference between extrusive and intrusive igneous rock?

Projecting skilled student work for all to see and exit tickets serve as purposeful endings to class.

| | |
|---|---|
| **Adapt for K–5** | • Create visual reminders for what students need to do when packing up for the day. Expect to practice and review these routines until they need few or no reminders.<br><br>• Aim for total independence. Keep practicing end-of-day routines until students can complete them on their own, and resist the urge to step in and rescue. |
| **Adapt for 6–12** | • Stay at the door to say goodbye whenever possible. Older students still need and deserve this powerful recognition. Also, you will gain valuable information as you observe how they carry themselves, who they're leaving with, and what last-minute questions they may ask.<br><br>• A middle or high school art or lab science class will likely need more end time built in than a math or English class. Consider what procedural time you will need to allow for collecting supplies and cleaning up so you're not rushing to do this on your own before the next class walks in.<br><br>• Resist the urge to cram in one more piece of material if you notice the class is about to end. Protect the closing time as students are already mentally "packing up" and that material is unlikely to be remembered.<br><br>• Go over homework and assignments at the beginning, not the end, of class. Students will be more attentive and you guarantee you won't run out of time to answer important questions.<br><br>• After a test, ask students to write down how they prepared in a few sentences. Make a slide-by-slide comparison with overall scores to help students understand the science of learning and what helpful study habits look like. |
| **How to try this with others** | • Talk to other teachers who feel confident about their classroom ending routines and who have classes where students move efficiently and independently through them. Even better, go visit and see routines in action.<br><br>• At a staff meeting, have everyone quickly share out their routine for ending class. List them. Circle back and ask people to share in more detail routines that are new to others. |

*Want to know more about this strategy and others like it?*

**Check out:** Anderson, Mike. 2015. *The First Six Weeks of School.*

# 3.5 Teach Students How to Do Things So You Don't Have to Do Them

**Try This**

Envision your dream classroom running like a well-oiled machine. In this fantasy, you are never interrupted with questions, every student knows exactly what to do, and you are able to facilitate learning from the sidelines while independent work flourishes.

Now, what would students need to know how to do for that to happen? List out everything students might possibly need to know, down to when and how to book shop, where to get notes from yesterday's class, what to do if a partner is absent, how to find something to write with or on, and so on. Treat each of these as an essential aspect of being an independent learner, and think through how you will teach your students to be successful in managing everything they need to know all on their own. Decide when and how you will teach those, and be as explicit as possible.

Use end-of-class and share times as opportunities to reflect on how things went with level of independence. You might model aloud how you weigh the options, such as, "I'm out of this particular kind of paper. Hmm . . . I could sit and do nothing and waste my writing time, or I could go get blank white paper and use that. Then, I could tell the teacher after writer's workshop that we are out of that paper choice." Seek the ideas of the classroom community and talk through possible solutions. Share out and highlight when you see a student solving problems and/or working independently.

Don't forgo the "why" behind these moves. If you are teaching students not to interrupt the teacher every time there is a problem, explain that interruptions take away from the learning time of the student and other students that the teacher is working with. Even older students need to understand this is not because we don't care or want to help.

**How do I know if this idea will help?**

- Independent work time is frequently interrupted by comments such as, "Where do I get . . . ?" or "I need . . ."
- You end up helping students with things they could manage on their own.
- It feels difficult to stick to your plan for helping a group or other scheduled instruction, because things take longer than expected.
- You find yourself explaining routines again and again or answering the same question several times.

- You finish what you started. Class activities go as planned, and the time you allocate for various parts of the class is consistent.

- When you are working with a student or small group, your attention is solely focused on them, and you are not pulled away with distractions or questions.

- You overhear students answering questions for one another, such as where to find something or what to do next.

- During independent work time and transitions, you see students taking care of themselves.

- When a student misses class, they know how to get caught up without asking you for help.

- Students can easily explain to visitors what to do, and a substitute teacher is able to supervise authentic independent work time.

- You hear from students who moved to the next grade band (such as middle school if you're in elementary, or college if you're in high school) that they felt ready for the transition and amount of independence expected therein.

## What should I do if I miss class?

☐ Go to the catch-up binder and get any handouts. I will try to put them there with your name on them. If I forget, just ask for them at the end of class.

☐ Take a copy of the lesson plan/notes. It is a rotating person's job to put them there each day.

☐ Make sure you have the contact info for at least two classmates. You can ask them for additional notes, too, or have them fill you in. Or, come to me at lunch. We all look out for each other in this class!

☐ Go to the class website on Edmodo. You'll find links to any videos, web pages, or additional resources there.

☐ Schedule a time to come see me if you miss more than one class. I'll want to make sure you're doing OK.

This eighth-grade teacher's syllabus clearly outlines what to do when students miss class. They review this the first week and again as needed so everyone knows just what to do.

**I finished my book, so I can...**

Retell · Reread · Search the · Choose

- Devote abundant time to teaching classroom procedures as essential—not add-ons.
- Kids are often able to do much more than we think. Take a day to note all the little things you do for a student that they could physically manage on their own, such as opening juice boxes or wiping up a spill or answering a question about how to spell a word.
- Pose questions back to the student, or the class if necessary: "How could we fix this?" or "What could you do next?"
- Expect to reteach—once is rarely enough.
- Visual reminders belong next to the relevant part of the room: for example, a chart on how to use the writing center should be next to the writing center.
- Asking students to approach at least three classmates with their question before asking you ("three before me") works only if any three random students have clear and consistent answers, and even then, those questions can serve as a distraction. Give enough support and visual reminders so that students can answer procedural questions in their own heads without interrupting others.

- Ask team members and administration to be as consistent as possible. For example, it will make everyone's lives easier if every seventh grader knows to check the class website for assignments when they miss class.
- Anticipate reteaching the routines of independence throughout the year.
- Middle school is a time when students can fall through the cracks if they need support with organization. Pull small groups of those who need additional support in remembering to hand in homework or other routines of independence.

- Consider the independence required in college. Ideally grade teams will meet so that the transition between ninth and twelfth grades builds up to a high degree of independence.

- Designate "office hours" during select lunch periods or before and after school. Coming to you for personalized questions and follow-up will help teens learn how to self-advocate and take initiative.

- At this point it is less essential that you align all expectations of independence with grade team members. Students will benefit from differentiating among various teachers and adults, just as they will later in life. Still, teach them how to successfully keep track of those various expectations in their notes—and by explicitly writing out what to do and when in the syllabus and on the class website.

*Want to know more about this strategy and others like it?*

**Check out:** Anderson, Mike. 2015. *The First Six Weeks of School.*

# 3.6 Three Steps to Cooperation

Try This

Although it makes me cringe, I can easily recall times I've tried to correct behavior and failed. I lectured, punished, yelled, and fixed in attempts to turn things around. It often backfired, leaving me bitter and students embarrassed or mad. Try this set of steps instead. Witness turnarounds that stick. When you follow these steps, it's remarkable how often resistance melts and cooperation ensues.

1. **Describe what you see** or describe the problem, keeping your words as objective and succinct as possible. "I see a YouTube video up on the Chromebook screen" or "The books are in a pile on the floor." No blaming, attacking, or sarcasm.

2. **Give information.** "The assignment is to look up articles. There are five minutes left for this activity" or "The books go back in the appropriate baskets."

3. **Say how you feel.** "I'm concerned when your time to learn is wasted" or "Books are important to all of us. I get frustrated seeing them on the floor where they can be stepped on."

Although these steps seem simple, they're not always easy. It's important not to convey a tone of disappointment or condescension. Make it clear that you see each student as capable and lovable and that there's simply a problem that needs fixing. Once you have named the problem, supplied relevant information, and shared how you feel, you create a space for the student to take care of it. Let them do so by walking away.

If you try this and it's not enough, consider:

- Are most of your interactions with this student requests or pointing out problems? Do they hear positive, inquisitive, and neutral comments from you as well?

- Is what you're asking them to do realistic and reasonable for their age, ability, and the time of day? Is there an adjustment that can be made?

- Are you sure they heard you and understood? Ask them, "Would you say back what I just told you?"

- Give choices. "There are five minutes left of work time. Do you want to quickly find two articles now or find one now and one during study hall?" "These books go back in different baskets. Do you want to pull those baskets first or take one book at a time over to shelves?"

- If the same misbehavior happens repeatedly, resist the urge to lecture or reexplain the issue in any detail. Say it in a word. "YouTube!" "Books!" They know what you mean.

*Want to know more about this strategy and others like it?*

**Check out:** Faber, Adele, and Elaine Mazlish. 1996. *How to Talk So Kids Can Learn at Home and in School.*

- Write a note. This works well for older students especially, but anyone may benefit. Reading the issue in writing can make it easier to absorb. "Books in baskets please."

- Channel humor or lightness. This often makes requests more palatable.

**How do I know if this idea will help?**

- Students act out frequently.

- The same rules are broken again and again, often by the same students.

- You lose your temper with students by yelling, shouting, or doling out punishments.

- Students tune you out when you try to deal with misbehavior.

- You consider certain students "problem" students.

**How do I know if this idea is working?**

- Students listen to you.

- You are working less and students are working more at following procedures and meeting expectations.

- Students who used to break norms are changing their behavior.

- There are still behaviors that you don't like, but you don't feel as anxious or unsure how to deal with them.

**Adapt for 6–12**

- Is there anyone who radiates more hostility than a teen about to be lectured? Expect some mild disbelief or outright shock when you do short and sweet, then move on.

- It is tempting to quickly correct or punish, but punishment and lecturing interfere with teens' ability to take responsibility, which they'll sorely need in the world. Keep that in mind to help you from regressing to less successful methods.

- Give teens chances to generate their own "fix." It might not be what you would do, but they will own it. For instance, you might immediately withhold technology access if you find several kids on games instead of reading an assigned article. See what they suggest. If they say they'll try again with an app to track computer usage, give it a chance.

**How to try this with others**

- If you have kids of your own, try this at home first. Our own children have seen us "fail" many times before!

- With a colleague or group of colleagues, commit to trying this a few times before you meet again. Jot down an informal transcript of how it goes so you can share and get feedback when you meet.

# 3.7　Teacher Notebook, Parts 1 and 2

Try This

**Part 1:** As a sanity-saving resource, keep a notebook on hand at all times. If (or really, when) you feel at the end of your mental rope, stop and get out your notebook. In full view of students, write. Rant or despair if you need to, and then write ideas for turning the situation around. Will you transition everyone into a few minutes of quiet reading time? Put your voice at a whisper volume? Dim the lights? Start over? Strategize your reset plan for a minute or two. You can give a simple explanation if anyone asks: "I just need a minute." It's OK if students wonder what is going on and need to wait for you.

Close the notebook and redirect the class as needed.

Escaping in a notebook for a minute or two serves two purposes. One is that you "count to ten" by creating some quiet space for yourself, and you're better able to hit the reset button when you stop writing. Another is that it shifts the tone of the room and can disrupt student-generated chaos. Students may wonder what you are writing. You might reassure them that you need to collect your thoughts so they see this as an option when they are at the end of their ropes, too.

**Part 2:** When you are ready to do more with your notebook, you can take it to the next level and use it for anecdotal notes.

Designate one page per student. Make it easy to find each student by alphabetizing, organizing by class, or using coded tabs. Let students know what this notebook is and show them the blank pages with their names. Explain you are using the pages to record both positive and negative observations. If they ask, tell them that each student's page will be kept confidential from other students and that although your notes aren't in service of a particular project, their actions help you to get to know them and what they need.

Use the notebook to record actions, small and big, positive and negative. Using a simple code will increase the chances you use it regularly enough to see patterns—*H* for helpful, *I* for including others, *OT* for on time, *L* for late, *T* for talking off task, and so on. Negative isolated incidents shouldn't merit much attention, but repeated behaviors are worth examining. Positive behaviors can be celebrated and noted anytime. Use these records to inform your follow-up with students, conferences, written recommendations, and more.

- You frequently feel stressed.

- You look at the clock and wonder how you'll get through X more minutes.

- What you're trying is not working.

- You've resorted to techniques that don't reflect your intentions.

**How do I know if this idea is working?**

- When things feel chaotic, you don't despair. You take a minute to jot and then regroup.

- Students may see the notebook as a signifier that things are past "acceptable," and you sense a quieting when it comes out.

- Your notebook is always handy and pages are filling up with quick jots.

- When it's time to head into a conference, individualized education program meeting, or to write a recommendation, you have anecdotal notes at the ready.

Hector

| | |
|---|---|
| 9/19 → | Helped Julia put markers back |
| 9/23 → | Hard time sitting at circle - got drink of water |
| 10/7 → | Cleaned up tables after Andrew's birthday celebration without asking |
| 10/8 → | Got restless during assembly - out of seat 3-4 times |
| 10/20 → | Easier time sitting during entire math center when it happens after recess |

Keeping note of students' small behaviors across the school year means this teacher focuses on authentic data, and she can see patterns of growth and need.

**How to try this with others**

- After trying notebooks for a week or two, bring them to a meeting. Share out and discuss what you're writing and how it's helped. Spend some time sharing what you've planned on paper to reset the class and which of those methods were most successful. When you're ready, commit to trying Phase 2 of the notebooks. Make them part of grade team meetings about students and see who else you can get to join you.

*Want to know more about this strategy and others like it?*

**Check out:** Gonzalez, Jennifer. 2017. "Notebooks for Classroom Management, Part 1." *Cult of Pedagogy.*

# "Call In" Hurtful Comments to Create a Safe and Kind Classroom Culture

Don't let hurtful comments go. Students are watching you to see if they can feel safe in your classroom. If you don't address hurtful words, racist or homophobic comments, and more, you become an adult who doesn't have their back.

However, outing such comments by immediately reprimanding the offender in front of others risks alienating or shaming students. Instead, call those students "in." When you hear racist comments, or anything unkind or offensive, take note and say something privately to the student in a nonblaming way: "You may not have meant it this way, but saying X is hurtful" or "I don't find that joke funny—let me explain why." Then, make sure the victim of the comment also knows you addressed the comment.

Later, teach the class about why such a comment is hurtful, without making any mention of the student who said it or the student it may have referred to. The lag time is to protect the victim so they are not publicly exposed. This also gives you time to decide how best to support this person who has been harmed.

Bring up the issue in a nonblaming way—operate on the assumption that the comment was made of ignorance, even if you suspect otherwise. Explain that you care about having a classroom that is a safe zone, free of words that hurt others. Empower students to be vigilant about such words outside of class, too.

Do your best to be honest with yourself about your own blind spots. Maybe you're highly alert to racist comments but sometimes don't react as quickly or don't hear the comments about trans or queer students. Make an effort to become mindful of the viewpoint of every student or potential student in your room. Trans students, queer students, immigrant students, disabled students—they are listening for your reaction to obviously hurtful comments like "that's so gay/retarded," "white trash," "ghetto," "loser," and less obviously hurtful phrases like "illegals," "good English," "terrorist," "you people," and "boys and girls."

Imagine the pain of not knowing you'd be safe in the bathroom, not being able to hold hands with a partner without fear, having your name frequently mispronounced. Consciously keep those perspectives

| Instead of saying . . . | Try . . . |
|---|---|
| Boys<br>Girls<br>You guys | Friends<br>Class<br>Readers, Writers, Scientists, Mathematicians, Artists, Athletes, etc. |
| Mother/Father<br>Parents | Caregivers<br>Families<br>Grown-ups<br>Guardians |
| Those students<br>Diverse students | All students |
| ELL student, dyslexic student, autistic student, ADHD student | Student's name |

in mind. This will help you be alert to the subtle microaggressions that our students are sadly subject to over and over again.

**How do I know if this idea will help?**

- You overhear obviously or subtly hurtful comments in class or in the hallways.
- You don't hear the comments, but students are reluctant to pair up with certain people or don't work well together. Comments are probably happening.
- One or more students stay isolated from others. They may put up physical walls such as hoodies, headphones, heads down on the desk, or simply not want to join the group. It may be that student has been the recipient of comments.
- You have called out comments publicly, and the comment maker has retreated or become less engaged.

**How do I know if this idea is working?**

- Students come to you about hurtful comments.
- You and your students identify microaggressions as such.
- Students call each other out on microaggressions and macroaggressions.
- You identify fewer comments as students are learning to rephrase their wording or censor insults completely.

**Adapt for K–2**

- It is vital that we are vigilant about addressing hurtful comments; however, remember that young children in particular often don't understand the power behind what they say or repeat.
- An age-appropriate desire for fairness can sometimes lead young children to overpolice classmates and exhaust your goodwill and patience. Since you likely teach explicit lessons on kindness already, reserve stepping in for times when the victim of the comment is not speaking up or when students are not aware of the damaging effect of their words.

**Adapt for 3–5**

- Every student knows curses and name-calling are mean. You (and they) may need to be more aware of how subtle comments can hurt. Referring to caregivers as "moms and dads" or separating students into groups of "boys and girls" makes assumptions about heteronormative families with two parents or that every child identifies as the gender they were assigned at birth. Explain what microaggressions are and what they sound like. Then hold students accountable for not using them.

**Adapt for 6–12**

- Don't be intimidated by older students' eye-rolling and scoffing at hearing you address comments that they feel are fairly innocuous. Microaggressions are never white noise to the person they insult.
- By middle school, students may delight in crude comments, inappropriate language, or racist/sexist/homophobic jokes. If you hear it, stop it in its tracks. If students try to defend themselves saying that it's just a joke, take the time to explain why it is hurtful to others.
- Watch these videos to jump-start an important discussion on microaggressions: "Microaggressions in the Classroom" by Dr. Yolanda Flores Niemann and Carla LynDale Carter (2017) and Ashante the Artist's, "I, Too, Am Harvard" (2014).

- Read about common microaggressions by teachers—Google "common microaggressions in the classroom" for some helpful lists—and discuss.

- As a staff, search online for the videos "Microaggressions in the Classroom" by Dr. Yolanda Flores Niemann and Carla LynDale Carter, and Ashante the Artist's, "I, Too, Am Harvard." Watch together and discuss.

- Use a prep period to sit in on a colleague's class, listening in on student conversation. It will be easier for you to hear the hurtful words because you aren't paying attention to everything under the sun. You and your colleague can decide if you or they will address the comments.

- Involve students by asking them what terms and words they hear that are hurtful to them, or to anyone. Learn what terms are used that you might not recognize.

*Want to know more about this strategy and others like it?*

**Check out:** Rademacher, Tom, and Dave Eggers. 2017. *It Won't Be Easy: An Exceedingly Honest (and Slightly Unprofessional) Love Letter to Teaching.*

Finley, Todd. 2019. "A Look at Implicit Bias and Microaggressions." *Edutopia.*

## 3.9 Deescalate Then Restore: How to Diffuse Conflict Then Set It Right Again

Try This

The first time I saw restorative justice in action, a group of eighth graders gathered in a circle to discuss a fight that had broken out earlier. Each student had a turn to talk about who had been hurt, what their needs were, and what steps needed to be taken to protect the community. Teachers in this building understood that the most egregious behavior comes from a place of hurt and need.

Indeed, the most exasperating and sometimes harmful student behavior is its own communication to us, telling us, "I don't know how to deal with this. I'm out of my league. I feel out of control." It's up to us to help. Ideally, you'll first do some reading about restorative justice practices and think how this could look across your school. But for now, think about how you can try a move that's aligned philosophically to restorative justice practices in your classroom.

**Deescalate:** If you encounter a student or group of students emotionally, verbally, or physically hurting others or the space, try this series of steps:

1. If it's only one student, call them off to the side or out of class. If it's a group, try to isolate a pair or, better yet, one student at a time. Avoid talking to them in front of their peers.

2. Speak in a low tone. Name your own feelings in the situation. "I feel/am _____ (emotion) when/that you _____ (behavior) because _____ (reason)."

3. Let them recount their own feelings using the same sentence frame or simply saying their emotion.

4. Listen. Try not to interrupt or correct. Circle back to helping them name their emotion if needed.

5. You might stop there and thank them for talking to you. Let them know you will revisit the conversation with them later that day and name the time the conversation will happen. Do this if you need to get back to the class or if you or the student are too emotionally fragile to calmly look at next steps.

6. Help the student reenter the class. Give them a task they can work on by themselves if reentering the group is likely to reignite the feeling and behavior.

7. If you have the time and mental bandwidth, move on to the next set of steps, or simply use this sentence frame: "I need you to _____ (request)." Let the student know what you need them to do to turn the situation around and make amends.

**Restore:** Try this series of steps to restore a sense of safety and trust and to restore appropriate behavior:

1. Help the student to acknowledge their behavior and how it might have affected others. Encourage specific language. Instead of "I acted out," help them get to "I threw my papers on the floor." "I ruined someone else's drawing." "I called a classmate mean names."

2. If appropriate, ask them to apologize to others. If this is likely to be a hollow gesture, however, you can skip this step. What is most important is that the student sees a vision for how to change in the future and makes amends when needed. A gesture or action might mean more than an apology.

3. Ask the student what they can commit to changing and doing in the future.

4. Create a plan for how the student can make amends by asking them to figure out how to make things right. Offer suggestions if needed.

5. Help follow up on the plan for making things right.

**How do I know if this idea will help?**

- When students hurt others, the behavior is either ignored or punished.
- Challenging behavior isn't occasional or isolated—it continues.
- You are unsure what to do when a student hurts others.

**How do I know if this idea is working?**

- Students are able to talk to you about their feelings and calm down.
- You feel able to deal with misbehaviors, even if the outcome isn't always ideal.
- Students take responsibility for their actions by finding ways to repair and restore.
- You see improvements as students learn new ways to handle frustrations and fears.

| Not a big deal: Try our problem-solving steps! | Big deal: Get an adult to help you |
|---|---|
| * Mess or spill | * Hurting yourself |
| * Not taking turns | * Hurting others |
| * Cutting in line | * I'm in danger |
| * Making loud noises | * Others are in danger |
| * Writing on your paper | * Breaking things |
| * Not sharing | |

← Saying mean things →

This chart helps younger students decide if a behavior warrants getting adults involved, if they can try to work it out on their own, or if they should simply let it go.

- Pick your battles. Not every situation warrants a full deescalation and restorative discussion. The ones, however, that are repeated, severe, or hurting others do warrant more than "Cut it out."

- When students become dysregulated, address it, but then quickly move on. Encourage students to see that tomorrow is a blank slate and a new day.

- Use the phrase "big deal" and "no big deal" to help students differentiate between times when an adult needs to be involved and when students can work on it themselves.

**Adapt for
6–12**

- Consider restorative justice practices that involve classroom communities and circles. Check out San Francisco's Unified School District's "Restorative Practices Whole School Implementation Guide" (2013) or the Schott Foundation's "Restorative Practices: Fostering Healthy Relationships & Promoting Positive Discipline in Schools" (2014). These are more involved but can be game changers in terms of helping students create and protect caring communities.

- Unless your school is using restorative justice practices, this may feel foreign to you and to students. Expect some surprise and push back from others. Be ready to explain the why and how of your new approach. Invite others in to try it with you.

**How to try this
with others**

- Read about restorative justice practices together. Discuss how these practices could look across a school.

- Commit to intervening with upcoming misbehaviors (the big ones, not the little ones) with restorative justice practices. Take notes on how it felt and what happened afterward. Come back together and share notes.

- Try restorative justice practices as a staff or department, addressing issues among yourselves and reflecting on how it felt.

- Include other school staff in using deescalation and restorative practices, including security guards, cafeteria workers, and more.

*Want to know
more about this
strategy and
others like it?*

**Check out:** Smith, Dominique, Douglas Fisher, and Nancy Frey. 2015. *Better Than Carrots or Sticks: Restorative Practices for Positive Classroom Management.*

# 3.10 Help Students Problem Solve

Try This

This strategy works when you and a student have a problem, when students have a problem with one another, or when there is a class-wide issue. When moving through these steps, remember that a student is not a problem that needs fixing, and you do not supply the answer on your own. Both parties take equal part. Yes, it takes longer than giving the fix yourself. But the payoff is well worth it: empowered and motivated student problem solvers.

1.  Talk about the student's feelings and needs. Don't discount them.

    a.  *This small step alone often calms meltdowns, dissolves tempers, and opens up space for the student to move on.* If a student is crying over a broken crayon, don't jump in with, "It's just a broken crayon! It still works!" Instead try, "That's frustrating when a whole crayon breaks. You can't hold it the same way, and it's harder to draw." Or with an older student, simply saying, "Uh-huh. That's tough," when they're upset. Even if you're thinking, "How do you not see this is your fault?" or "How can you be upset by this? It's not a big deal!" resist the urge. Letting students have their feelings can be a magical step in defusing and giving them the space to problem solve on their own.

    b.  If there is a bigger issue that still needs fixing, problem solve together. Head to step 2.

2.  Talk about your (other students' or teachers') feelings and needs. If it's yours, keep it brief.

3.  Generate a list of ways to move forward or solve the problem together. Write down *all* the suggestions.

4.  Review the list. Focus on solutions that all parties are willing to try.

5.  Write out the steps everyone will take as a plan of action.

This approach keeps students from being victims or enemies. It eliminates power struggles and the sense that one person is the winner and the other is the loser. It says, "We can problem solve together so that both of our needs are met."

Some tips to help you avoid common pitfalls and experience success:

*   Spend sufficient time acknowledging the student's feelings. They may need to hear their feelings discussed and named for a while before they feel calm and ready to move on. That said, you're the adult. It's appropriate and best to keep *your* feelings brief or you risk them tuning you out.

*   Let the student come up with the first solution. Welcome all of their ideas, and don't evaluate any of them. Every idea goes on the list. Make sure to write them down.

- If the student(s) can't come up with any solutions right then, circle back later. Give them time to think.
- When working through the suggestions, avoid any put-downs or judgments. Just say, "I wouldn't be comfortable with . . . because . . ."
- Follow through! "What steps do we need to take to get this going? What will we each do and when?" Write down the plan. Choose a time to follow up if needed.
- Remember that this takes much more time than just announcing a fix. But the long-term benefit of empowered students is well worth it.

**How do I know if this idea will help?**

- When problems arise, you rush to come up with a fix on the spot.
- Students come to you with problems big and small, and they expect you to solve things for them, even if they don't always like or follow up with your answer.
- The same problems occur again and again.
- Students are not sure how to take action when they have a problem.

**How do I know if this idea is working?**

- Problems often dissipate quickly as soon as you name the students' feelings and hear them out.
- Students come up with solutions to problems that never would have occurred to you.
- Students are facing problems on their own sometimes, without even coming to you.
- You hear less blaming of others for problems and more solution generating.
- It's taking more time to come to solutions, but the solutions work and stick.
- Students take pride in solving their own problems.

When you <u>ripped my book</u>,

I felt <u>mad</u>.

I would like <u>you to tape the pages</u>.

Provide sentence frames to help younger students voice their issue and a way to solve the issue.

When problem-solving with students, especially for bigger, long-term, or class-wide challenges, it can help to write down all the possible solutions.

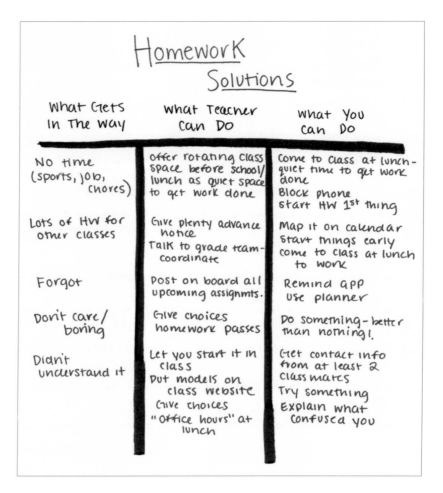

| What Gets In The Way | What Teacher Can Do | What You Can Do |
|---|---|---|
| No time (sports, job, chores) | Offer rotating class space before school/lunch as quiet space to get work done | Come to class at lunch-quiet time to get work done<br>Block phone<br>Start HW 1st thing |
| Lots of HW for other classes | Give plenty advance notice<br>Talk to grade team-coordinate | Map it on calendar<br>Start things early<br>Come to class at lunch to work |
| Forgot | Post on board all upcoming assignmts. | Remind app<br>Use planner |
| Don't care/boring | Give choices<br>homework passes | Do something-better than nothing! |
| Didn't understand it | Let you start it in class<br>Put models on class website<br>Give choices<br>"Office hours" at lunch | Get contact info from at least 2 classmates<br>Try something<br>Explain what confused you |

**Adapt for K–3**

- Younger students' stamina for talking through the entire problem will be short. Rely on the very first step as often as possible and see if that is enough. Frequently just hearing their emotions validated is enough to calm a younger student and allow them to move on.

- Try naming feelings for each student in a conflict and see if that lets them move on. Don't be surprised if their solution is wildly different than what you would have suggested. For example, "Sam, you want Elliot to listen to you. You really want him to play the game the way you like to play it. Elliot, you don't like it when Sam talks to you like he's the boss. You want to play the game your way sometimes." This exact scenario happened recently with two six-year-olds, who in sixty seconds went from tears to deciding to let Elliot be "boss" that time. They were perfectly happy with this solution and moved on.

**Adapt for 4–8**

- **Peace table.** Students involved in a disagreement with another student(s) can write out a structured response or draft that must include:
  - a brief summary of what it was about
  - how the writer feels ("When you _____, I felt _____. I would like _____.")
  - how the other person may feel ("When I _____, you might have felt _____. Maybe you would _____.")

- At a later time (that day if possible) the teacher meets with both parties. Often the time in between writing the conflict statements has been enough. Other times, the teacher may need to help name the feelings for each party. Then the teacher can say, "This is a dilemma! What can we do to make this better?"

Adapt for 9–12

- Try sentence starters that students finish in writing before meeting with you to discuss. These can help older students do some prethinking and get some emotions out of the way. For example:

  - "I'm angry that . . ."
  - "It hurt me when . . ."
  - "I'm afraid that . . ."
  - "I'm sorry about . . ."
  - "I wanted . . ."
  - "I understand that . . ."
  - "I appreciate you because . . ."

  If there is a pair of students with an issue, encourage them to use each of the sentence starters as a way to get past their own emotions and think about the other's perspective as well.

- If you have a problem with a group, consider assigning some work on the board for the rest of class while you meet with this group. This brief interaction can prevent a public scolding (which leads to resentment), and it is faster than waiting until they can join you later on.

- You can also use this method for impromptu conferences in class. Make sure you express that you are on this student's side. Saying, "I care about you, a lot! I want you to love science/math/Spanish as much as I do" isn't cheesy. It's a way to open up a teen to talking and participating in problem-solving.

How to try this with others

- Experiment with this approach by addressing a problem among staff, in your family or relationship, or even on your own. See how it feels to go through this process and take notes on what comes easily and what's harder. This will help you feel prepared to try it with your students, and it will engender empathy for the awkward or tricky parts.

- Commit to trying this for a conflict in your classroom this week. Keep notes and come back together with a colleague to reflect. If a colleague is feeling comfortable with this strategy, ask to visit and listen in during a prep session so you can see it in action. Make sure to let students know you are observing because they have expertise in problem-solving and that you are learning from them.

*Want to know more about this strategy and others like it?*

**Check out:** Smith, Dominique, Douglas Fisher, and Nancy Frey. 2015. *Better Than Carrots or Sticks: Restorative Practices for Positive Classroom Management.*

Faber, Adele, and Elaine Mazlish. 2017. *How to Talk So Kids Will Listen and Listen So Kids Will Talk.*

# Management, Part 2 *Relationship Building*

## Why is this important, and what do you need in place first?

It is hard to overstate the importance of building relationships with your students. This is the game-changing step in creating a classroom of thriving learners. Students won't learn unless they know we care about them.

And we do care about them! Students are why we are here. But that deep affection can get muddied or diluted when we are stressed, overwhelmed, or focusing on other things. That's why we start with taking care of ourselves, getting our rooms ready to welcome in students, and putting essential routines in place. Without those elements, you'll be half listening to your students with a distracted eye on what's next and preventing chaos. Now we are ready to turn to our kids and mean it when we say "I'm so happy you're here."

## What does the research say?

Taking time to show our students we care isn't an optional "extra"—it's the priority. When students feel valued by us and by one another, everything else becomes possible. John Hattie's research shows that teachers who have strong relationships with students have a strong impact on achievement (Hattie 2009). If we want to make a difference, we must foster positive relationships with all of our students. Every one. Years from now, this is what they (and we) will remember most fondly.

Relationship building isn't about being permissive and fun—it's about taking time to get to know students, believing they are each capable of success, fostering connections among them, and having empathy for who they are and what they feel.

Stay with this goal as long as you need. Return to it anytime. It will never be time wasted.

## Is this the goal for me?

- Do you respond "yes" and "sometimes" for most statements? Consider moving to the next chapter. You've got this!

- Do you have a mix of "yes," "sometimes," and "not yet" answers? This might be the goal for you.

- Do you answer "not yet" for most statements? Go back and try the checklists from previous chapters. You're likely to enjoy greater success and see quicker results by focusing there.

## What do you notice?

| | Yes | Sometimes | Not yet |
|---|---|---|---|
| I know at least two things about each of my students, neither of which have to do with grades or academic performance. | ☐ | ☐ | ☐ |
| I feel comfortable arranging my students into almost any group structure, knowing they will treat one another with respect. | ☐ | ☐ | ☐ |
| I'm confident that I'm saying everyone's name the way they want it to be said and that every student can do the same for one another. | ☐ | ☐ | ☐ |
| Students are deeply aware that I care about them and their well-being. | ☐ | ☐ | ☐ |

# 4.1 Say Their Name and Get It Right

**Try This**

Saying a student's name wrong isn't a little thing. It can be a microaggression, a potential embarrassment, and a substantial roadblock to helping students feel valued.

- Before meeting students, review their names. Use Google Translate's text to speech to hear unfamiliar names. When you meet students, have them say their name the way their family says it. Jot it down phonetically next to their name on your list. When you write their name, check that it's spelled correctly, including hyphens and accents.

- Make sure students can say and write each other's names correctly as well. Give them many opportunities to practice. Have them use tent cards the first week of school, with names and phonetic spellings on both sides so everyone can see.

- Use NameCoach or another online voice recorder so students can record their name to help others practice. Make it one of the first week's goals that everyone in the room can say (and write) each other's names correctly.

- Join the #mynamemyid campaign, which seeks to ensure every teacher gets every child's name right and respects each individual, language, and culture in this way.

- Practice asking every student, "Did I say your name correctly?"

- Remind students of their right to have their name pronounced correctly and to ask those around them, including adults, to say it the way it should sound.

- If you hear other teachers or students saying someone's name incorrectly, explain how to say it. Have them repeat it back to you. Write it out for them phonetically if you think they need it.

- Have students ask caregivers if there is a story behind their name.

- Double-check with caregivers at back-to-school night or fall conferences to make sure you're saying student names the way their families say them.

- Leave a phonetic list of student names along with the regular attendance list for substitutes and visitors. Make sure everyone is able to address others by name correctly every time.

**How do I know if this idea will help?**

- You hesitate to say certain student's names.

- Students don't use each other's names correctly or consistently.

- You have a hunch that not everyone knows everyone else's name.

- Students respond when you say their name.
- Students correct you and others when their name is mispronounced.
- English language learners and other students don't frequently change or modify their name from what is on the roster.
- Students all say each other's names the way they are meant to be said.
- You know stories and meanings behind student names.

Jesus
pronounced: Heh-soos

Kirsten
pronounced: KEER-stin

- As a staff, do this with your own names first. Share the way your name is said and written. If there's time, everyone could share a brief anecdote about their name, or what it means.
- After the first week of school, read through every student's name. Note any names that you can't universally agree upon in terms of pronunciation. By the next staff meeting, everyone should know those students' names.

*Want to know more about this strategy and others like it?*

**Check out:** Kay, Matthew R. 2018. *Not Light, But Fire: How to Lead Meaningful Race Conversations in the Classroom.*

# 4.2 Start Before the Start— Greet Them at the Door

**Try This**

Take a few minutes to greet students in the hallway before class. Make a mental note of who they're walking with, if anyone, and take a quick scan of their mood. This brief observation time will provide you with a wealth of information.

Don't be shy to show that you care and that you're happy to see students. NBA teams that do the most high fives also cooperate more, work better as a team, and win more games (Wagner 2019). It stands to reason the same gesture can work with kids, too. Give a high five, tell a corny joke, ask a question, or simply smile and say hi to each student as they enter. So that you don't worry about what is happening inside your room without you, create an established routine for what students should do until class officially begins (see Strategy 3.3, "Beginnings That Welcome and Set the Tone"). Taking out a book to read is always time well spent.

**How do I know if this idea will help?**

- Students have difficulty transitioning into your room.
- Students sometimes have a hard time working in pairs or groups.
- Some students are withdrawn. They may avoid contact with you or with others.
- Students may not acknowledge you or classmates outside of class.

**How do I know if this idea is working?**

- Students respond to your greeting.
- Students look for you as they come down the hall. They're expecting it!
- Students greet one another as they enter.
- Students ask you a question or initiate a greeting.
- You are able to use the insights gained by scanning who is walking with their head down, who is no longer walking with their friend, or who is eager and bounding into the room.
- You modify groupings and reach out to certain students according to these observations.

**Adapt for K–5**

- There are videos on YouTube of students entering classrooms, letting the teacher or a classmate greeter know if they want a fist bump, high five, hug, dance, or handshake. Letting students choose how much physical contact they want is a way to communicate that they are in control of their bodies and how others touch them, and it's a wildly popular way to set the tone for the day.

- If you have to switch classrooms throughout the day, do your best to have things prepared in advance (charts up on board before school starts, materials ready to go) so you can catch students entering the room. If logistics make this tough, create a few minutes in another part of your day when you can see students outside of the classroom setting. Stop by the cafeteria during lunch to circulate and say hi, choose a couple of afternoons to hang out by the front doors during dismissal, or make a point of following your students out of class at the end. The important thing is to create a small window of time to observe students and to greet them warmly outside of the demands of regular instruction.

- Resist the tendency to feel rejected or wounded if teens don't acknowledge you in return. Being dissed by a teen doesn't actually mean they don't want you there. Keep offering your hand or a smile, and eventually they may respond. Letting teens know you're out there because you care about them, and not because you're policing the hallways, is important.

**How to try this
with others**

- Invite your hallway colleagues (or the entire grade/school) to join you in making this greeting a routine. You will bear witness together to student behaviors that add to or contrast with what you notice in class. Also, you may get to greet a colleague or two as you occupy common spaces.

- If you share students with a colleague, compare notes about your observations of particular students.

- If you can't do this every day or for every class, establish a rotating schedule with a colleague. Maybe you will take turns standing outside your room after your prep and lunch. Or, you will greet students as they come in for the day, and your colleague will walk out with them.

# 4.3 Identity Webs

Try This

I remember seeing my teacher, Ms. Jackman, at the town pool. "She swims?" I thought with astonishment. Students often don't know their teachers as people, and sometimes they don't know much about one another. Identity webs are a great tool to counteract that anonymity and grow connections among students (and teachers!).

Start by making your own identity web to share with students. You can do this in front of them or create it in advance. Draw your name in the center of the board and then make connections to yourself around your name. You might include:

- family
- traditions
- celebrations
- hobbies/interests
- nationality/ethnicity
- gender
- physical traits
- personality traits
- passions
- favorite foods, books, sports teams
- how you treat others
- opinions, beliefs.

After seeing your example (and getting to know you a bit better!), have students create their own identity webs. You can keep adding to yours as they work to model the process and spark ideas. Challenge them to add as much they can in a specific time frame so they feel a sense of urgency.

Circulate, noting less obvious traits and courageous additions. Ask if anyone wants to be brave and share out something that is unique to them. Thank them for taking the risk. Have students keep adding to their own webs as others' spur their thinking.

After students have worked for a bit, ask them to circle two things that feel most important. Do the same on your own web.

As an adaptation or next lesson, you might discuss how the way we're seen by others can feel different from the way we see ourselves. Share some examples, and model adding this layer, in another color, to your own web. Ask students to do the same. Discuss how both viewpoints shape our identities.

Students can choose to share their webs, or they can opt out, depending on their comfort levels.

Revisit the identity webs across the year to help students reflect on how they see themselves, how others see them, and how both may shift over time.

**How do I know if this idea will help?**

- You don't know much about your students—or not much beyond the immediately obvious.
- Students don't know a lot about one another.
- Students assume they don't have much in common with others, based on qualities such as clothing choices, race, or gender.

**How do I know if this idea is working?**

- Students share surprising or brave details about themselves.
- Students establish new connections with classmates, discovering common ground they didn't know before.
- Students comment on aspects of your web and classmates' webs in later days, remembering details that stood out to them.
- Students articulate differences in the way they see themselves and the way others see them.

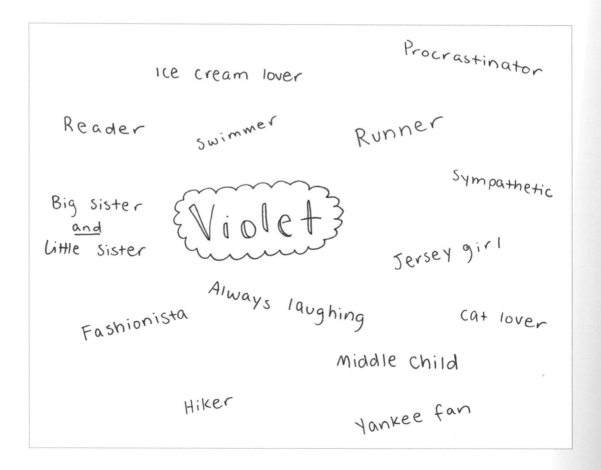

| | |
|---|---|
| **Adapt for K–5** | • If you teach K–1, include lots of sketches as opposed to words to represent details about yourself. You might add labels, but keep words limited so students feel comfortable drawing. |
| | • Have students ask a family member to create an identity web. This can be a good way for you to establish connections with caregivers and for young students to get to know their family members in new ways. |
| **Adapt for 6–12** | • Watch Chimamanda Ngozi Adichie's TED Talk, "The Danger of a Single Story" (2009) to enrich your discussion about the multiplicity of identity. |
| **How to try this with others** | • Create your own with other teachers. Share out. Do one each year to see how you are evolving. |
| | • Bring student identity web examples to your colleagues. Discuss what new information emerged. |

*Want to know more about this strategy and others like it?*

**Check out:** Daniels, Harvey, and Sara K. Ahmed. 2015. *Upstanders: How to Engage Middle School Hearts and Minds with Inquiry.*

# 4.4 Go to Them, Outside of Class

Try This
Commit to visiting your students outside the classroom at least once a week. Vary where you go so that you see everyone and explore different contexts. Observe, participate, socialize, and show enthusiasm. Make sure they see you, and introduce yourself as a guest in their world. Take mental notes of anything that you might bring back to the classroom. Bring back actual artifacts if appropriate.

- If your schedule is tight that week, make it an in-school visit during a prep period or lunch. Buy the school lunch on a day that students speak favorably about the menu choice and sit with them. Notice who sits with whom and who might need support in finding a tablemate. Stop by a class such as music or gym. Hang out at recess. Start a game with anyone who is by themselves. Stop by the basketball court on your way to your car and shoot hoops or cheer players on. Visit the aftercare facility and play a board game. These are fifteen-minute investments with guaranteed and substantial returns.

- When your schedule allows, go bigger. Get a ticket to the school play and take time to visit backstage and high-five the stage crew. Join a volunteer group. Attend a game, and not just the championship team but the junior varsity team with a losing streak. Consider home visits as a way to make a deeper connection with this student and their family.

- Finally, go into the community at large, especially if you don't live in the school neighborhood. Patronize the pizza place that students frequent, the barber shop or hair salon, the church, the bodega, the skateboarding park. Don't just buy a coffee and leave, though. Watch the interactions of people there. How are these places welcoming? What makes them inviting and safe for your kids? Recreate any of those aspects that you can in your classroom.

**How do I know if this idea will help?**

- You can't readily list an outside-of-class interest or frequented space for most of your students.

- You don't know where students go after school.

- Most of your "data" on students are numbers-based.

**How do I know if this idea is working?**

- Kids mention seeing you the next day in class.

- You receive invitations to anything: a barbecue, a game, a poetry slam. Remember, an invitation from a student is unlikely to arrive as an engraved document in the mail. It's more likely to sound like, "Hey, did you know there's a debate after school?"

- You know something about each of your students out of school life and interests.

Rosie makes a point of getting out on the playground and interacting with her students outside of class.

Stephen hasn't eaten lunch in the staff room in years. His classroom is a place where anyone can come eat and hang out.

**How to try this with others**

- Brainstorm a list of school activities and places. Decide which ones you'll each attend or visit and agree to meet up afterward and compare notes, or email/text each other a picture and notes.

- Find colleagues who live in the neighborhood. Ask for their suggestions of local spots. If you're lucky, get an invitation to join them, or skip the formalities and invite yourself.

*Want to know more about this strategy and others like it?*

**Check out:** Milner, H. Richard. 2012. *Start Where You Are, But Don't Stay There: Understanding Diversity, Opportunity Gaps, and Teaching in Today's Classrooms.*

# 4.5 Games and Sentence Starters That Build Connections Among Classmates

**Try This** Use a variety of warm-up exercises with students each day or class period until it feels like students all know and feel comfortable with one another. No need to limit these activities to the start of the year—they are valuable all the time. Once the game or activity has been done, it will take less time to repeat it another day.

## Games/Moving Activities

- **Formations:** A leader rings a bell, names the kind of grouping students need to create, and students form those groups as quickly as possible. As soon as students have formed a group, the leader calls out a new formation and students change groupings. For instance: "Get in groups of three." "Get in groups where everyone is wearing the same-color shoes." "Get in groups where everyone has the same number of letters in their name."

- **Giants, wizards, and elves:** This is a variation on rock, paper, scissors but is team based and involves more movement. It works best outside or in the gym. Create a centerline as well as a safety zone at the far end of each side. Before starting the game, the class decides on a posture that will signify giants, wizards, and elves. Each team takes one side. Teams huddle and choose a posture they will all create. Then they go to the centerline. At the count of three, each team performs the posture. Wizards beat giants, giants beat elves, elves beat wizards. Whoever loses has to run back to their safety zone before the other team tags them. Anyone tagged joins the other side.

- **Nonverbal lineup:** Students silently line up according to their birthdays (month and day), using hand gestures to communicate where each person should stand.

- **Famous pairs:** Generate a list of age-appropriate famous pairs with students, from Batman and Robin to Kim and Kanye. Write each name in the pair on each card, then tape one name to each student's back. Send students to circulate and ask one another questions about their unseen card until they find their partner.

- **Two truths and a lie:** Over the course of several days, students take turns telling the class two things about themselves that are true and one thing that is not. The class guesses which is the lie before the student reveals it.

- **One thing you like to do:** Taking turns, students go in front of the class or group and act out something they love to do without talking. The class guesses what activity it is.

- **Name tags plus:** Give students name tags every day for a few days or a week, and each day ask them to write something beyond just their name. Their favorite place on earth, someone who taught them something, something they love to do . . . Give them time to circulate and read each other's name tags.

> Alexis
> Favorite thing to do outside of school:
>
> Bake cookies and cakes with friends

> Maya
> My favorite Youtuber is Emma Chamberlain

- **Three-question interview:** As a class, generate three interview questions. Favorite movies, activities, and foods are all good, but see what they come up with. Assign partners and have students interview one another and record answers. Then, students introduce their partner to the class. This demands good listening skills! Add new questions and shift partners another day.

- **A warm wind blows:** Place chairs in a circle so there is a chair for each student, minus one. One student stands in the middle of the circle while everyone else sits. The student in the center says, "A warm wind blows for anyone who . . ." Anyone who matches the category comes to the center of the circle and then finds a new chair. Anyone who doesn't find a seat does the next sentence: "A warm wind blows for anyone who . . ." It may help to generate a few categories in advance, especially ones that will help them get to know one better.

- **Gesture name game:** Everyone stands in a circle. Each student says their name while making a gesture that shifts for each syllable of their names. The group repeats the student's name and gestures. The activity continues around the circle, doing each student's name and gestures before adding one more.

## Writing and talking routines that build connections

- Ask students to jot down and/or share happy news.

- Have students finish the sentence: "I'm looking forward to . . ."

- Set a time for students to recognize each other in positive ways. Students can use the sentence starters: "I really like how (classmate) . . ." "Something (classmate) did that helped me/others was . . ." "I appreciate (classmate) because . . ."

- Do a status check of what's on people's minds. Let students write for a few minutes, then share a line or two in pairs or as a class. Unloading on paper can help students transition to the work at hand, plus it builds empathy.

*Want to know more about this strategy and others like it?*

**Check out:** Anderson, Mike. 2015. *The First Six Weeks of School.*

Wilhelm, Jeffrey D., Rachel Bear, and Adam Fachler. 2019. *Planning Powerful Instruction, Grades 6–12: 7 Must-Make Moves to Transform How We Teach— and How Students Learn.*

**How do I know if this idea will help?**

- Class time is all work and no play.

- Students don't know each other well, or you don't know all of them well.

- There are not many opportunities for movement in your class—if so, choose the games here that get them up and out of their seats.

- Students are hesitant to pair up with any and all others in the class.

**How do I know if this idea is working?**

- You and students know each and every person's name and something about them.

- Students are comfortable being grouped with any other class member.

- Students enter class with a smile—they know there is often some fun at hand.

- Games can be run quickly, because students know the routines.

**Adapt for K–5**

- Ask what games students already know and play. Chances are many of them know a few of these, and that will save you time in teaching them the rules if your schedule is tight. Then, decide which new ones you'll introduce so you can build excitement and interest for all.

- Remember that dysregulated behavior is often a sign of feeling bored or restless. Bring out a new game anytime you sense students can benefit from a break, some movement, and some fun.

- Most of these games can be played outside, too. If you're concerned about taking away from class time, find students at recess and play then.

**Adapt for 6–12**

- Middle and high school students may seem reluctant to play "babyish" games, but know that they crave structured ways to connect. It is hard for them to overcome social anxiety or shyness, so trust that games are needed and wanted even if body language says otherwise. The more you can project an all-in attitude and ham it up, the more students will feel license to indulge their playful side too.

- Explain the rules to two or three games and then let students vote, or ask some of the shyer students to choose that day (just make it seem random that you asked them to choose). This will increase comfort levels at an awkward age.

- On the off chance you're wondering, they are *not* too old for this. Tweens and teens need playful and structured ways to move, to get to know one another, and to associate school with something other than stress or boredom.

**How to try this with others**

- Choose one or two to start off a professional learning community or staff meeting. See how it feels, how you might have encountered some anxiety or awkwardness, and what helped alleviate that.

- With a colleague, choose the same game to play in your separate classrooms. Report back on what went well and what may have been tricky. Which one will you try next?

- Consider visiting a colleague's class to "run" a game if you've done it and know it well. They can watch you and feel more comfortable running it on their own the next time.

# 4.6 Dot Activity: Find Out Which Students Need to Be Better Known

**Try This**

Ideally, gather with colleagues who share the same students as you. Put every student's name on a piece of paper, or have every teacher bring their class list. Teachers walk around, putting a dot next to any student's name with whom they have a strong relationship. To determine whether you have a strong relationship, ask yourself if you know at least three nonacademic things about that student.

Then, look over the lists. Where are the gaps? Which names have few or no dots? Commit to learning more about those kids over a specific time frame. Find out those students' interests, goals, and histories. Notice who those kids walk with in the halls, what books they're reading, and what they talk about. Take time to greet them and ask questions that don't have anything to do with academic content. Listen carefully. See other strategies in this chapter for getting to know students if needed.

At a following meeting, try this again. Share out your findings—how have things changed? Make a point to share positive findings as much as possible. Look for any remaining gaps on the list. Decide how to continue to minimize those gaps or how to raise the "dot" requirements before an upcoming meeting, such as being able to list three specific strengths per child.

**How do I know if this idea will help?**

- Most of your data on kids have to do with scores.
- You work in a large school or have a lot of students.
- Almost all or all of your interactions with students have to do with academic content.
- Even before doing this activity, you can foresee blank spaces next to student names.

**How do I know if this idea is working?**

- Students greet you outside of class.
- You can list 3–5 things about every student that have nothing to do with scores.
- Students come to your room outside of official class time (stopping by during lunch or after school).
- You are surprised to find out that one student helps her family in their restaurant after school, that another student loves anime, that another student is the oldest of five boys, that another student wants to try out for the play . .
- Students know similar details about you.
- You have a list of new information gathered about certain students, none of which relates to grades or scores.

**Put a dot if you know 3 things that __aren't__ academically related**

Carlos • • •
Danielle • • • •
Julia •
Ethan
Aniyah • • • • • • • •
Gabriel • • • • •
Fatima • • •
Taylor • •
Jaylen • • • • •

| Names w/out dots from last months meeting: | New information we've discovered: |
|---|---|
| Julia | * Best friends with Raquel<br>* Goes to art club<br>* Little sister in grade 3 |
| Ethan | * Loves Karate<br>* Helps dad at family store after school<br>* Always shares his snack |
| Taylor | * Huge Harry Potter fan<br>* Sits by herself at lunch some days<br>* Thinking about joining dance team |

After placing dots next to student names, teachers realized they needed to make more of an effort to get to know specific students.

A few weeks later, teachers were able to share out details about these students, before committing to keep adding to the list for even more names and with more personal details.

**Adapt for K–5**

- If you see the same group of students across the day, aim to learn one new thing about every student each week.
- As you work to connect with students, try to find them at recess, specials, lunch, or aftercare if you want to really delight them.

**Adapt for 6–12**

- You likely see a great number of students across the week, so realistically, aim to learn one thing about each student a month. Jot your learnings down in a little file on each student. This will help you remember these details, and it will help you track whether you learn about everyone.
- Older students are better skilled at being invisible, but don't take that as a sign that they don't want to be noticed. Keep at it so your students know you care, and don't let them fall off the radar even if they're putting up walls in every direction.

**How to try this with others**

- Designate a professional learning community or staff meeting for this purpose. Schedule a follow up within 2–4 weeks.
- If there are a high number of students without dots, or students share a large number of teachers, split up names. Make a point of choosing students that you personally may avoid or harbor sour feelings for (unconsciously, of course!) in order to reframe that relationship.

*Want to know more about this strategy and others like it?*

**Check out:** Fisher, Douglas, Nancy Frey, and Russell J. Quaglia. 2018. *Engagement by Design: Creating Learning Environments Where Students Thrive.*

# 4.7 Spread Good Gossip About Students

**Try This**
Every day for a week, choose a student to spread positive gossip about. Make sure you rotate through all of your students. When you hear a student's name frequently attached to negative reporting, make a point of starting with them.

Once you've determined who you'll gossip about, be on the lookout for positive anecdotes. Also, look back to any recent successes by that student. Then, sprinkle those into chitchat with other adults in the building. Tell the secretary about the kid who remembered his book every day that week, buzz at the staff meeting about the student who wrote five pages in one sitting, or mention to your principal that a student helped his classmate on a math problem. Make sure that student shines!

If you hear something good about a student from a colleague or another student, spread it like wildfire. Bring it back to the student, "Do you know what a little birdie told me?"

**How do I know if this idea will help?**

- Students are often brought up in conversation for what they're doing wrong.
- Some students have negative reputations.
- Already existing good gossip tends to reflect academically successful, nondisabled, white, cisgender students and neglects those in marginalized groups.
- You sense that some students don't feel like school is a place where they belong.

**How do I know if this idea is working?**

- Good gossip gets back to the student on its own.
- You overhear others spreading positive information about students, especially those who are not typically noticed for good things.
- You see new interest, energy, or attitudes from students.

---

Third-Grade Teachers

Good News of the Day

Hi All,

Some happy news to share: Aiden took our new student everywhere today, even giving up his time on the four square court to show him around the playground. If you see him, tell him Ms. G was so proud!

Ms. G

---

To guarantee good gossip gets around, an email to colleagues and/or caregivers is always an effective way to spread positive news. Do make sure you're not sharing information in this way that's considered private under the Family Educational Rights and Privacy Act.

| | |
|---|---|
| **Adapt for K–5** | • Go right from the positive moment to an adult, so that it gets back to kids quickly. |
| | • Include caregivers on the gossip first and foremost, and start with those who might feel particularly heartened to hear their child recognized. |
| | • Don't wait for something huge. Quick tidbits count! |
| **Adapt for 6–12** | • Praise can sound false if it isn't meaningful. Rather than sharing that a student remembered her book, share that she invited a lonely classmate into her group. |
| | • Older students' caregivers deserve to hear the good, too, and if your school does not do regular conferences, they may know very little about their child's academic life. Get working phone numbers and emails for caregivers during the first week of school so finding contact information is not a tedious task. |
| | • You have large numbers of students, and it will be only natural to find it easier to collect good gossip for some students more than others. Document who you talk about in this positive light to ensure you get around to everyone at least once during the year. |
| **How to try this with others** | • Decide on a number of students you will each commit to spreading gossip about until you meet next. At your next meeting, share out notes that you gathered, how you spread the gossip, and what you noticed from others and the student as a result. |
| | • Try this with someone on your staff who is frequently the subject of negative gossip. Start with an administrator, as they are common recipients of negative bashing. See what happens as you make a point of saying only positive things. |
| | • After trying it for a while with students, share out with the entire staff or grade team what you have tried and what results it garnered. Enlist more people to choose a student for good gossip. |

*Want to know more about this strategy and others like it?*

**Check out:** Moore, Eddie, Ali Michael, Marguerite W. Penick-Parks. 2018. *The Guide for White Women Who Teach Black Boys: Understanding, Connecting, Respecting.*

# 4.8 Know Students Better in Two Minutes

Because we all know there's never enough time, here's a two-minute strategy to use over ten days, twenty minutes total, that pays off big. Carve out two minutes and give this a try.

Dedicate two minutes a day to talking to students about anything other than school for ten days straight. Set a timer and let students know that after two minutes are up you will switch gears, and do so. But for those two minutes, get them *all* talking (or writing) about totally unacademic, completely non-curriculum-related stuff.

Try to hear as many voices a possible by asking a nonacademic question and having students jot then talk to partners while you circulate, listening in. Or, use an online survey. Or, ask a question that requires a one-word answer and have all students quickly share out. Post a longer student interest survey as a class assignment and share out one answer from the whole group each day. Do these all-in protocols so your two-minute time investment pays off for every kid, not just the quick and confident talkers.

Give a choice of questions whenever possible—it doesn't matter that they all have the same thing to share, just that they're sharing something! Share your own answers, too, so they're getting to know you as well.

Some questions you might pose:

- What's your favorite breakfast?
- If you could live anywhere, where would it be?
- If you could only eat one meal for the rest of your life what would it be?
- What makes you laugh the most?
- What's the last movie you saw?
- What's your favorite holiday?
- What's the strongest of your five senses?
- What makes you happy?
- What annoys you?
- What would you uninvent if you could?
- What's your favorite smell?

Be mindful of questions that would embarrass anyone, and for that reason, again, give choices. Even seemingly innocuous questions about favorite vacations or restaurants are uncomfortable if your family doesn't take trips or go out to eat.

After ten days, reflect on how it worked. What did you learn? What surprised you? How did the students react? If it felt good, keep doing it. If you worry about the time, make it a Friday thing.

**How do I know if this idea will help?**

- One hundred percent of class time is spent on curriculum and task management.
- You know your students academically, but that's about it.
- Students don't know much about you.
- You couldn't tell someone what your students watch, play, listen to, or love to eat.

**How do I know if this idea is working?**

- When you see a student outside of class, you have something to talk about other than schoolwork.
- You know things about your students that don't have to do with their academic performance.
- Students enjoy hearing one another's answers. New connections or friendships are forming.
- Students joke with you using their new knowledge—teasing you that your favorite breakfast is boring oatmeal or that you love Thanksgiving for the Macy's Day parade. Those jokes are made with affection, truly!

For the two-minute approach, choose a question or two from an interest survey such as the two surveys that can be found online at hein.pub/JoyfulTeacher (click on Companion Resources). Or, if you can afford it, take the time to ask all the questions and revisit them throughout the year.

**How to try this with others**

- Try this at a staff meeting, noticing how much information you're able to offer and glean about one another in just two minutes.
- You and a colleague each commit to trying this for a week. Join up afterward and reflect on what you learned, who you know better, and who may still be a bit of an unknown. Decide how you will keep relationship building using this or other strategies.

*Want to know more about this strategy and others like it?*

**Check out:** Smith, Dominique, Douglas Fisher, and Nancy Frey. 2015. *Better Than Carrots or Sticks: Restorative Practices for Positive Classroom Management.*

# 4.9 Reach Out Early On and Find Common Ground with Caregivers

My first year of teaching, I promised myself I would call every home weekly with positive feedback. This promise lasted about one week, before my "free" time became filled. Optional tasks dropped to the bottom of my to-do list. I regret, however, that I wasn't able to reframe those calls home as equally essential as lesson planning or going to the vending machine for a very needed candy bar. Opening up lines of communication with caregivers can create entry points with students that no other efforts can, and making calls is a small time investment that pays dividends for the rest of the year.

Make it a priority to open communication lines with caregivers at the beginning of the year. It will make the equally necessary follow-up so much easier and more effective when big stuff happens.

First, establish contact with a neutral greeting, a little bit about yourself, and how to best to contact you. Use the templates provided online for phone calls and written communication. Try to replicate what the school uses most often. If the school sends paper notices home in folders, do the same. If they send emails, do the same. The consistency ensures higher success rates of reaching every caregiver and that caregivers will see it as important communication.

In your communication with caregivers, emphasize your shared priority—their child! Refer to your students with respect, curiosity, enjoyment, and high expectations.

After a month or so, do your best to follow up with a quick note/email/text about something positive. It helps if you've kept a notebook where you've been collecting concrete details for each student (see Strategy 3.7, "Teacher Notebook, Parts 1 and 2").

Throughout the year, use your established communication to keep working together for your shared priority: that student and child. Some tips for communicating with caregivers:

- Defuse angry communication by acknowledging caregiver's feelings, no matter how irrational they seem. The simple phrase, "I'm so sorry that happened" works wonders. It does not say that you did something wrong, but it does say that you are sorry something happened to make the caregiver or their child feel hurt.

- Wait a day if at all possible to respond to emails if you are angry, hurt, or scared. If you must, compose a response, but wait until the next day and reread it before sending. Sometimes I haven't waited because I'm just so sure I'm right. And every time, I'm reminded why I should have waited.

- Use the home language whenever possible. The closer home language and the language of school align, the higher the chances of academic success. Don't just hit Google Translate—work to find someone who is fluent in the home language who can translate for you.

- Use a conversational tone and language. You aren't out to intimidate with academic acronyms and jargon. You want to invite caregiver's input and efforts by making it easy to understand and comfortable to respond. Have a colleague or family member read it over before you send. Ask what tone they think is being established. If it's anything other than respectful and inviting, try again.

- If you're calling with a concern, state the action as objectively as possible. Never name call or label. Words like *rude, lazy,* and *uncooperative* will create a wall between you and the caregiver and won't work to problem solve. See the online template to help you with communicating concerns in a productive way.

- Whether using email or calls or in person, listen more than speak—you may find out important information that sheds new light on the situation. Let caregivers feel your respect. Giving caregivers space to talk, even vent, will help them calm down if they're upset. If you are white and caregivers are people of color, it's especially important to recognize any uneven power dynamic by focusing on listening and asking questions. When caregivers are done talking, paraphrase what you heard to make sure you got it right.

- Offer up specific and student-friendly actions you will take, not just what the student can do to improve the situation. Make a plan of action for everyone involved and decide how you will follow up.

- Notice the term *caregivers* throughout this strategy. We can't assume moms, dads, or blood relatives are the main people in our students' lives. *Caregivers* is an all-encompassing term that includes any adult who takes part in raising that child. To that end, ask if there are others who should be included in emails or invited to conferences. Sometimes an older sibling, a grandparent, a coach, a babysitter, or a neighbor plays a big role and can add a needed perspective.

**How do I know if this idea will help?**

- Your first contact with a caregiver is often when things go wrong.

- You don't know who your students live with.

- You rely on the guidance counselor, homeroom teacher, or administrators to deal with caregiver communications.

- You dread talking to caregivers because they're often angry or upset.

**How do I know if this idea is working?**

- You can connect students to specific adults in their lives.

- You hear from caregivers who don't speak English, who haven't had much formal education, or who otherwise might be reluctant to communicate with teachers.

- Caregivers reach out to you with positive feedback and/or genuine and nonaccusatory concerns (in addition to the other stuff!).

- You initiate communication as often as caregivers do.

- You find yourself greeted more frequently around town or at school events.

 - Visit hein.pub/JoyfulTeacher and click on Companion Resources to access templates for phone calls and written communications.

*Want to know more about this strategy and others like it?*

**Check out:** Anderson, Mike. 2015. *The First Six Weeks of School.*

Souto-Manning, Mariana, and Jessica Martell. 2016. *Reading, Writing, and Talk: Inclusive Teaching Strategies for Diverse Learners, K–2.*

**Adapt for K-5**

- Some K–5 teachers communicate with caregivers on a daily basis regarding students' behavior. So that this doesn't become a reporting out of behavior, consider a system in which students take part by self-assessing, setting goals, and reflecting:
  - Students use reflection sheets they fill out with emoji-like symbols of how they felt that day.
  - Seesaw (kind of like a private social media account for you, students, and caregivers) is a way to message caregivers, post student work or pictures, have students record themselves reading their work, post their goals, and so on. You can post to everyone or just to specific students. You can print QR codes so each caregiver gets access to their child's work.

**Adapt for 6-8**

- You likely see a great number of students each week. Decide how you will reach caregivers regularly without letting it pile up. Will you call two families each day during your prep or right after school? Five or six each Thursday and Friday morning?
- Don't wait until you have big concerns before calling.

**Adapt for 9-12**

- Depending on your school size and culture, caregivers are probably less accustomed to hearing from individual teachers without a major concern. Calling with a specific and positive detail will make their day. Don't neglect this opportunity to spread goodwill!

**How to try this with others**

- Share notes with colleagues about students you have in common: Who you have reached out to and what was discussed. Are any students' families hearing from an overwhelming number of teachers? Is anyone hearing only negatives? Is anyone not hearing from teachers at all? Work to even out the balance and ensure caregivers are hearing positives more than negatives as much as possible.

---

## *Tech Integration Tip*

### CREATE A CLASS WEBSITE

A class website can improve communication with caregivers and students in addition to being an eco-friendly way to disseminate information. Weebly is a popular platform for many teachers, but there are also lots of options for free sites. Or, your school may provide something that is consistent for all classrooms. Don't be intimidated if you're not tech-savvy. This process can be done in less than an hour. Check out any simple web publishing platform for simple instructions. Make sure that all parties have internet access before designating this as your sole form of caregiver communication.

# 4.10 Uncover Brilliance in Students Who May Be Seen as "Less Than"

**Try This**

Use a strength-based approach to help everyone in your room feel valued and to see the positives in all of their classmates. It takes careful thought and an open mind, however, to work against the labels that can demean or pigeonhole students in negative ways. Think through the following for all of your students, but start with those who are most likely to question if school is a place for them, or whether they belong.

- What's unique about this student? What might they need support with? How might those challenges also be strengths? For example:
  - They speak another language and/or may be an expert about another country or culture.
  - A child with autism may be able to focus on small details and can remember those details well.
  - A student with dyslexia may have strong artistic skills.
  - A student with attention deficit disorder may not be afraid to seek novel experiences and brings creative skills to any group project.
  - A student with Down syndrome may be a wonderful greeter to any newcomer because of their contagious smile and warm personality.
  - A quiet, shy student may take their time to formulate answers and bring new thinking to conversations after others have spoken.
  - A talkative student may break the ice and jump-start conversations.

Let these students know that their unique strength adds to the classroom and can help others. Do this in a one-on-one conversation as you point out a specific strength in their work or behavior. You can also use written feedback, but make sure there is also a face-to-face acknowledgment.

Let the students know about each other's assets. Show them that there are aspects of brilliance in each one of their classmates. As you wrap up each class, you might make a point of highlighting a few students' unique strengths.

Keep your eye trained and tuned to authentic and unexpected assets in each and every student. But make sure you start and stay with those who are accustomed to hearing deficits and gaps. They need this the most.

- Students subtly or outright communicate that they are not good at certain skills, and those skills are associated with a difference.
- You teach inclusion classes.
- Students do not treat everyone in the room with equal kindness and respect.
- You hesitate to let students form their own groups because you suspect some students would be left out.

- Students light up, smiling or sitting up straighter, at hearing their unique strengths noted by others.
- Students mention their own or others' strengths.
- Students are discussed by other teachers or staff members in specific and objective ways, not by reputation.
- Students are not referred to or automatically labeled by their difference or disability.

This teacher takes some time each month or so to think through specific, individual strengths about each child. Getting in the mindset of looking for positives as opposed to falling back on negative labels has helped her genuinely reframe the way she looks at students.

| Students | Stand Out Qualities from January |
|---|---|
| Maya | Enjoys entertaining others with jokes & stories |
| Christian | Remembers tons of details from the books he's reading |
| Angelo | Loves to help others during math & at snack time |
| Marco | Keeps great track of time |
| Jamie, Kate | Both work well by themselves and can stay really focused |
| Jenn, Abigail | Get along well with others in groups |
| Adam | Organizes thoughts & materials well (backpack & desk) |
| Jaiden | Focuses on his work even when hallways are loud or announcements are on |

- Start by listing shared students with known disabilities or differences that aren't typically seen as strengths. Generate as many assets as you can about those students in advance.

- Ask special education, bilingual, paraprofessionals, or other support staff to join you as they often have intimate knowledge about these students, including specific strengths.

## Want to know more about this strategy and others like it?

**Check out:** Lenz, Laura. 2016. "A Strength-Based Approach to Teaching English Learners." *Cult of Pedagogy.*

Solomon, Andrew. 2012. *Far from the Tree: Parents, Children, and the Search for Identity.*

# 5 Independent Practice

## What is independent practice, and why is it important?

Students become better scientists, artists, readers, athletes, writers, historians, and mathematicians by *doing* those things. The ones doing the most (whether discussing, reading, writing, performing, painting, problem-solving) are the ones learning the most. If students are passively observing and listening while we do the heavy lifting, we have not granted them the opportunity to really learn. But simply handing over the reins is rarely that easy.

When timing myself speaking in front of the whole class, I'm dismayed to realize I typically talk far more than I planned. Sometimes the student eyes glazing over clue me in. But other times, the adrenaline of being in front of other people means I talk too much, despite knowing it's not effective. We all tend to grossly underestimate just how much our voices fill up class time. Whether we are pressured to cover more information, reluctant to cede control, or unsure how to get students engaged, we stay at the helm. Unless we get students independently doing and trying, there's no space for us to really pay attention to them—we're too busy talking! But with less leading comes more listening. Not to mention, student engagement soars.

And selfishly, wouldn't it be nice if students were the ones who needed a chocolate or caffeine fix at 3 p.m. instead of us, because they've been so actively engaged in learning all day?

## What does the research say?

Students may feel as though they're learning in a teacher-driven classroom when there's a great deal of content delivered in a captivating way. However, the truth is that students, across levels and content areas, learn more when they are actively engaged in the process (Reuell 2019). Students must be the ones doing, then, to be learning.

John Hattie's (2009) research shows that independent work time has a significant impact on learning outcomes. All students, no matter what age, are hardwired to want independence. We need to grant them the space to make choices and do things within safe boundaries. And we need to support their independence so they can truly learn.

Maria Montessori believed in helping children to help themselves in all aspects of learning (Montessori 1995). John Dewey's pedagogy was based on the idea that learning is doing (not passively listening) (Dewey 2018). Vygotsky's theory of teaching to the zone of proximal development is based on helping students move from supported learning to independence (Karpov 2014). The gradual release of responsibility (Pearson and Gallagher 1983) is also designed to incrementally move students toward independence. More recently, we see the movement toward project-based learning (Larmer, Mergendoller, and Boss 2015) and inquiry circles (Harvey and Daniels, 2009) as ways to shift to students' independence in the classroom.

## What do we need in place before independent practice can work?

Nurturing independence means helping students to feel both valued and capable. If we stay at the helm, we don't show students we believe they can do more than sit and listen. When our classrooms are communities with routines in place, we can loosen the reins! And, when we've developed relationships with students, they will be ready to take part in the learning. Without knowing we care about them, students are unlikely to dive in.

Although you can work on this goal along with the planning or formative assessment chapters (6 and 7), it will help if you prioritize independence and student time on task beforehand. This chapter will show how to shift the balance so that students take the reins, whether in reading a text, swinging a bat, painting a portrait, or solving a problem.

## Is this the goal for me?

- Do you answer "yes" and "sometimes" for most questions? Consider moving to the next chapter. You've got this!

- Do you have a mix of "yes," "sometimes," and "not yet" answers? This might be the goal for you.

- Do you answer "not yet" for most of these questions? Go back and try the checklists from the previous chapters. You're likely to enjoy greater success and see quicker results by focusing there.

## What do you notice?

| | Yes | Sometimes | Not yet |
|---|---|---|---|
| The bulk of class time is students working on their own or in groups. I am "on" in front of the whole class briefly, if at all. | ☐ | ☐ | ☐ |
| Students transition into independent practice smoothly and efficiently. | ☐ | ☐ | ☐ |
| Students work as hard or harder than I do during class time. | ☐ | ☐ | ☐ |
| Most students produce a high volume of work on a consistent basis. | ☐ | ☐ | ☐ |
| I'm able to use independent practice time to coach students and provide immediate feedback. | ☐ | ☐ | ☐ |
| Most of my students are able to focus on the work at hand for at least as many minutes as their age, be pulled back for a quick refocusing point, and jump back in again for as many minutes. | ☐ | ☐ | ☐ |

# 5.1  Ask Yourself: "Can They Do This?"

**Try This**

Tying our students' shoes, reminding them of due dates, checking their work . . . these are all the moves of well-intentioned adults. But ultimately, doing these things for our students robs them of the opportunity to do it themselves. Confidence comes from competence. Teaching our students how to do things themselves is the first step.

But, speaking from experience as a parent who caught herself pouring cereal for her six-year-old just this morning and brushed his teeth last night, we first need to take a hard look at what our students can start doing.

For as little as a period, or as long as a school day, track everything you do for students and whether they can do that thing on their own. Passing out papers, greeting a visitor, getting out supplies, cleaning up a mess, as well as more challenging tasks like managing a conflict, determining next steps—these are all doable by our students, even though it's tempting to just do it ourselves. This is similar to Strategy 3.2, in which you teach basic routines. This time, however, you're keeping a keen eye out for those processes that you've been taking care of on your own—things you handle, but don't need to. Students are ready for more!

Each time you catch yourself doing something for your students, ask yourself: "Can my students do this on their own?" If yes, then you will decide:

- **Can they be shown how to do it on their own in a step-by-step model?**
- **Can a classmate show them how to do it?**
- **Can a visual show them how to do it?**

If your list reveals how much you're doing, choose just a few things to start turning over to kids. Start with the simplest of tasks that will have the highest success, such as gathering materials or cleaning up supplies. Decide how you will allow students to do this thing for themselves and how much you will guide and supervise. As in Strategy 3.2, resist the urge to rescue!

When you announce students' new role, speak with utter confidence in their abilities. Watch them as they try, to see where they need support, but don't jump in and fix right away.

You might announce their new roles by making today's arbitrary date of delegation seem planned: "Since we are five-eighths of the way through the year, it's time for you all to start being the ones to (greet visitors/distribute materials/collect materials/record notes for anyone who was absent), and today I'll show you what that looks like." Talk to them about why they are given new responsibilities so they know it's not punitive—it's because you care about them and value their growth in all aspects of life.

> *Never help a child with a task at which he feels he can succeed.*
>
> —MARIA MONTESSORI,
> *The Absorbent Mind*

Enjoy hearing students say, "I did it!" If they're less than enthusiastic, trust the process and enjoy any newfound time on your hands to do things like give meaningful feedback, plan, and get a cup of coffee.

**How do I know if this idea will help?**

- You do for students what they can do for themselves.
- You find yourself jumping in to fix problems, thinking, "It's easier if I just do it myself."
- You find yourself frustrated by how much you take on.
- Students ask you for help frequently.
- Your plans for independent work time are often interrupted by questions.

**How do I know if this idea is working?**

- Students take on new responsibilities.
- You have a game plan for what you'll help students take on in the coming months.
- If you share these new roles with caregivers, you may hear surprise and delight that their children are so capable.
- As you watch students try doing things for themselves, you discover modifications and supports that will help them each succeed, such as a step stool to reach the upper shelves or a digital clock to help everyone watch the time.
- You hear, "I did it!" or see students taking on roles that you used to play.

| What I'm doing that kids can do for themselves | How they can do it on their own |
|---|---|
| Asking everyone what lunch choice they want | Put clipboard sign-up by door or pass it around |
| Collecting homework | Show them marked bin & do reminders first week |
| Tying shoes | Have Ryan & Gavin teach others during snack time |
| Refilling supplies in writing center | Add this to job chart - show them supply closet and how to let me know when supply is low |

**Adapt for K-5**

Reminder that students can:

- Clean up messes.
- Tidy up desks, backpacks, and classroom areas.
- Distribute materials, snacks, handouts.
- Write thank-you notes.
- Ask for help at appropriate times.
- Notice when others need help and offer it.
- Open and hold doors for others.
- Greet visitors.
- List and assemble items they'll need rather than you putting everything on tables for them.
- Be resources for one another.

**Adapt for 6-8**

Reminder that students in these grades can do all of the above, and:

- Create invitations and plan classroom events.
- Organize and clean up classroom spaces.
- Volunteer in and out of the school building.
- Come talk to the teacher if they are unhappy or confused about a grade or assignment.
- Speak up for themselves.
- Convey gratitude.
- Be resources for one another.
- If they have the same responsibilities as the year before, determine what else they can do. Set the bar high.

**Adapt for 9-12**

Reminder that students in these grades can do all of the above, and:

- Plan across their week for assignments and due dates.
- Seek help and advice.
- Find appropriate adults in the building for information regarding schedules, requirements, coursework, and so on.
- Fill out forms that need to be signed.
- Make arrangements for any planned absences such as games or field trips, as well as gather work after an absence.
- Be resources for one another.

- Seek out teachers known as tough *and* admired, or whose classrooms seem to run like well-oiled machines. Ask them, or better yet, observe the students in action to see what their students take care of on their own.

- Involve special education staff to find out what supports they suggest for students with different needs. Special education teachers, therapists, and support staff often bring a treasure trove of suggestions that will help any child feel successful in taking on more responsibilities.

- As a grade team, decide what you will collectively turn over to students each month for the remainder of the year. Keep ramping up students' independence across the year, and know that when students are asked to do these things on their own in every class, they will fall into habits with more ease.

# 5.2 Build Up to Longer Stretches of Independent Work

**Try This**

Without prompting or encouragement, time how long the majority of the class is able to work independently, staying focused on the task at hand. Pencil to paper, fingers to keyboard, paintbrush to canvas, hands to instrument, or eyes to print. How many minutes? Jot that number down.

Before moving on to the next thing, explain to students that this number is now the number to beat. Make it an explicit goal that every member of the class writes, plays, scrimmages, sketches, problem solves, or reads more and focuses for longer stretches of time on their own. Every day, keep track of the number of minutes as you all work to reach that goal. Celebrate growth and keep the expectation high and consistent. Twenty minutes of independent work is doable for first *and* twelfth graders!

**How do I know if this idea will help?**

- Students run out of steam after just a few minutes.
- You hear "I'm done" early and often during independent work time.
- Students are producing low volumes of writing, or they are reading at low volumes.

**How do I know if this idea is working?**

- You have specific data on how independent work time is used, such as minutes per day of time on task across a month or more.
- Data show an increasing amount of time on task.
- Students are filling up pages in notebooks, racking up page counts in books, completing more labs, or doing more in-depth math problems than before.
- You are able to work with small groups and individuals because the rest of the class is engaged and on task.

## How Many Minutes Focused, Independent Work Time?

| Date | # minutes | Notes |
|------|-----------|-------|
| 9/9 | 11 | Research & note-taking |
| 9/10 | 14 | Drafting essay - focused! |
| 9/11 | 9 | Lots of announcements |
| 9/12 | 13 | A few distracted - once we met they got back on track! |
| 9/13 | n/a | assembly |
| 9/16 | 10 | some forgot notebooks → quickly off-task |
| 9/17 | 19 | resources on edmodo helped a lot |
| 9/18 | 14 | Letting them choose groups → un-successful |
| 9/19 | 17 | Seating chart helped ☺ |
| 9/20 | 20 | Great day! Celebrated w/ Hershey kisses!! |

- Compare initial time frames for independent work. What factors contribute to longer times of engagement? Was it time of the day? Hunger level? Did students have choice in what they were doing? What did the teacher do to help them get there?

- Set goals for increasing the time across classrooms and grade teams. Compare new numbers after a week or two. Discuss progress and what contributed to jumps in time for independent work.

- As a test group, track your own engagement. Grade a set of papers together, or read articles about your chosen topic of interest. Time how long you all can pay attention, what made your mind wander, and what helped you to keep focus. Share those findings with your students.

## Tech Integration Tip

### FLIP IT *IN* CLASS

Record your lesson in advance and have students watch it at the start of class, instead of as homework. This gives you breathing room at the start of class so you can circulate and see students one-on-one. It allows students the autonomy to review the material at their own pace and revisit it later on. Plus, watching the lesson in class helps correct the inequity of traditional "flipped" lessons, which reward those for whom doing work outside of school is possible.

Use the Chrome extensions Screencastify or EDpuzzle (or a similar app) to make a three- to five-minute video of your lesson. This will allow you to record your screen, embed a video of yourself talking, and upload it to YouTube or your classroom website. If you are using slides or images, include a sidebar video of your face as you narrate over the material. This makes a difference. If you don't need to record your computer screen, you can record yourself in front of the easel or whiteboard. EDpuzzle allows you to embed formative assessments throughout, which you may include.

When students access the video at the start of class, give them a few minutes longer than the actual video so they have time to pause and replay parts as needed. If appropriate, students may take notes on a separate Google Doc or paper. Those who finish first can move on to other work. After everyone has finished, or after ten minutes total, transition to the next part of class. Provide in-person follow-up to the whole class, small groups, or individuals as needed. You'll be able to quickly view the EDpuzzle formative assessments to determine these needs, in addition to simply asking them who needs help.

*Want to know more about this tech tip and others like it?*

**Check out:** Petty, Bethany, J. 2018. *Illuminate: Technology Enhanced Learning.*

# 5.3 What Questions Do They Need Answered?

**Try This**

Before any stretch of independent work time, reserve a few minutes for Q and A. Explain the task, then ask, "What questions do you need answered to engage in the (photosynthesis lab/ algebraic word problems/independent reading/self-portraits/brainstorming activity) for the next fifteen minutes?"

Give students a moment to think through the entire time frame and anticipate any needs or potential frustrations. If questions can be quickly answered in a few minutes, address them right there. If a few students have questions that deserve longer support and others are ready to go, have question holders stay with you as the rest get started.

**How do I know if this idea will help?**

- Independent work time frequently starts with the teacher circulating to those with hands raised.

- Independent work time rarely sticks to the time frame you allotted, or students do not accomplish what you had hoped.

- You hear the same questions from multiple students.

**How do I know if this idea is working?**

- Transition into independent work time is smooth and efficient. Work gets started right away.

- You circulate to students on your terms, not according to who has their hand raised or who isn't on task.

- Your planning includes supports that you can readily anticipate, based on previous feedback from students.

Students can be involved in building up to longer stretches of independent work time, too. Help them reflect on and set goals for how they'll stay focused and busy during independent work time that day.

> 11|14
>
> My class time plan (25 min)
> - Finish problems from chapter 3
> - Ask Kiara for help if stuck
> - Start outlining project
>   → use model to help
> - If time, research graphing examples

| **Adapt for K–6** | • Students may not be able to articulate questions without repeated practice. Expect a learning curve. |
|---|---|

- If you send kids off to work and immediately many hands go up, encourage them to try *something* before you go to them. You might busy yourself with a task or work with a student to let them know you're unavailable for the moment, so they'll have to get started with something before you'll come to them.

- Sometimes students pose questions more for the gratifying audience of their classmates than having a genuine inquiry. Send students off to work and keep question holders with you on their own to help counteract this.

- As students get more skilled at asking questions, encourage them to think through their own plan for independent work time, including how they might handle any questions or issues on their own.

**Adapt for 7–12**

- It can be more intimidating to pose questions in front of classmates, so create safe ways for students to do so, such as posting anonymously on a Google Doc or Padlet or jotting questions while you look over shoulders. You can also show students the content, topic, or text for the following day and have them pose questions in advance electronically.

- In addition to having them anticipate questions, teens are ready to make a plan for how they will manage their independent work time. Model this for them at first so they see how it looks to set ambitious but realistic goals, have backup plans, and anticipate challenges.

**How to try this with others**

- Present your upcoming independent work/task to a colleague, without qualifiers or explanation. Ask them to anticipate what questions they need answered. Have you already anticipated such questions?

- Try this with a small group of students in advance. Poll them for questions, then plan answers before working with the entire group.

- Visit a colleague's classroom during the transition to independent work. Help them by observing off-task students and then doing on the spot conferences with those kids. What's getting in their way? Is it a question that could be answered, or another roadblock such as lack of interest, stamina, or motivation?

*Want to know more about this strategy and others like it?*

**Check out:** Martin-Kniep, Giselle O., and Joanne Picone-Zocchia. 2009. *Changing the Way You Teach, Improving the Way Students Learn.*

# 5.4 Stop and Jot, Turn and Talk

Try This

To learn rather than regurgitate, students need to *do* something with new information. In the big picture, that might be inquiry projects, discussion, choice assignments, and project-based learning. In the small picture, however, it can be as simple as stop and jots and turn and talks.

## Stop and Jot

Teaching (or discussion, reading, or other activity) stops for a brief moment, and students jot down their thinking. You might provide sentence starters or question prompts for students to choose from. Students write for one to three minutes—this isn't essay writing; it's a way to process, reflect, and quickly hold onto their thinking. When they are done jotting, you can ask for responses, have them share in partners or groups, or move on.

## Turn and Talk

Similar to the stop and jot, pause in your instruction and provide a sentence frame or other prompt so students can discuss and process new information, develop their ideas, and so on for a minute or two. This will work best if students are seated with assigned partners and don't need to spend time finding someone to talk to. After half the allotted time, remind them to switch so both partners get a chance to talk.

Stop and jots and turn and talks can also go hand in hand. Sometimes talking first primes the pump for writing and vice versa.

While students are talking or writing, you are circulating to see what kinds of responses they have. This will help you to know what questions they need answered, where to go next, and to better frame the information to their thinking.

## Sample prompts

- "I wonder . . ."
- "I have a question about . . ."
- "I learned that . . ."
- "This reminds me . . ."
- "I'm surprised that . . ."
- "I noticed . . ."
- "I think . . ."
- "What's interesting is that . . ."
- "I used to think . . . but now I think . . ."

Notice none of these prompts ask students to recall or spit information back out. And that makes sense, because none of our standards ask students to do that! In fact, you can use the standards to help inform even quick stop and jot and turn and talk questions.

How do I know if this idea will help?

- Only a few hands are raised when you pose questions, and it's often the same students' hands.
- Students aren't always retaining or understanding the material. Or, you're not sure whether they are or not because, again, you hear from only a few voices.

How do I know if this idea is working?

- Everyone participates when you pose a question.
- After turn and talk or stop and jot, you can call on anyone. They all have thoughts to share.

---

2/12    Stop + Jot

I noticed the author of this article included a lot of quotes from people who work in the pharmaceutical industry.

I wonder what people who can't afford this drug would have to say?

---

*Want to know more about this strategy and others like it?*

**Check out:** The Teacher Toolkit. "Stop and Jot." www.theteachertoolkit.com/index.php/tool/stop-and-jot.

**124**   THE JOYFUL TEACHER

# 5.5 Sentence Starters That Set Up Students to Do More on Their Own

**Try This**

A wonderful way to scaffold students' independent work is to provide them with sentence starters or frames. Sentence starters steer students' thinking and writing for short answers or discussion, remove pressure of getting it "wrong," save time for those who find writing difficult or intimidating, and often clarify misunderstandings. Anytime you anticipate students struggling to get their thinking across in writing or in discussion, you might create sentence starters.

1. Create 3–5 sentence starters that students can choose from.
2. Introduce the sentence starters and model how you would finish one or two. Let them try it as well.
3. Ask them to choose at least one when writing or speaking. Share out which worked and which were nonstarters.

## When starting a new unit or introducing a new concept
- "I understand that . . . "
- "I already know that . . ."
- "This is similar to/different from what we learned before because . . ."

## When working through a problem
- "First, I . . . Then I . . . Finally I . . ."
- "It's tricky when . . ."
- "One thing I can try is . . ."

## When talking in a group
- "To be clear, you're saying that . . ."
- "I hear you saying that . . ."
- "I agree with you because . . ."
- "I see it differently because . . ."
- "_____ mentioned that . . ."
- "Adding to what _____ said . . ."
- "More than anything else, I believe that . . ."
- "Could it also be that . . ."
- "I have a question about . . ."
- "I wonder . . ."
- "On the other hand . . ."

### After reading a nonfiction text

- "The purpose of this article is to . . ."
- "The author wants us to think . . ."
- "I think . . ."
- "One of the most interesting things about . . . was . . ."
- "What surprised me was . . ."
- "A key player in this situation was . . . and they had an impact because . . ."

### To cite text evidence

- "On page _____ it said . . ."
- "This shows that . . ."
- "According to the text . . ."
- "We can infer from this . . ."
- "We know this because . . ."
- "Based on this example . . ."

### Goal setting

- "I intend to . . ."
- "I will begin by . . ."
- "Following that I will . . ."
- "To do this I will . . ."

### When summarizing a story

- "Somebody wanted . . ."
- "But . . ."
- "So . . ."
- "Then . . ."

**How do I know if this idea will help?**

- Students are slow to get started with their writing work.
- Students ask lots of questions including "Is this right?" when they are assigned writing work.
- Student writing can reflect confusion, but you don't catch it until they're done.

| **How do I know if this idea is working?** | • Students get started on the writing work right away. |
| | • Student writing reflects the sentence stems—they're using them. |
| | • Student writing reflects the understanding you intended—they used the sentence frames to orient their thinking. |

| **How to try this with others** | • Collect student work after introducing sentence frames and see which frames students used the most. How did the process impact their work? Which new frames will you introduce. and why? |
| | • Try reflecting on a teaching article or on your own teaching goal using the frames. How did it help you? |

*Want to know more about this strategy and others like it?*

**Check out:** "Language Supports for Number Talks." 2018. *Teaching Channel.*

# 5.6 Anchor Charts as Silent Teachers

Try This

Store-bought charts packed with tiny text or cute posters of kittens saying "Hang in There" don't help our students all that much. What can and should go on our walls are charts with bold graphics and text that serve as silent teachers—reminding students of key information so they can try things out on their own.

Create (or cocreate with students) large, poster-size charts to serve as references and easy reminders for the skills you teach. Keep an easel pad of chart paper at the ready or create a rough draft chart on an 8.5 × 11-inch piece of paper using the document camera. If you do the smaller version in front of the students as you teach, you can make it larger and user-friendly later, when you don't have a group of students to manage.

To make the anchor chart:

- Break down the skill you are teaching in a series of concrete steps. What are the essential "need to knows"? Include those basics on the chart so students can refer to them anytime they need that reminder.

- Use graphics, bright colors, and visual reminders for these steps so students can easily remember the skill and steps.

- Err on the side of less text, more images/graphics, even for older students. It will "pop" and be easier to read from anywhere in the room.

- Whenever possible, create this with the students, allowing their input to guide what goes on the chart. Have a clear idea in advance what it will include, but involve students in "filling in the blanks" so they are engaged in the process.

To post and use the chart later on:

- Before posting the chart, look it over to make sure it can serve as a silent teacher. A few weeks from now when the strategy may be long forgotten, will a student be able to look at the chart and remember exactly what to do?

- Tons of anchor charts posted on the walls can serve as proud mementos of all the important concepts we are teaching, but they can also veer toward visual clutter. Rotate charts every marking period and keep up only the most essential.

- Organize displays of charts so students know where to look for what. Will they be organized by steps in the scientific process? Genre of writing? Math concepts? Keep them in order so students can access them easily.

- Refer to anchor charts, old and new, as you teach so students are reminded of their presence and so they see them as tools and not just decoration.

| | |
|---|---|
| **How do I know if this idea will help?** | • You find yourself reteaching lessons as reminders.<br>• Students are unclear how lessons and units are building on one another.<br>• Class walls are bare, or what's on them is seldom referred to or used by students. |
| **How do I know if this idea is working?** | • Students visually scan the walls for help with what they're working on.<br>• Students refer to the charts on a regular basis.<br>• A visitor can look at the walls and know what the class is learning. |

Solving Word Problems

1. Read the entire problem slowly and carefully.

2. Make sure you understand what the problem is describing. You may need to re-read the problem.

3. Draw bars or a picture to match the problem.

4. Re-read the problem to make sure the bars or pictures match the problem.

5. Write an equation to match the unknown. give it a letter!

6. Solve the problem.

7. Check your work.

8. Write your answer in a complete sentence.

This kindergarten chart provides easy visuals to explain and remind students what to do with their reading partner. It can be referred to anytime students need a reminder, rather than relying on the teacher for instructions.

This eighth-grade chart reminds students of the specific steps for word problems, and the students refer to it often.

| | |
|---|---|
| **Adapt for K–2** | • Use symbols and images more than words and sentences.<br>• Keep text at a minimum by using a large font.<br>• Create charts in advance if students lose focus or the lesson takes too long when you do it with them. |
| **Adapt for 3–6** | • You can increase the amount of text and involve students more in the creation process as attention spans allow. Still, keep the process and the text streamlined. |
| **Adapt for 6–12** | • Google Docs are great for storing images of previous charts and allowing students to access them later.<br>• Older students still benefit from things on walls. Their minds and eyes are going to wander. Why not have them space out on things that matter?<br>• Older students also enjoy graphic charts with illustrations as well as text. Don't deny them the visual pleasure of charts that pop. Consider enlisting an artistic student for help. |
| **How to try this with others** | • Do a learning walk through classrooms to see one another's charts. Jot down notes and share when you regroup. Which charts popped the most visually? Which were most clear in terms of breaking down the work of a skill? What could you tell about what the class was learning, based on the charts? How was the organization clear or unclear? What do you want to try, based on what you saw?<br>• Look ahead to your upcoming lessons. Draft anchor charts on regular-size paper as guidelines. Share them out. What do you notice? What will be clear to students? What might be unclear?<br>• Do another learning walk after everyone has worked on their charts. What has changed?<br>• Survey students about anchor charts. What do they like? Not like? When do they use them? When are they just wallpaper? Share out findings in a group. |

*Want to know more about this strategy and others like it?*

**Check out:** Mraz, Kristine, and Majorie Martinelli. 2014. *Smarter Charts for Math, Science, and Social Studies: Making Learning Visible in the Content Areas K–2.*

# 5.7 Track Independent Work Time for Those Who Need It Most

Try This

Students who need the most independent practice often get the least. Their days are packed with important interventions that support their learning, but that also take them away from time to practice learning skills. These students need protected time to practice, all on their own.

Think of two or three students who would benefit from support with some aspect of the content in your class. On a given day, track how much time they have to work independently. Count only the minutes they have all by themselves to work—no aide or paraprofessional at their side, no pullout time, no small group, no teacher conference, no distractions.

If those students have thirty to sixty minutes a day of solo, consistent, protected time to work on their reading/science/history/art/writing/math (fill in the blank), pat yourself and your colleagues on the back for protecting the time students need most and move to another strategy.

Students benefit from substantial chunks of time for independent reading and writing, ideally 30–60 minutes a day. It doesn't have to be all at once, but it has to be while students are in school, with us. Designating independent work as homework is unfair. We can't control what happens after school.

Make weeklong schedules for the students in your class who receive pullout and push-in services. See how much independent time they have compared to their peers, and carve out more for them. It's important that kids who receive academic intervention services (AIS) for math or literacy aren't always missing private work time. Try to be proactive before the problem occurs. If you notice a big gap in time for independent practice, call a team meeting to make necessary switches.

Make every effort to protect every students' independent work time. Is there a fire drill? Skip something else. Is there an announcement? Allow an extra minute for students to refocus. Were students pulled out for speech or occupational therapy (OT) while others were independently working? Find another part of the day to give back that time. Add it up: Did everyone get 30–60 minutes? Did the students who are struggling with content get as much or more time than others? If not, look to tomorrow to see where you will make it happen.

How do I know if this idea will help?

- Students are pulled out for AIS.
- You and/or aides give extra support in the form of side-by-side presence and verbal coaching during independent work time.
- Students, especially those performing below grade level, don't do homework or don't do it well.
- You are "on" for the bulk of class time.
- Students rarely get more than thirty minutes of time to work on their own.

- Students who receive pullout or push-in AIS are getting independent practice time during other parts of the day.

- The volume of student work is higher.

- Students regularly get thirty minutes or more of independent practice.

- If independent work time gets cut short, students complain.

If a child leaves for speech during independent reading, then the teacher finds thirty minutes across the day to give them that time back. This teacher takes time to see what her students are missing and then is creative in finding places to reclaim that time, knowing that those who benefit from extra support often get the smallest amount of independent time.

| | Monday Class Schedule | Monday Stella's Schedule |
|---|---|---|
| 7:45-8:00 | Unpack/<br>Morning Work | Unpack/<br>Private Reading<br>(Additional 5 minutes) |
| 8:00-8:30 | Morning Meeting | Morning Meeting |
| 8:20-8:30 | Writer's Workshop | Writer's Workshop |
| 8:30-9:00 | Writer's Workshop | Writer's Workshop |
| 9:00-9:30 | Shared Reading | Shared Reading |
| 9:20-9:30 | Reading Workshop | Reading Workshop |
| 9:30-10:00 | Reading Workshop | SPEECH |
| 10:00-10:20 | Phonics/Word Study | Phonics/Word Study |
| 10:20-10:30 | Prep for Lunch | Prep for Lunch |
| 10:30-11:20 | Lunch/Recess | Lunch/Recess |
| 11:20-11:30 | Quiet Time | Private Reading<br>(Additional 10 minutes) |
| 11:30-12:00 | Read Aloud | Read Aloud |
| 11:50-12:00 | Math Workshop | Math Workshop |
| 12:00-12:30 | Math Workshop | Math Workshop |
| 12:30-1:00 | Art | Art |
| 1:00-1:30 | Snack | Snack |
| 1:15-1:30 | STEM Activities | Private Reading<br>(Additional 15 minutes) |
| 1:30-2:00 | Science/SS | Science/SS |
| 2:00-2:10 | Pack Up | Pack Up |

- Check whether you have pockets of time built into the schedule for catching up. Try to add 10–15 minutes of quiet time after lunch, for example, for kids to do additional writing or reading and for you to deal with recess issues or to complete assessments. This quiet time can be used flexibly depending on the needs of individual kids.

- When there are emergency interruptions, try to revise on the spot. Explain you're going to extend private reading today and not have partner reading or share so that everyone has more time to practice on their own.

- You might occasionally enlist the kids' help as you work to reshuffle a schedule—this shows them how valuable independent time is. "We need more time for you to practice, so how could we move the schedule, or what can we push off until next week?"

- It's easy to forget how little time certain students have to work on their own, because we don't see them all day. Check in with your colleagues to find out which of your students get pulled out, and when. Take a look at the student's entire day, even if you only see them for one small part of it.

- Buying back time for students who get pulled out for extra support is hard when you may only see your students for forty-five minutes a day. Work to protect their independent time by not overconferring with those kids. Remember that solo time helps them too.

- Offer a rotating room during lunch where students can work quietly. The only rules are no talking and clean up your lunch. Students can read, do homework, or catch up on classwork. This space can also serve to provide a safe respite from the fraught cafeteria. Or, if you regularly come to school early or stay in your classroom after school, you could provide the same quiet space then.

- Help older students navigate their time. Ask them, "We need more time for you to practice. How might you move something in your schedule, add more time, or push something to next week?"

- Ask grade-team colleagues who share your students to weigh in on how often and for how long they offer extra support in the form of one-on-one conferences or small groups with that student.

- As a start, designate a few students to track. Log the exact minutes of their independent work time each day for a week. Compare notes. Troubleshoot together to keep increasing those minute goals. Consider adding 2–3 students to track the next go-round.

# 5.8 Remove Obstacles for One and All: Tools That Help Everyone Achieve Independence

**Try This**

Protecting kids who have disabilities or who are learning English benefits all students. Every student needs support at different times—when they face personally challenging content, when they're tired, when their parents go through a divorce, when they've been out sick for two weeks, and on and on. When support tools are used by those other than students getting Tier 3 support, we level the playing field and destigmatize difference.

There are easy-to-include tools for your classroom that foster independent success for all. Encourage students to see such tools as resources for everyone. Model using them yourself when you are teaching. Provide access to these tools and allow students to choose what works for them.

## Tools that foster students' independence during and after class

- **Keychain recorders.** You or a classmate can record information on these small devices for nonverbal students. Verbal students can record themselves. They can record reminders such as bringing a library book or permission slip, content such as vocabulary terms of periodic elements, homework assignments, and more. For older students with devices that go home with them, consider the Remind app.

- **Rubber stamps, preprinted stickers with words, and word cards.** Use these tools for students with OT issues or who benefit from support with handwriting so they don't always have to write out entire answers.

- **Speech-to-text dictation software** for independent keyboarding work.

- **Video tools** that capture thinking (gosynth.com) and audio-recording tools so students can share thinking and access it later on without needing to write.

- **Communication boards** with images and words for selecting among choice responses.  For example, during a guided reading, students can choose from symbols on a board such as "I love this story," "Read that part again," "I have a question," and "Turn the page."

- **Open Dyslexic font** or other sans serif fonts. Use these fonts for anything you write and share, and suggest students use these fonts.

- **Sentence starters and sentence frames** help students independently work on their writing or discussion skills and keep that work focused. Provide the basic structure of the sentence with key components blank so students can insert their thinking. Entire templates are also helpful for students to get the work done without worrying about the organization at first.

- **Before-and-after photos** help students independently access the information and concepts. Show students what the work looks like during key stages. Let them refer to these models as they work. Don't worry if they rely heavily on the models. If they do, it's because they needed them.

- **Calculators, geometric sketch pads, preformatted graph paper.** Virtual or concrete math manipulatives such as base ten blocks or algebra blocks can increase students' ability to take on math work on their own.

**How do I know if this idea will help?**

- Students rely heavily on you for getting started and keeping going.
- There are tools now, but they are only used by the students with individualized education programs.

**How do I know if this idea is working?**

- Everyone uses the extra supports at varying times, not just students with designated needs.
- Students use the tools some days and not others, seeing them as optional supports when needed.
- Students report using these tools in other classes or at home.

**How to try this with others**

- When your students hear that their teachers have tried these tools and rated them as "helpful," they will be much more willing to give them a go. Choose a few to try together and decide which will be most helpful and inviting for your students. Let students know that the tools are preapproved, and that others are to come!

*Want to know more about this strategy and others like it?*

**Check out:** Kluth, Paula, and Sheila Danaher. 2010. *From Tutor Scripts to Talking Sticks: 100 Ways to Differentiate Instruction in K–12 Inclusive Classrooms.*

Muhtaris, Katie, and Kristin Ziemke. 2015. *Amplify: Digital Teaching and Learning in the K–6 Classroom.*

## Tech Integration Tip

**GIVE *ALL* STUDENTS THE TECH TOOLS THEY NEED TO SUCCEED**

Protecting and supporting kids who have disabilities or who are learning English benefits *all* students. Universal learning tools related to tech can offer support tailored to students' needs. Make tech tools available to everyone, and allow students to choose what works best.

### If students need extra access to content or background knowledge
- Flipped lessons—record the same lecture on photosynthesis.com and anyone who forgets a stage can go watch it on the class drive.
- Use internet searches for content they forgot or don't know: kiddle.co is helpful for younger students.
- Use digital bins (put websites, articles, images, videos all in one folder).

### If students need support with writing legibly
- Let them use word processing (Google Docs, Word, Pages, etc.).
- Let them use TalkTyper or Dragon or any speech-to-text dictation.
- Use digital publishing apps for infographics (Canva, Smore); for book-style presentations (Book Creator, Creative Book Builder); for presentations (Google Slides, Emaze); for comic strips and comic panels (Toontastic, Make Beliefs Comix, FriendStrip, Pixton).

### If students need support with spelling and grammar
- Try the Word Dynamo app.
- Spell-check, but show them how to use it so they know what word to choose.
- Use Slick Write (see settings to modify so it doesn't highlight the entire text).
- Use Grammarly.
- Use Co:Writer.

### If students need support with reading digital texts
- Try E Ink screen layovers.
- Use Open Dyslexic font (sans serif font that is easier to read).
- Natural Reader is a Chrome extension that will read web pages and Google Docs to you. Also consider Voicepods for multiple languages. You can adjust the speed, replay parts, pause, and more.

### Want to know more about this tech tip and others like it?

**Check out:** Kluth, Paula, and Sheila Danaher. 2010. *From Tutor Scripts to Talking Sticks: 100 Ways to Differentiate Instruction in K–12 Inclusive Classrooms.*

Cruz, Colleen. 2018. *Writers Read Better, 50+Paired Lessons That Turn Writing Craft Work into Powerful Genre Reading.*

## If students need support with stamina

- Do a physical activity right before something mentally challenging.
- Use timers. Show students how to set themselves up for short bursts of work, then take a quick mental break using Time Timer or another timing app.
- Using apps that provide white noise or other soft background noise can help students focus. Show them myNoise or Noisli to start.

## Other tools

- Use calculators or geometric sketch pads.
- Try virtual math manipulatives such as base ten blocks or algebra blocks.
- Use the Scribble app—they can take notes on online sources, highlight, and put virtual sticky notes onto the article.
- Try Rewordify.

# 5.9 Be Brain Scientists

Try This

Our brains change based on the way they are used—not just as infants but across our entire lives. Students may look at a classmate's ability to focus on a book for a long time, solve math word problems, or paint a portrait as a genetic talent or gift. The truth is, repeated practice creates new pathways in our brains so that skills become embedded and therefore less taxing to complete. Let students know that the brain's malleable nature means we get better at anything with repeated practice.

Teach students age-appropriate brain science so they are aware of the reasoning behind independent practice, so they feel less discouraged by roadblocks, and so they feel empowered to keep trying.

Provide a short explanation and use a real-life example that connects to your students. Some teachers have shown the one-minute Under Armour commercial showcasing well-known athletes Misty Copeland, Stephen Curry, and Jordan Spieth repeatedly practicing their moves. It's clear these celebrities were not only born with athletic gifts but devote hours and hours to practice. Share your own experience with repeated practice. Ask an older student who may have some school-wide fame for being talented at something to come in and share out how much time and practice they devote to that skill. Or, record them in an interview and play it for the class.

You might share more empowering brain science, too. Brain research gives ample evidence for our need to eat nourishing food, to get plenty of sleep, to move our bodies, and to get off screens. Use powerful data to teach students why they will benefit from choosing the healthy lunch option, going to bed earlier, doing ten jumping jacks before a quiz, or putting their phone in another room when they go to bed. These are easy-to-do life skills toward independently succeeding at any goal.

You can also share a goal you're setting for yourself that reflects this brain research. After providing a brief amount of brain research to back up the need for independent practice (or going to bed earlier, etc.), ask your students to tell a partner or jot down a goal that will protect and boost their brain for learning ahead. In a week or so, have them revisit and adjust their goals. Model yours, too!

**How do I know if this idea will help?**

- You hear comments such as "I'm not good at math," "I give up," "Writing isn't my thing," or "I'll never understand this."
- Students place value on "knowing" how to do something on the first try.
- Students give up easily when things feel hard.

- Students continue to try things after failing or making mistakes.
- Students set goals and try to meet them through research-backed methods, such as continued practice.
- You hear students citing brain research to one another.

After/Before (current practice), I will (new practice)

* Brain research tells us that we increase the odds of getting to new habits by making a specific plan for <u>when</u> & <u>where</u>, and linking that to something you already do

Study for SAT : <u>Before</u> I eat breakfast, <u>I will</u> do 15 practice problems.

Read more : <u>After</u> I shower, <u>I will</u> read one chapter of my book.

Finish homework. <u>Before</u> I go to soccer On time. practice, <u>I will</u> start homework for 20 minutes at the writing center.

- Ask students how they have learned to do something in the past, and connect it to how our brains develop.
- Let them know that their brains are most plastic right now! The more they practice something, the more their brains will hot-wire themselves so that action becomes second nature.
- Don't underestimate younger students' capacity to understand brain science. Explain how this "machine" works just as you would any other—using visuals and age-appropriate vocabulary. There are great resources for doing just that at NatGeoKids. Just search for the science of the human brain.

- Tell students about the enormous brain growth that happens throughout adolescence (Lorain n.d.).

- Share research on the amazing new skills that grow as teen brains develop, such as moving from concrete to abstract thinking and growing in metacognition, deductive reasoning, problem-solving, critical thinking, and, yes, impulse control.

- Check out the "Brains On!" website for podcasts about brain science (brainson.org).

- Check out the "Science News for Students" website (sciencenewsforstudents. org) and search for "brain."

**How to try this
with others**

- List out possible brain research topics that are relevant to your students. Among your group, choose topics of interest to report back on at a future date. Be ready to share tips and extensions for students.

- Share the brain research that's age-appropriate for your students with a colleague. Think of a learning goal you can each apply it to in your own life. For example, you will turn off all screens by 9 p.m., based on what you read about blue light exposure interrupting sleep patterns.

## Want to know more about this strategy and others like it?

**Check out:** Clear, James. 2018. *Atomic Habits: An Easy & Proven Way to Build Good Habits & Break Bad Ones.*

Hammond, Zaretta. 2015. *Culturally Responsive Teaching & the Brain: Promoting Authentic Engagement and Rigor Among Culturally and Linguistically Diverse Students.*

# 5.10 Wonder Hour

Invest just an hour in supporting students' independence and curiosity. We can all find an hour when we know that in learning and in life, students need to cultivate a sense of agency and independence.

Choose a low-stakes hour or period so you don't feel like you're sacrificing essential time. Maybe it's the day before a break, a Friday, or when the whole class will have just returned from a half-day field trip.

Give this time a name. Wonder Hour, Genius Hour, and Maker Challenge are all possibilities, or come up with your own (surely better) moniker. A few days beforehand, announce to students that it's coming and get them brainstorming questions. Model a few authentic questions of your own, and include a mix of playful and burning questions.

Some of mine might be:

- Why do sharks exist? They terrify me and keep me from enjoying the ocean. Do they really serve a purpose?

- How come people's laughs are all so different? Are we born with our laughs?

- I grew up thinking milk was the best (and healthiest) drink in the world. Now I hear people say the opposite. What's the real truth here?

- What are hiccups?

- Is it too late for me to learn a new language?

- What are the best natural cures for insomnia?

Set students to coming up with their own burning questions that are unlikely to ever be addressed in the official curriculum. Encourage their efforts and talk up the results. Let them know they can "share" each other's wonderings, either by partnering up or trying a version of the same question on their own.

At the appointed hour, send them off to start answering their questions using any and all resources provided. Make sure laptops are charged, Wi-Fi is on, the classroom library is open, and additional resources are provided. You can use kiddle.co to create predetermined websites in Google classroom, or add videos and links in advance to Seesaw so you know students will have access to sites you like. Maybe students collected or checked out books in advance, or you did a quick survey of questions and checked some books out for them. Maybe a guest expert or two is on hand—if many students had questions about sports, can the gym teacher stop by? Maybe you allow some students to travel to other areas in the school such as the media center or computer lab.

Ten minutes before the hour is up, gather everyone. Ask students to share out something they learned that surprised and/or interested them.

That's it! You did it—you gave students agency, and you let them pursue learning that mattered *to them*. Now that you took a nibble with a Wonder Hour, reflect and consider if you and students are hungry for more. If so, you can expand on it later on.

For now, reflect: How did it feel? Did anyone or any moment surprise you? What was the energy level like? What would you do to modify this in the future?

**How do I know if this idea will help?**

- Thought-provoking questions might come up in class, but it feels like there's never time to explore them.
- You want to incorporate more independent work, but overhauling the current daily structure feels overwhelming.
- You are rarely able to observe your students in the act of learning—most of class time you're "on."

**How do I know if this idea is working?**

- Students are buzzing about their topics and questions.
- Students bring in questions in advance—they're thinking about the Wonder Hour throughout the week.
- The answers students discover are unexpected and often promote more insightful questions.
- You have at a minimum an hour or so a week during which you get to observe your students in action.

## Wonder Wall Question Stems

Why do you think...?
What can we do about...?
How is it possible...?
What caused...?
What are some ways to solve...?
How come...?
I wonder if... why... how...?

| | |
|---|---|
| **Adapt for K-2** | • Devote some time to modeling and supporting questioning. Start with, "What do you love? What do you want to know more about?" |
| | • For very young students, have them draw something they love first and ask them to come up with questions about it. |
| | • Students don't need to research much—give them time to create, make, and tinker instead. |
| | • Expose them to the Wonder Hour through a learning lunch with older students. |
| | • Record all of their questions throughout the day on a chart paper. |
| | • Model by showing your own questions first. |
| | • Read them the picture books *What Do You Do with an Idea?* by Kobi Yamada (2014) or *The Most Magnificent Thing* by Ashley Spires (2014). |
| **Adapt for 3-5** | • Expect some organized chaos. You might have students interviewing others, researching in books or online, or building things. |
| | • If students do Wonder Hour on an ongoing basis, have them start a folder to keep their notes and questions in one place. |
| | • Designate a quiet space if there is a lot of talking and sharing among others, so everyone has the ability to focus. |
| | • Wonderopolis is a great resource for students this age. |
| | • Students can reflect in paired discussion or in writing: What did they do today? What sources did they use? What surprised them in their learning? What are their goals for next time? |
| **Adapt for 6-12** | • You know your students best, so find a video on a topic that would interest them. Choose a TED Talk or a video from the website: "The Kid Should See This" (thekidshouldseethis.com) to spark questions. |
| | • Keep a "status of the class" board where students can see what questions and activity is going on. |
| | • If students are getting off task, you may suggest they go back to the question or help someone else. |
| | • Consider creating a website where students can share their discoveries. |
| | • Saving time for students to share out their findings will up engagement and motivation. Let them know in advance what this will look like so they feel some accountability. |
| **How to try this with others** | • Commit to devoting an hour to this in a designated time frame, and then come back to share out and reflect. Use the reflection questions to guide your discussion: How did it feel? Did anyone or any moment surprise you? What was the energy level like? What would you do to modify this in the future? |

*Want to know more about this strategy and others like it?*

**Check out:** Daniels, Harvey. 2017. *The Curious Classroom: 10 Structures for Teaching with Student-Directed Inquiry.*

# Formative Assessment and Feedback

## What you have in place, and what you're ready for next

Although ideally we'd assess what students know and need from the get-go, this isn't always realistic. Years ago, while doing a demo lesson in a wholly unfamiliar ninth-grade classroom, I did a classic formative assessment, a KWL chart (What do you know? What do you want to know? What did you learn?). Essentially, these teens answered, "I don't know anything, I don't want to know anything, and I didn't learn a thing." Once I dusted off my bruised ego, I saw this as its own feedback— it was a loud and clear reminder that I didn't have essential components in place yet: routines, structures, or trusting relationships. Time to go back to the drawing board.

If you do have those building blocks in place, you're ready to focus on what students know and what they need! To dig into formative assessment, most of your students should be able to work independently so that you can watch, listen, and respond to what they're doing. It's important that they are producing enough work for you to study and assess. And it's crucial that you've developed relationships with them, that you value their individual strengths, and that they know you believe in them. All meaningful feedback is "underpinned in the belief that all students can improve" (Hattie 2012).

## What is formative assessment, and why is it important?

First, what it isn't: grades. Assessment is often thought of as a final evaluative number in the grade book. That is *summative* assessment, which comes at the end of a unit, marking period, or assignment. It is an inevitable part of teaching, and we'll take a good look at this kind of assessment in Chapter 10.

Because it comes at the end of our teaching, however, summative assessment doesn't inform our teaching across a study, and it doesn't impact student learning as we go.

Formative assessment happens throughout, and when done well, it drives student learning. Let's take a closer look at just what formative assessment entails.

Formative assessment:

- **is an ongoing process** where you continually check in on what students are doing, what they're ready for next, and what they need to get there

- **is used immediately** to make changes and provide quick feedback to students

- **typically happens in class** in your observations of what students are doing right then and there

- **drives our instruction** (Based on what students know, need, and are ready to do, you adjust all necessary elements of your instruction, from where students sit, to what lesson you deliver, to who you pull for extra help and for what, and more.)

- **involves students.** (Students are privy to this information and also make adjustments to what they're doing to learn.)

## How are formative assessment and feedback linked?

Formative assessment informs our feedback so that every student gets what he or she needs to learn and grow. We assess what students need, and then we provide feedback to students so they know what to keep doing and what to try next. Without feedback, we lose students in the process of learning. With feedback, we create a collaborative learning process. Feedback lets students take part in and have ownership of what they are doing and learning.

## What does the research say?

Formative assessment is one of the highest-impact processes we can engage in as educators in terms of driving student learning (Black and Wiliam 1998). When done on an ongoing basis, it allows us to adjust our instruction so we are meeting the needs of every learner in the room.

John Hattie (2009) says feedback is "one of the most powerful influences in learning and achievement." When students receive ongoing, specific feedback, they can progress through a year and a half's worth of learning in one academic year.

Feedback is not just saying "good job" or providing a numerical grade. Feedback *is* including students in the questions and answers of where they are in the learning process, where they can go next, and what they need to get there.

# Is this the goal for me?

- Do you answer "yes" and "sometimes" for most questions? Consider moving to the next chapter. You've got this!

- Do you have a mix of "yes," "sometimes," and "not yet" answers? This might be the goal for you.

- Do you answer "not yet" for most of these questions? Go back and try the checklists from the previous chapters. You're likely to enjoy greater success and see quicker results by focusing there.

## What do you notice?

| | Yes | Sometimes | Not yet |
|---|:---:|:---:|:---:|
| My lesson planning reflects where students are at and where they can go next. | ☐ | ☐ | ☐ |
| I have a clear sense of what my students are able to do in relation to the grade-level and unit expectations. | ☐ | ☐ | ☐ |
| Students have a clear sense of their strengths and what to work on and toward. | ☐ | ☐ | ☐ |
| I spend more time doing formative assessments and providing feedback than on grading. | ☐ | ☐ | ☐ |
| I have an organized system for keeping data and feedback on my students (that isn't just grades). | ☐ | ☐ | ☐ |

## 6.1 Feedback at a Glance

**Try This**

After a lesson, gather quick written feedback that you can look over later that day and use to inform the next day's lesson. Have students write their name on a sticky note, and answer one or all of these three questions:

- What did you learn?
- What question(s) do you still have?
- What don't you understand?

After you collect these, sort them based on various understanding levels and questions. Decide who you will follow up with tomorrow. Determine what material you will reteach or explain anew to the whole class.

Vague responses provide their own feedback. Minimal responses might mean minimal understanding. Short, blunt, or sarcastic answers may also reflect disinterest or embarrassment at admitting confusion.

If students need it, model with your own sticky notes that show detailed and honest answers. Make admitting confusion appealing by acknowledging those who do so. When appropriate, say so that others can hear you as well, "It's so helpful to know that you really didn't get all the parts of yesterday's lesson. Now I've got an idea for how we can try this again . . ."

**How do I know if this idea will help?**

- Summative assessments reflect a wide range of grades, or the entire class is confused about concepts.
- Your lessons and groupings rarely veer from what you originally planned.
- You discover late in the unit that students have been confused.
- Students are producing a low volume of work.

**How do I know if this idea is working?**

- Your teaching points may stick to the original plan, but the groups of students you meet with and the way you modify and reteach content varies on a daily basis, according to what you know about specific students' needs.
- You know who needs support and with what.
- There are few or no big surprises toward the end of a unit regarding understandings and skills.
- Students are clear about their progress toward unit goals.
- Outside of this exercise, students ask for help, admit to misunderstandings, and let you know when they're confused.

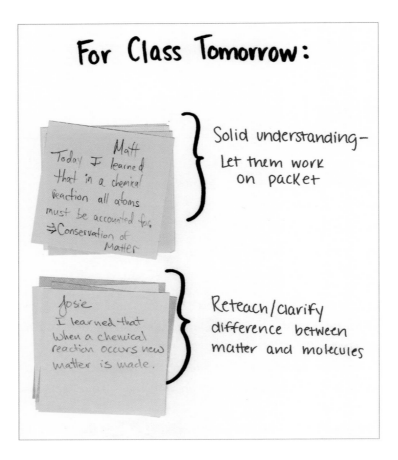

**Adapt for K–2**

- Since public information gathering methods like thumbs up or down can lead to inaccurate results because children might mimic what a friend does, you might opt for gathering information on paper. If print work is still coming along, use tally marks or a simple yes or no. This can still take time, however, with young students, so consider saving these methods for the essential check-ins, not as an every-concept strategy.

  - They write numbers 1–3 down the left side of a sticky note. They place a tally mark next to any statement they agree with.

    1. A square has four sides that are the same length. _____

    2. A rectangle has four sides that are the same length. _____

    3. A circle has no sides. _____

  - Give them preprinted questions or sentence starters. For example, after a lesson on the water cycle:

    » I can tell a friend the three stages of the water cycle. YES NO

    » Water is lost in the water cycle. YES NO

    » Ice is solid water. YES NO

- Collect feedback immediately after a lesson or activity.

- If you confer regularly with students, use this only on days when you anticipate confusion or know the material is challenging.

| | |
|---|---|
| **Adapt for 6–12** | • You have a lot of students and likely not enough time to meet with them individually on a weekly basis. Use this or a similar procedure at least once a week if not more. Get ahead of misunderstandings that can derail a unit. |
| | • Try it as homework. You'll see greater gaps in understanding than if you do it directly at the end of class when it's fresh, but this will help you see if they're retaining concepts. |
| | • Use SurveyMonkey, Nearpod, Plickers, or a Google Form exit ticket in the form of a QR code. Let students use phones or tablets to answer before leaving class. |
| **How to try this with others** | • Look over an upcoming unit. Choose a day early in the unit that you and a colleague(s) will collect sticky notes. Look at them all together. What do you notice? What are the gaps in understanding? How will you address them? |

- Look over an upcoming unit. Choose a day early in the unit that you and a colleague(s) will collect sticky notes. Look at them all together. What do you notice? What are the gaps in understanding? How will you address them?

  ○ Email a quick update after meeting with groups and/or reteaching parts of the lesson as necessary. Did you see growth? Were misunderstandings cleared up? What did you do to make that happen?

  ○ Look ahead. How can you use what you learned proactively for a future lesson? Did you discover any "preventive medicine" for getting ahead of confusion next time?

  ○ Strategize together.

- Visit the classroom of a colleague who is successfully incorporating what they learned from this process. What do they do to support every student?

*Want to know more about this strategy and others like it?*

**Check out:** Fisher, Douglas, Nancy Frey, and Russell J. Quaglia. 2018. *Engagement by Design: Creating Learning Environments Where Students Thrive.*

# 6.2 Kidwatching

**Try This**

"Assessing" kids from a distance can provide incredibly useful information in any unit. Without interacting with them or looking at their work, observe and take objective notes on their actions—what they are or aren't doing, where they go, who they talk to or don't—and use that data to make informed decisions for next steps.

You don't have to watch every student each time you do this. Sometimes you'll watch a group as they collaborate on a task or perform a lab; other times you'll watch just one or two who you aren't sure about how to help. And sometimes, yes, you will take a look at every student and jot down notes on what everyone is doing.

Choose an easy note-taking method. To assess who appears engaged during independent work time and for how long, you can try any of the following:

- An engagement inventory (See Jennifer Serravallo's [2015] *The Reading Strategies Book* for a good example.)
- A seating chart with space for notes
- Two columns with student names on the left and space to note take on the right
- A sticky note with each student's name on it whom you plan to watch (This will help you remember to fill out the notes by the end of class.)
- For a discussion, a seating chart for each discussion group, as well as space for direct quotations

Expect to play around with various options and find out what works for different scenarios. Keep it simple and easy.

For bigger numbers of students, create a code for predictable or repeated behaviors: *R* for reading, *W* for writing, *TT* for talking on task, *TO* for talking about something other than class, *DD* for daydreaming, *H* for raising their hand, *M* for gathering materials. It is also useful to jot down the time. You may pick up on a pattern—students who are focused right after lunch but highly distracted before recess, for example. These data might help you shift to placing easy, choice-based work before recess and more challenging tasks after lunch.

Look over your kidwatching notes later and decide how you will use that information to plan the next lesson, to group differently, to provide extra support, and more.

**How do I know if this idea will help?**

- Looking at student work isn't providing enough information to help you know who needs what.
- All of your information on student learning comes from "official" assessments such as tests, papers, homework, and projects.
- Your instruction isn't tailored to individual strengths and needs.

- You have in-depth information on every student that extends beyond their written work.

- Your lessons and support tools have changed according to what you notice students are doing in class.

- You analyze your observational data and can share it with students, caregivers, and colleagues as a way to empower them in being more effective.

- Try kidwatching in your own classes and then reconvene to share your findings. Discuss together how you will use this information to enhance your upcoming lessons and teaching.

*Want to know more about this strategy and others like it?*

**Check out:** Owocki, Gretchen, and Yetta M. Goodman. 2002. *Kidwatching: Documenting Children's Literacy Development.*

| Morgan | Sydney |
|---|---|
| R, R, Th | H, R, R |

| Allie | Will |
|---|---|
| R, O, Th | R, R, R |

R = reading
W = writing
H = hand raised
T = talking
O = out of seat
Th = thinking
9:20, 9:27, 9:35 am

| Jackson | Vanessa |
|---|---|
| R, T, T | T, T, O |

| Claire | Angie |
|---|---|
| R, T, T | H, T, O |

| Liz | Darian |
|---|---|
| O, R, R | R, R, H |

| Jose | Maya |
|---|---|
| R, R, R | R, H, R |

| Jacob | Eric |
|---|---|
| R, R, R | R, R, Th |

| Kayla | Meredith |
|---|---|
| R, R, Th | W, R, R |

| Haru | Isabella |
|---|---|
| R, R, R | Th, R, R |

| Luis | Ben |
|---|---|
| R, R, R | W, R, R |

# 6.3 Surveys—Don't Wait Until June

Try This Why wait until the last week of school for thoughtful suggestions, surprising insights, heartening praise, and frank critiques in a survey? Do it now.

Create a student-friendly set of questions and get feedback while there's still time to make relevant adjustments—not to mention to bask in students' compliments when you need them the most, not when summer vacation is days away.

Make your surveys brief and ask for feedback that makes a difference. In other words, ask to hear the hard stuff. Those bits stand to impact your teaching in the most important ways.

Include questions that get to students' sense of safety, value, and fairness; their grasp of content; interest in the materials and assignments; and more. Some questions to use and adapt are:

- **What is hard and what is easy about the class/content?**
- **When and how have you felt shut down or celebrated by the teacher or classmates?**
- **When and how do you feel your voice matters?**
- **Are assignments fair? Why or why not?**
- **What do you like about this class? What don't you like?**
- **What do I do that helps you understand what we're learning? What gets in the way of understanding?**
- **What else should I know?**

Make sure to include a version of this question: "What else should I know?" Trust me, this helps you discover enlightening and surprising feedback.

Announce that these are for your eyes only, and that you will use their answers to help you be a more effective teacher. Anonymous surveys might elicit greater honesty, but they also prevent you from following up with specific students on what they need.

Model what a helpful answer looks like. But let it go when their answers aren't the work of a skilled diplomat. Read between the lines. "Pop quizzes suck," can be just that—who likes a pop quiz, especially if you're unprepared? But think deeper—are pop quizzes getting in the way of students wanting to be part of your class?

Don't read these at the end of a long day when a negative comment might be harder to hear. Put on your Teflon suit and remember students might not have much experience tactfully or clearly expressing their needs.

Look for repeated responses, not outliers. When students answer consistently regarding any concern or frustration, that's important. Start there for immediate impact.

Let students complete these in class, not as homework. Sit apart so they won't worry you are checking their answers. Thank them for their feedback.

After reading results and making a plan for adjustments to your class, explain that the changes are based on their feedback. *Let them know that you listened.* Remind them their voices are important to you and that they don't need to wait for the next survey to give you constructive feedback.

**How do I know if this idea will help?**

- You're struggling to connect with all of your students.
- Things aren't going smoothly, and you don't know why.
- There's been a shift in student energy, enthusiasm, or engagement.
- You find yourself trying new things all the time in an effort to "right the ship."
- When you ask questions in class like, "Does this make sense?" you get perfunctory answers.

**How do I know if this idea is working?**

- You have new insights into what students are thinking about the class and content.
- You plan according to what you now know about students and their needs.
- Students aren't waiting for the survey to give you helpful feedback—they come to you at lunch, after school, or communicate it otherwise.
- Students let you know their needs in constructive and clear ways, not by acting out.

---

## Survey

Complete the survey below!

---

What adjectives would you use to describe how you feel in your favorite class?

Your answer

---

What adjectives would you use to describe how you feel in your least favorite class?

Your answer

---

What happens to make you feel engaged and interested in a classroom?

Your answer

---

| | |
|---|---|
| **Adapt for K–2** | • Naming feelings and emotions can be hard at this age. Keep it very simple. Surveys should simply ask them to circle an emoji or number that corresponds to a statement. |
| | • When you introduce the survey, keep it simple—say that you want to hear how they're feeling about school or in class so you can help them even more, and leave it at that. |
| | • Adults are very much "in charge" at this age and that is a security to kids, not a threat to their autonomy. Explain that this check-in is just so you can learn what they need, not to open the class up to an overhaul—scary! |
| **Adapt for 6–12** | • Try this after assignments and units, especially when performance was not what you expected. |
| | • Set the climate for a feedback-friendly classroom early on. Let students know that you welcome their thoughts. This will be an important step to establishing mutual respect. |
| | • Always follow up after you've solicited feedback. Students need to know that you listened to it, even if you can't make changes to accommodate everyone. |
| | • If students do approach you with feedback, remember the courage it took for them to come to you. Thank them for being brave. |
| | • Don't get overly invested in outlier comments that are harsh. Remember that teens are often subject to cruel comments (and therefore often pass it on). |
| **How to try this with others** | • Create a survey together that makes sense for you and your kids. Review as you go—are you opening this up to hear the hard stuff, the stuff that will matter? |
| | • More importantly, read the results together. This feels vulnerable, but it helps to have a buddy around. Highlight the positive comments and praise for your friend. Those are easy to dismiss. Be problem solvers together. |
| | • Help your friend look for patterns. Repeated, consistent frustrations or concerns are the place to start. |
| | • Set a goal together for what you will try in moving forward, based on this feedback. |
| | • Make a date for when you will administer the survey again, and decide what specifically you hope to see changed. |

*Want to know more about this strategy and others like it?*

**Check out:** Seeger, Chris. 2017. "Improve Your Teaching by Asking for Student Feedback." *Teaching Tolerance.*

# 6.4 Checklists

Try This

Checklists are different from rubrics, although you might refer to a rubric when making a checklist. Rubrics can be visually overwhelming, they are designed for teachers, and they can focus on the negative, i.e., "More than five grammatical errors." Checklists are user-friendly, are visually accessible, and help students self-assess for strengths and places to grow.

To create a checklist that helps students self-assess progress toward end-of-unit goals, list skills you have explicitly taught that you'll assess at the end of a unit. Break them down into concrete, measurable steps. Create a table so each skill goes on a line, along with three columns to the right: yes, starting to, and not yet.

| Math Unit #3: Multidigit Whole Numbers | | | |
|---|---|---|---|
| | Yes | Starting to | Not yet |
| When I write numbers, I know that a digit in one place is ten times the value of the place one over to the right. | ☐ | ☐ | ☐ |
| I use base ten numerals, number names, and expanded form to help me write multidigit numbers. | ☐ | ☐ | ☐ |
| I compare two multidigit numbers using <, >, and = to show the values. | ☐ | ☐ | ☐ |
| I can round multidigit whole numbers to any place correctly. | ☐ | ☐ | ☐ |

Before having students self-assess, demonstrate how to check your work for specific and consistent evidence before checking off "yes." You can also encourage students to go a bit further with this self-assessment tool by circling the skill that they feel most confident in or the one that is the greatest challenge for them.

Narrate aloud: "I almost always use paragraphs when I introduce new ideas, speakers, or changes in time or setting. But when I look back over my piece, I see I didn't do it every time. So even though I know how to do this, I don't see it here. So, I'm going to check 'not yet.'" Students tend to overestimate their regular application of skills, so help them see that when we are honest with ourselves, we nudge real growth.

When students have finished filling out their checklist, have them set a manageable goal based on gaps their checklist revealed. Your feedback and support, then, will be tailored to that individual goal.

| Self-Assessment Checklist Chemistry Lab | | | |
|---|---|---|---|
| **Did I do it like we learned?** | **Yes** | **Starting to** | **Not yet** |
| **INTRODUCTION** | | | |
| I used the sentence frames from class to write the purpose statement. | ☐ | ☐ | ☐ |
| I articulated the question that I was attempting to answer with the experiment. | ☐ | ☐ | ☐ |
| I wrote the purpose statement after I finished the lab. | ☐ | ☐ | ☐ |
| Someone who did not conduct the experiment would still understand the statement. | ☐ | ☐ | ☐ |
| I stated a hypothesis that is based on the research. | ☐ | ☐ | ☐ |
| I included a prediction in the hypothesis that is testable. | ☐ | ☐ | ☐ |
| I included a title to the lab that is relevant and names the topic clearly. | ☐ | ☐ | ☐ |
| **OBSERVATION/RESULTS** | | | |
| I included two graphs and/or tables to show our findings. | ☐ | ☐ | ☐ |
| I labeled the graphs with the terms from our notes. | ☐ | ☐ | ☐ |
| I added a description below each graph/table so the reader can see trends. | ☐ | ☐ | ☐ |

| **How do I know if this idea will help?** | • Students are unsure of how they are doing in relation to the learning goals. |
| | • If you use grades, students are surprised at the grades they received, either positively or negatively. |
| | • Students want to know "what they got" or how they're doing academically. |
| | • You currently grade or assess without having students self-assess first. |

| **How do I know if this idea is working?** | • Students are able to set goals for themselves. |
| | • Students' self-assessments match your own assessments. |
| | • No one is surprised at report card time. |

| **Adapt for K–5** | • Use familiar language. Don't pull phrases directly from standards, for example, unless you know students understand those terms. |
| | • Make the checklists visually simple, keep language brief, and include no more than 3–5 skills at a time. |

| **Adapt for 6-12** | • Remind students that being honest about their challenges will help them grow, and that we improve by taking an objective look at what we are and are not doing, not by being overly forgiving. |
| | • Extend the lesson by showing students how to set goals and then move their work forward toward that goal. Show them how to get support: mentor texts, peers, outside resources, looking at models, coming to you after school, setting up a conference in class, and more. |

| **How to try this with others** | • Together, work to rephrase the standards you need to address in an upcoming unit into student-friendly, first-person statements. |
| | • Create a list of appropriate tools and resources that will help students shore up the "not yets" in their work. Think of classroom, school, and out-of-school resources that you will suggest. |

*Want to know more about this strategy and others like it?*

**Check out:** Calkins, Lucy, with Kelly Hohne and Audra Robb. 2015. *Writing Pathways: Performance Assessments and Learning Progressions, Grades K–8.*

Gawande, Atul. 2014. *The Checklist Manifesto: How to Get Things Right.*

# 6.5 Make Praise Count

Try This

Praising students with comments like "Great job!" or "You're so smart!" is a bit like eating a sugary granola bar with all the nutritional benefits of a doughnut. Praise that feeds long-term success is specific and process oriented and doesn't include evaluative language. This kind of positive feedback will nourish students in the long term.

Psychologist Carol Dweck's (2016) research on growth mindset looks at the long-term impact of praise that focuses on students' efforts versus end results. When students feel that their success is tied to their effort (something they feel they can control), they stick with and perform better at challenging tasks than students who associate success with innate ability. The way we praise, Dweck points out, plays a big part in creating children's growth (or fixed) mindset.

Evaluative praise can do the exact opposite of what we intend. Specific, process-oriented praise instills confidence and motivates students to keep trying, even when they face tough challenges.

So how do we get to the productive kind of praise?

- **Note students' efforts as opposed to the final product.**
- **Point out what students *did* to be successful, so they can employ those same strategies again in the future.**
- **Keep comments specific and avoid generalities such as "Great job!"**
- **Make the focus on the specific action and avoid tying praise to who they are as a person: "You went back and read over your answers. Then you noticed something you could change," as opposed to, "You're such a good student!"**

This *is* praise—despite not being gushy or evaluative.

You might say, "I noticed that you went back to your notes from the last unit and you used that information to help you with the concepts in this unit. That reuse of earlier concepts helped you understand the new work in this unit." This compliment feels rather simple because it is simply restating what the student did. Do not underestimate, however, the power in pointing out and explicitly stating these precise moves back to the student. The student now knows what to do again, and they feel acknowledged and heard for their efforts. There is great power in that "simple" restating, even if it may not initially feel as glowing or effusive as our previous form of praise.

One teacher I know in Ritenour, Missouri, told her students (after reading the research around praise) that she was trying to stop using the word *awesome* after they do legitimately great things. She reminded them that she wanted to provide specific feedback that helped them see what they were doing well, not just general or "empty" praise. Knowing this, they loved helping "correct" her mistake.

| How do I know if this idea will help? | • Students who receive high scores are reluctant to challenge themselves or to make mistakes.<br><br>• Students give up quickly when they get to difficult material.<br><br>• Students look to you for approval and praise or to determine if their work is "good." |
|---|---|
| How do I know if this idea is working? | • Students keep trying, even after making mistakes or getting to challenging material.<br><br>• Students look to you less for approval and praise.<br><br>• Students are able to reflect on what they did to succeed and make those same efforts again. |
| How to try this with others | • Collect a pile of student work and bring it to your next meeting. Look it over with an eye for what *is* working. If you are stuck looking at the gaps, ask a colleague to help you out. Share out how this felt, what was hard, and how you'll share your praise when you see students next.<br><br>• Visit a colleague's classroom and observe together what students are doing well in their behaviors and in their work. Aim to do this for every single student, but start with those who are most accustomed to hearing what still needs work. |

**Want to know more about this strategy and others like it?**

**Check out:** Dweck, Carol S. 2016. *Mindset: The New Psychology of Success.*

Hammond, Zaretta. 2015. *Culturally Responsive Teaching & the Brain: Promoting Authentic Engagement and Rigor Among Culturally and Linguistically Diverse Students.*

# 6.6 Quick Writes to Tell You What Students Know and Need

Try This

Use quick writing prompts to check understanding and to invite inquiry at the start of class or to let students reflect and solidify thinking at the end of class. Make this writing low stakes (ungraded), short in time and length, and public (students share in pairs, groups, to the class, or even among classes.)

## Before the content is presented, or at the beginning of class

- **Entry tickets:** Get students to consider an upcoming topic by answering a related question: "What does water look like in different forms?" "How did the Revolutionary War impact our lives today?" "If you divide something, do you make more of it, less of it, or the same amount?"

- **Prediction:** Students write predictions about an upcoming text or topic: "If they were Macbeth, how would they react to the events of the last act?" "After learning about torque yesterday, what will happen if they rotate their body before they swing?"

- **What I know and what I wonder:** Present the topic briefly. Ask students to list what they already know about this topic and questions they have about it.

## After the content is presented, or at the end of class

- **Postcard:** Write a postcard to a student who was absent today, explaining what the key ideas from today's class.

- **1–10:** Rate your understanding on a 1 out of 10. Explain your number.

- **Sum it up:** Summarize the big idea of today's lesson in ten words or less.

- **Verbal exit ticket:** Stand at the door as students leave. Let them know they must each share something they learned that day, but that they must each be different answers. Give them some time to generate thinking so they are ready with backup answers.

- **3-2-1:** Answer three questions:

  1. What new thing did you learn in today's lesson?

  2. What question do you have about the content or anything else?

  3. What is something you don't understand?

Most important is that you collect these and read them over. You don't have to do any more than simply look at them (no comments or grade), and then you can decide what you'll do tomorrow. How will you add to these understandings, clarify misunderstandings, answer questions, and celebrate growth?

| **How do I know if this idea will help?** | • A lot of content and material is covered in class, but there isn't a lot of time allotted to reflect on that content. |
| | • You feel rushed to cover a lot of content each class. |
| | • You are unsure if everyone is getting the concepts. |
| | • Students are struggling with a skill or concept, but you're not sure why. |
| | • Some students seem bored. |

**How do I know if this idea is working?**

• You have a solid sense of what students understand and what they don't understand on a regular basis.

• Students are honest about admitting confusion on the quick writings—they know it means you will offer additional support and clarification the next day.

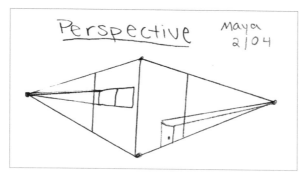

Students were asked to demonstrate their understanding of perspective.

Students quickly jotted words with a short e sound.

**Adapt for K–2**

• Many of these can be modified to involve less writing, which will take time and effort for some of your students. You can have them rank with numbers, choose along a scale of understanding, or select from pregenerated answers to assess understanding.

**Adapt for 6–12**

• If devices are allowed during the school day, consider creating exit and entry tickets as QR codes that students can complete quickly (and typically more eagerly) on their phone. Google Forms allows you to get exit ticket response back immediately, already graphed to show you the complete data.

**How to try this with others**

• Bring quick writing responses to look at with others. Decide together how you can use these data to better inform tomorrow's lesson or even upcoming assessments and units.

*Want to know more about this strategy and others like it?*

**Check out:** Fisher, Douglas, and Nancy Frey. 2014. *Checking for Understanding: Formative Assessment Techniques for Your Classroom.*

# 6.7 Set Your Timer: Partner Feedback

Peer feedback sounds student-centered and productive—and it can be—but it can also be the opposite. Sometimes, advice can be lackluster, and talk can be monopolized by one confident voice. Avoid these pitfalls with structured feedback that empowers students and enriches learning in just ten minutes.

Model this exercise with a student or colleague, and then let students use the same protocol in partnerships. Suggest students use a timer to keep the pace swift and the feedback focused, or set the timer yourself and announce minute breakdowns until students are able to manage on their own.

1. Minutes 0–2: Partner A gives a brief summary of the work to Partner B, who listens. Partner A describes their idea and what they're trying to do and hoping to produce.
2. Minutes 2–4: Partner B asks clarifying questions to A. A answers.
3. Minutes 4–6: Partner B provides feedback while A listens to the suggestions and thoughts.
4. Minutes 6–8: Partner A recaps what they heard, making sure they understand. Partner B affirms and/or clarifies as needed.
5. Minutes 8–10: Partner A creates a plan for moving forward. As Partner A charts an action plan, Partner B provides input and support.

Switch! Roles are reversed so Partner B receives the same attention and feedback.

After students try the protocol, give time for them to reflect and self-assess. They might consider:

- What was helpful?
- What felt comfortable and productive?
- What felt uncomfortable or frustrating?
- What will they try next time to make it go better?
- What could the teacher do to make this go better?

Share out your own observations and suggestions and decide how you will support students in using the protocol again in the near future. Give an opportunity for students to try it again, using their ideas for making it work even better.

- Students frequently ask you, "Is this right?" or request your feedback and approval.
- Students volunteer to share their work with the class or with you, but they are not as eager to listen to others' ideas and work.
- Peer feedback is only written and/or doesn't produce helpful suggestions.
- Listening skills are in progress.
- Feedback can be one-sided in that some students ask for and receive it, but they are not as likely to provide it thoughtfully for others.
- Students see the teacher as the sole provider for feedback.

- You are solicited less and less for feedback at every stage of the work.
- Students ask one another for feedback, using the protocol or otherwise.
- You see revisions and changes to work due to peer feedback.
- Partners are able to listen to one another's work ideas and to one another's thoughts and suggestions.
- Student work reflects ideas from one another.

- Give time for students to practice each step while you offer feedback.
- Provide sentence frames for each phase of the process. For example:
  - "I'm trying to . . ." "My idea is . . ."
  - "Can you explain . . . ?" "What do you mean . . . ?"
  - "I like how you . . ." "I notice . . ." "I wonder if . . ." "You might try . . ."
  - "You're thinking I could . . ." "One thing you're suggesting is . . ." "I like your idea that . . ."
  - "I'm going to try to . . ." "Next I'm going to . . ." "I'm going to need . . ." "Another thing I'll work on is . . ."

| **Adapt for 6–12** | • Students will benefit most when this is done in person. Logistically, however, using Google Docs or FaceTime provides students with an easy way to get feedback outside of class, too. |
|---|---|

- Sentence starters may help older students, too, if they're new to this.

- Start with low-stakes work so egos are protected. Students may shy away from providing feedback or admitting to their challenges if the work is overly personal, of low quality, or at risk of receiving a damaging grade.

**How to try this with others**

- Create a model for students by doing this with a colleague. Talk about your teaching goal and describe what you're trying to do. Go through the minute-by-minute breakdowns, listening to and answering your colleague's questions, hearing their feedback, and then creating an action plan together. Make it genuine. Be able to share with students what was hard, what worked, and what to look out for.

*Want to know more about this strategy and others like it?*

**Check out:** Spencer, John, and A. J. Juliani. 2017. *Empower: What Happens When Students Own Their Learning.*

# 6.8 Immediate, Personalized Feedback: Conferences

**Try This**

Use independent work time to talk with students individually about their learning. Sit next to them, one-on-one. Listen to how they're doing, what questions they have, and what they need help with before offering suggestions.

Although often used in reading and writing workshop classrooms, conferences are a way for *any* teacher to assess students' needs and strengths on the fly and to teach into just what that student needs, then and there. Conducting conferences is a practice that many teachers devote decades to improving, so for now, keep it simple.

1. Ask the student open-ended questions about how they're doing and how the work is going.
2. Listen to their successes, struggles, questions, and goals.
3. Tell the student something specific they are doing well and should continue doing.
4. Offer one specific suggestion to lift the level of their work.
5. Write down a note so you remember what you discussed and can follow up in your next conversation.

## Tips

- Start with an open-ended question, such as, "How's it going"? Then listen.
- If the student says little, you can follow up with, "Tell me more about that." Or you might offer to come back in a few minutes so they have a minute to think of what to say.
- Let students know what a conference looks like so they're prepared. Give them ideas of what they might talk about, such as something they're proud of in their work, something they're not sure about, or something specific they want help with.
- It may help to let students know when they'll meet with you. This gives them time to think about what they want to talk about.
- Let students do most of the talking.
- Don't forget to say what's working well.
- Limit your suggestion to one thing. Any more risks overwhelming the student or muddying the goal.
- Conferences usually last about 3–5 minutes.
- Keep track of whom you talk to and when. These records provide essential information about what your students know and need to know, and ensure you get to everyone evenly.

- Students rarely have one-on-one time with you unless they're in trouble or come to you for help.

- You're unsure what individual students know and need to know.

- You base your lessons and plans on the curriculum only, not on what students may need.

- Students have personal goals as well as class goals that they're working on.

- Your relationships are stronger across the class.

- Students ask to meet with you to talk about their work.

- You can see students' varied needs within the overall unit.

- You are able to track individual goals and progress using conference notes across weeks and months.

- You become less invested in students' final products and more invested in their individual progress.

| Teacher's Job in a Conference | Student's Job in a Conference |
|---|---|
| Let students know they're coming. | Be ready to talk about their work and what they're trying to do. |
| Ask questions. | Ask questions. |
| Listen carefully. | Show what they're proud of and why. |
| Take notes. | |
| Tell students what they're doing well. | Show where they're struggling and why. |
| Tell them a way to grow. | Keep notes on what the teacher shows them. |
| Show them what that looks like. | |
| Ask them to try it. | Try the suggestion after the teacher leaves. |
| | Stay quietly on task when the teacher is conferring with others. |

**Reading Workshop Workflow**

| Deep into their books | Organizing notes and listing questions for conference | Conference with Mr. Suarez | Priority for AR |
|---|---|---|---|
| • Angie | | | • Alex |
| • Sarah | • Angelina | • Brianna | • Anya |
| • Dylan | • Miguel | • Ben | |
| • Hailey | • Emma | • Amanda | |
| • Max | | | |
| • Roger | | | |

This teacher posts a schedule every day that shows who is working independently, who will meet with the teacher in a conference, and who is getting ready to meet with the teacher soon.

**Adapt for K–5**

- Safeguard one-on-one time by reminding students you can't answer questions when you're in a conference. One teacher has a stop sign on the back of her note-taking clipboard and she holds it up as a reminder.

- Ask students to recap what you asked them to try. This will help remind them that you're holding them accountable to try what you taught them.

- Provide a visual reminder of what you taught on a sticky note. Make sure the student keeps that visual reminder handy.

**Adapt for 6–12**

- Students can keep notes on conferences, too. You can ask them to jot down what you taught them that day and use their notes as a check for understanding. Did they "get" what you intended? If not, reteach it right away.

- Don't mistake one-word answers as lack of comprehension. Focus your first conferences on positive aspects of students' work to help them develop positive associations with this time.

- Consider sitting at bar-height stools or even standing up when you conduct a conference. When other students can see you they're less likely to get off task.

- If you see upward of 100 students in a week, it's unlikely you'll do one-on-one conferences with them more than once every week or two. That's OK. Don't sacrifice meaningful feedback for speed. Three to five students a class is plenty.

**How to try this with others**

- If someone in your building already confers with students regularly, go see it in action. Listen in and debrief with the teacher afterward. Look at their conferring notes and see if their note-taking system would work for you.

- Go online and watch videos of teachers and coaches conferring with students. Jot down what you notice the student and the teacher doing and debrief. How would this look in your classroom?

- Commit to conferring with each student you see in a week, and then come back together. What worked? What was hard? What resources will you use to address any challenges?

*Want to know more about this strategy and others like it?*

**Check out:** Serravallo, Jennifer. 2019. *A Teacher's Guide to Reading Conferences.*

Munson, Jen. 2018. *In the Moment: Conferring in the Elementary Math Classroom.*

## 6.9 Compliment Conferences

**Try This**

Focus your verbal feedback on what is working. Find one or two meaningful aspects of the student's work to praise, even if the work feels chock-full of errors or is well below grade level. You might rehearse by studying some of that student's work before meeting with them.

When telling the student what they're doing well, stay with it until you sense they absorb the compliment. They may be so used to hearing the "but . . ." that they can't hear what's working. When you see them nodding/smiling and you know they understand the compliment, end the conference or conversation.

**How do I know if this idea will help?**

- Students say, "I'm not a good math student/badminton player/artist/reader/writer."
- Students' enthusiasm for this subject is low.
- You find yourself focusing on or aware of what's not working more than what is working.

**How do I know if this idea is working?**

- The student nods or smiles during conferences.
- The student works with more gusto and volume after the conference.
- The student remembers what you noticed them doing well and takes pride in that accomplishment.

Sometimes your conference notes will reflect a conversation that focused only on what was going well.

Date: 1/17

General: Started new book— Elizabeth Acevedo's <u>With the Fire on High</u>

Compliment: Paying attention to multiple themes, not just one! Tracking all these ~~Next steps:~~ ideas in notebook with theme chart. Wow!

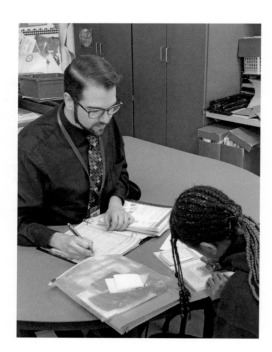

| **Adapt for K–5** | • Prepare to see a lot more of whatever you compliment. Therefore, go for high leverage and easily replicable qualities of work that the student can use frequently. For instance, purposeful elaboration of details that support a big idea, filling in all of the white space in a drawing, and inviting others in their group during an activity offer bigger pay-offs than, say, putting a comma in the proper place.<br><br>• Putting the student's work up on the document camera to share with the class will instill pride. Make sure to do this with *all* students' work. Remind them to tell their families, too, or send the work home so families can see it.<br><br>• Many younger students look for "fairness." Keep track so everyone gets a compliment conference at least once a month if not more frequently. |
|---|---|
| **Adapt for 6–8** | • Students may take longer to internalize the compliment. Find ways to keep reiterating what is working.<br><br>• Try to find aspects of the student work that are genuinely strong and have an impact, and avoid compliments that they brought their pen to class or remembered to title their piece. By middle school, students are keenly on the lookout for anything "fake." |
| **Adapt for 9–12** | • Prepare to spend time helping the student see what is genuinely working. They may not trust this at first.<br><br>• High school students often focus on the grade. If they ask about what this means for their grade, you can ask them to hold off on that discussion until they've spent more time on the piece, or show them on a checklist or rubric where that skill would be accounted for. You can also try Strategy 10.4 "Side-by-Side Grading," in which you grade the piece with them at your side, going through the rubric together. |
| **How to try this with others** | • Observe a colleague conducting a compliment conference. Invite them to your class to watch you, and debrief together afterward.<br><br>• Practice compliment conferences with colleagues by studying a stack of student work and noticing only what's working. Share out what you find. You might even create a running list of what you notice to praise for everyone's reference later on.<br><br>• Share out student strengths in your subject or content area for other grade team teachers to see. They can reinforce those strengths when they work with them or find others to add. |

*Want to know more about this strategy and others like it?*

**Check out:** Johnston, Peter, H. 2004. *How Our Language Affects Children's Learning.*

# 6.10 Learning Progressions

Learning progressions chart student's progress with a skill across a continuum. They aren't just assessment tools for teachers; they are also designed to empower students to see what they can do and how to move forward. Learning progressions are designed to match each student's entry point. They provide a road map based on what each student is able to do, so no one feels defeated and everyone sees clearly what how to improve.

Here's how to create a learning progression (also known as a progress map or learning ladder):

1. Name the skill you are assessing.
2. Choose or assign a piece of work that shows evidence of that skill.
3. Collect student work and read quickly through all it.
4. Sort the work into three piles, ranked according to your (as of now) holistic sense of skill development. Don't stress if some students fall in between categories. Just choose a pile for now.
5. Take the pile ranked as the beginning group. Reread a few of these in closer detail. Start a list: What can these students already *do*? Create a list of one to five bulleted phrases articulating the skill's qualities that are evident in student work at this stage. Keep the list objective and positive. Now go to the next pile, and the next, and do the same thing. This process will get easier as you start to see gradations of the skills and subskills.
6. Chart the qualities of skill work across a columned chart, leaving one column at the far right blank for now.
7. Now you have a delineation of what students are doing and how they can advance in a realistic and doable way.
8. For the open column, create a list of qualities of work that advances one more rung up the ladder so that students already skilled in this area have a vision for what to work toward.
9. Share the learning progression with students and show them examples of what each quality looks like.
10. Ask them to look over their own work and decide what column it matches. Then, how can they revise it to make it match the next column?

This self-assessment can also be done in peer editing. Students rank their partner's example on the continuum and make suggestions for how to advance one to the right.

- Students are dependent on you to tell them if their work "is right."

- Some students are bored or feel like they've mastered this skill. Others are frustrated and feel like they can't get it.

- All students are trying to get better at this skill.

- Students who are most challenged by this skill don't say they are "bad" at it— they look at the progression and see where they are and where to go next.

- You have concrete suggestions to give students for how to get a better at this skill.

- Students can give peer feedback using the progression, showing their partner where they are on the progression and offering suggestions for how to move one column up.

| 1 | 2 | 3 |
|---|---|---|
| I can explain natural selection or evolution in general terms. | I can define natural selection and evolution. I can give examples of both. | I can explain the process of natural selection and evolution and how they relate to each other. |

Understanding Natural Selection, Biology

| 1 | 2 | 3 | 4 | 5 |
|---|---|---|---|---|
| I wrote about how a character feels and why they feel that way. | I wrote about a character trait, not an emotion or feeling. | I wrote about more than one character trait, knowing that characters are multifaceted. | I compared different characters who have similar traits. | I analyzed how a character's traits changed across the book. |

Making Character Inferences, Language Arts

**How to try this with others**

- Create learning progressions with colleagues. Look at student work together and reflect on what students at various skill levels are doing and how they can move up the progression. Use the process across grade teams to develop an understanding of an even greater range of what students do when developing this skill.

*Want to know more about this strategy and others like it?*

**Check out:** Calkins, Lucy, with Kelly Hohne and Audra Robb. 2015. *Writing Pathways: Performance Assessments and Learning Progressions, Grades K–8.*

# 7 Planning Matters

## What you have in place, and what you're ready for next

The most important planning happens in response to the people in front of us each day—our students, who know and need a wide range of unpredictable things. Curriculum is a basic building block, but we need to plan responsively, in relation to where students *are*, not where they're supposed to be. To make your curriculum fit your students, as opposed to the other way around, you need to truly know students (relationships) and have an in-depth sense of what they know and need (formative assessment and feedback).

This chapter works on the premise that you will use your school community's relevant standards to inform your learning goals and curriculum. That is important. And now we will look at how to structure lessons and units so that they address those standards, and more importantly, address the needs of the people walking into your room each day.

## Why is planning important?

Over two decades into teaching, I never "wing" a lesson—this practice is mildly panic inducing and, despite my experience, rarely successful. A common thread among the most effective classrooms that I visit is that those teachers leave little to chance—their lessons are thought through each and every time. Ironically, thorough planning is what allows for spontaneity. The more time we effectively put into prep, the better our classes function. In a best-case scenario, the hard work happens before the kids set foot in the classroom. When we aren't busy thinking about what to do next in a lesson, we're better able to respond to kids as things come up. Planning, therefore, isn't a rookie practice that you outgrow but an essential, ongoing and challenging part of teaching.

The multitasking required in a room full of students means that we cannot afford to make decisions on the fly. Of course we can and should change gears or reroute as needed, but this should happen by *adjusting* plans, not creating them as we go. It is a kindness to your students and to yourself to put in the time beforehand. You will feel confident and competent in running a responsive classroom.

What we want to avoid, and I speak from experience, is spending time searching the internet for superficial activities to do the next day. Or, again speaking from experience, copying the plans of the fabulous teacher next door. This kind of desperate search for a quick fix won't empower you long term to plan with your particular kids in mind or to understand all parts of the planning process.

Solid planning also means that we are getting to essential learning goals and not just filling up time with activities. The best plans start with the end in mind, and then work backward, thinking through what needs to happen to get students to those long-range goals.

## What does the research say?

Planning is one of the four essential domains outlined by Charlotte Danielson (2007) in her book, *Enhancing Professional Practice: A Framework for Teaching* and for good reason. Being able to meet the standards and the needs of our students requires critical decision-making and top-notch skills.

And yet between 96 percent and 99 percent of teachers (secondary and elementary, respectively) are so flummoxed by planning needs that they turn to Google on a regular basis to download someone else's plan (Pondiscio 2016). When teachers are given a subpar curriculum, or not enough support to understand the curriculum, they turn elsewhere. It takes time and support to strengthen the planning process and to know that this will be a lifelong learning curve.

The most effective classrooms are ones in which teachers have a plan (and a reason for that plan) for each step of the day. Learning how to do that is a massive task but an essential one. When we have a plan, we teach more confidently and more effectively (Jensen 2001). Not to mention, it provides us with a record of where we've been and points where we can go next. Without effective plans, it's hard for us (and for students) to see the thread connecting the day to day that leads up to big understandings. And finally, in all likelihood, someone in your building will ask to see your plans, or you'll need them for a sub. There's no way around it—we have to plan, and we have to get good at it!

## Is this the goal for me?

- Do you answer "yes" and "sometimes" for all statement? Consider moving to the next chapter. You've got this!

- Do you have a mix of "yes," "sometimes," and "not yet" answers? This might be the goal for you.

- Do you answer "not yet" for most of these statements? Go back and try the checklists from the previous chapters. You're likely to enjoy greater success and see quicker results by focusing there.

## What do you notice?

| | Yes | Sometimes | Not yet |
|---|---|---|---|
| For each lesson and unit, I can state what I want students to know, understand, and be able to do by the end. | ☐ | ☐ | ☐ |
| Students can consistently answer: "What are you learning to do today? Why? How will you show what you learned?" | ☐ | ☐ | ☐ |
| All students are engaged in the lessons, not just the academic performers. | ☐ | ☐ | ☐ |
| Lessons build on what came before, and they lead up to what comes next. | ☐ | ☐ | ☐ |
| I feel confident in my knowledge of the content and can predict where my students might struggle with it. | ☐ | ☐ | ☐ |
| There are multiple ways for students to engage in and be successful with the learning goal. | ☐ | ☐ | ☐ |

# 7.1 Whatever They Do, You Do

**Try This**

Name the specific task or skill you want students to understand and be able to do in your upcoming lesson: shoot a layup, sound out multisyllabic words, write a thesis statement, generate a topic for a research paper, solve an algebraic equation. Do it yourself. As you do, spy on yourself. Ask:

- "What did I need beforehand (preknowledge, preparation, practice, safety, encouragement) to do this?"
- "What did I do to get ready?"
- "What did I do when I got stuck?"
- And most importantly: "What did I *do*, step by step?"

Now picture a complete novice doing it. Do it again, taking note of anything new that got in your way. Think through: What support would help ease that obstacle?

Now picture a student in your class who is unlike you. Do it again. Take note of anything that would present a frustrating challenge for that student. Think through necessary support.

Go back to your planning and assignments and adjust accordingly. Incorporate necessary supports so the task sets up everyone for potential success. Provide clear, step-by-step explanations for how to perform this skill. Break down the teaching into more than one class or day if the actual teaching of the task or skill takes more than ten minutes. Create or keep your work as a model to show students. Bonus points if you can show your own authentic struggle and how you problem solved. More bonus points if you explain how you adjusted your planning accordingly.

**How do I know if this idea will help?**

- Class assignments or work is often met with unexpected questions and concerns.
- The transition to independent work time takes a while.
- Students give up easily when they don't "get it" right away.
- Students do not always complete the tasks. Note that their answers of "It's boring," "I forgot," "This is stupid," and other excuses often mask a genuine confusion or fear of failing.
- Students are failing or performing the skill poorly, and you're not sure why.
- You were not challenged by this same skill, or you cannot remember how you were challenged by it.

- You see students nodding as you explain the task or teach the skill, and they are eager to try it themselves.
- You see new successes.
- A high percentage of students are willing to try challenging tasks, even when they don't get it right the first (or second or third) time.
- Students are using your breakdowns, explanations, and supports to help themselves problem solve.

- Ask a colleague or a student to help you. Show them your plans for an assignment or lesson, or actually deliver your planned lesson. Have them try the task, or simply ask them to think through any part that would be confusing, scary, or boring. Even if they don't have specific suggestions, you'll know to go back and look at those parts carefully.
- Listen to a colleague's lesson as a novice, or a specific student your colleague is unsure how to reach. Jot down any time you are confused, fearful, or bored. Troubleshoot how to clarify the skill, increase comfort levels, provide support, and engage and motivate.

*Want to know more about this strategy and others like it?*

**Check out:** Hertz, Christine, and Kristine Mraz. 2018. *Kids First from Day One: A Teacher's Guide to Today's Classroom.*

## *Tech Integration Tip*

### USE DIGITAL TOOLS AS YOUR STUDENTS WOULD

Before introducing an app, platform, website, or digital tool, make sure you've tinkered with it yourself and explored its potential value for every learner in your room. Sign in to the tool as a student. Use it just as a student would, going all the way through the process. Ideally, do it twice, keeping a different student in mind each time. What would a tech guru find? A technophobe? An English language learner? A student who knows this content well? A student who would benefit from extra support with this content?

Better yet, invite a few students to try it with you. Observe them and take notes. See how each student manages the tool. Ask for their feedback during and after.

Before introducing the tool to students, reflect on its usefulness, accessibility, and impact for every learner in your room. Is it a glorified worksheet, or does using this tool or platform actually increase engagement and learning?

# 7.2 Predictable Isn't Boring

**Try This**

Use daily and weekly templates when planning lessons. Instead of writing out every day's lesson, use the template to fill in the blanks with those components you know need to happen. Predictable templates ensure consistency and keep your instruction streamlined. When routines and structures are consistent, students' minds are freed up for learning.

Predictable chunks of time, both within a lesson and across a week, ensure that you get to everything, that you protect what's important, that you hold yourself and students accountable, and that you create a safe learning environment where students are set up for success. Students will be more independent and focused when they don't need to learn new processes each day. Put your energy instead into designing relevant and meaningful lessons—your energy and passion will be contagious!

To create a framework that you can replicate day to day, it's more important that you find what works for you and your students than adopting a specific template. Think of previous classes that flowed, that allowed for big chunks of time for students to be "on" as opposed to passive, and that felt productive. How did the time go? How can you use and adapt those time frames and structures on a regular basis?

When you have a template you like, go the next step and add sentence starters to help you plan with ease. Sentence frames that introduce each part of the lesson will help you stay consistent, frame the learning in predictable ways, and keep the guesswork out of the planning process.

**How do I know if this idea will help?**

- You plan day by day.
- Each day can look different.
- Writing out lessons takes a lot of time or feels overwhelming.
- Lesson language isn't routine or consistent.
- Students come into class and ask, "What are we doing today?"

**How do I know if this idea is working?**

- You can use concepts from the curriculum and insert them into your template.
- Lessons use consistent language such as, "Watch me as I . . . ," and, "Now it's your turn . . ."
- You plan across a week or unit, then fill in the smaller day-by-day components.
- You typically know what you'll be doing in a class on a given day or time.
- Students ask fewer questions about what is coming next.
- There is greater independence as students know what to expect.

## Ms. Maurantonio's Schedule – 2019–2020

| | Monday | Tuesday | Wednesday | Thursday | Friday |
|---|---|---|---|---|---|
| 7:45-8:05 | Unpack/ Morning Work | Unpack/ Morning Work | Unpack/ Morning Work | Unpack/ Morning Work | Unpack/ Morning Work |
| 8:05-8:20 | Morning Meeting | Morning Meeting | Morning Meeting | Morning Meeting | Morning Meeting |
| 8:20-9:00 | Writer's Workshop | Writer's Workshop | Writer's Workshop | Writer's Workshop | Writer's Workshop |
| 9:00-9:20 | Shared Reading | Computer 9:30 | Shared Reading | Shared Reading | Music 9:30 |
| 9:20-10:00 | Reading Workshop | Reading Workshop | Reading Workshop | Reading Workshop | Reading Workshop |
| 10:00-10:20 | Phonics/Word Study | Phonics/Word Study | Phonics/Word Study | Phonics/Word Study | Phonics/Word Study |
| 10:20-10:30 | Prep for Lunch | Prep for Lunch TEAM MEETING | Prep for Lunch | Prep for Lunch | Prep for Lunch |
| 10:30-11:20 | Lunch/Recess | Lunch/Recess | Lunch/Recess | Lunch/Recess | Lunch/Recess |
| 11:20-11:30 | Quiet Time | Quiet Time | Quiet Time | Quiet Time | Quiet Time |
| 11:30-11:50 | Read Aloud | Read Aloud | Math Workshop | Read Aloud | Read Aloud |
| 11:50-12:30 | Math Workshop | Math Workshop | Snack | Math Workshop | Math Workshop |
| 12:30-1:00 | Art | P.E. | Music | P.E. | P.E. |
| 1:00-1:30 | 1:15 Snack | Snack 1:20 | Library 1:05 | Snack 1:20 | Snack 1:20 |
| 1:30-2:00 | Science/SS Pack Up | Science/SS | Library 1:50 | Science/SS | Choice Time |

**Adapt for K–5**

- Routine helps younger students feel secure and maximizes their independence. If you have to introduce lots of new learning processes, expect students to be a bit dependent on you at the start until they internalize the new processes.
- Having a chart visible with the routines and time frames will help students know what's coming next.

**Adapt for 6–12**

- Considering your students see multiple teachers every day, don't worry that your lesson language is predictable. There is a comfort in that routine and knowing what to expect.
- Post an agenda so students can pace themselves across the period and they know what to expect. This will also help you hold yourself accountable to keep to those time frames.

Using a lesson-planning template with predictable and precise time frames helps to ensure a routine. It also ups engagement and streamlines our planning process.

PLANNING TEMPLATE—Class Period 45 minutes

| Time Frame | Daily Class Structure | Sentence Frame |
|---|---|---|
| 5 min | **Soft Start** | ***Remember as you come in to . . .*** <br> (Read your article/listen to podcast excerpt/complete the Google poll/write off today's quote.) <br> *We'll get started all together in five minutes.* |
| 1 min | **Name the learning for the day**—what this learning builds on and why we're learning it. | *Yesterday we learned to . . .* <br><br> *Today we're going to build on that by learning how to (skill) by (steps).* <br><br> *This is important because . . .* |
| 5–7 min | **Focused Instruction** <br><br> Repeat today's learning. <br><br> Teach and model one strategy that gets to a standard/skill. | *One way we get better at (skill) is by (steps) . . .* <br><br> *Watch me as I . . . and listen to my thinking as I share what I'm doing.* <br><br> *Notice how I . . .* |
| 2 min | Check understanding—did they "get it"? | *Now it's your turn!* <br> *Try this quickly as you turn and talk to a partner . . .* <br><br> *Stop and jot for just a minute and try to . . .* |
| 1 min | Remind them of the strategy as they set off into independent work. | *So today we're learning how to (skill) by (steps).* <br> *You're going to be working on this by . . .* <br><br> *I have these steps right here on the chart to refer to if you need it.* |
| 15–25 min | **Independent work** <br> Students are working individually, in pairs, or in groups on one or more parts of an ongoing project or task. They are applying today's strategy and previous strategies. <br> Teacher is helping individuals and small groups. | *Today you're going to continue working on . . .* <br><br> *Remember to keep in mind what we learned to do today . . .* <br><br> *As you're working, I'll be meeting with . . .* <br><br> *If you get stuck, don't forget you can* <br> *(three choices) . . .* |
| 5 min | **Closing, share** | *Talk at your table and share your best example of . . . along with two reasons why it is your favorite example. Everyone look up here on the document camera so I can share what . . . did so well . . .* <br> *Let's hear from everyone one sentence of when you tried . . .* |

**How to try this with others**

- Every teacher brings one of their lesson plans. Discuss what components of your lessons are essential each day. See what language you use in your lessons, and choose sentence starters that feel like a good fit to introduce each of those components.

- Modify the templates here as a starting point. Try planning out a few upcoming lessons together using the template. Alter as needed after a few weeks of trying it out.

- Save even more time by dividing up a unit's worth of lessons between grade team colleagues. Everyone fills out the template for their assigned lessons, then shares. Planning is done!

# 7.3 Incorporate Managed Choices

Choice, even between just two options, boosts buy-in and engagement. Think through the lesson you're planning with choice in mind. How can you provide a choice in topic? Or process? Or product? You don't need to incorporate choice in all aspects, but allowing for options in even a few places across a lesson will work wonders, and it won't cost you a thing.

Because your own choice matters, right now choose one aspect of the lesson where you'll add choice. Think about the content students work with, the way students will learn that content, or the way they will show their learning. Then, when you add choice, start with just a choice between two or three things.

For example, you might let students choose from one of three insects to study for their life cycle research project. Or, you'll let them decide if they'll work with a partner or do it on their own. Or, you'll offer the option of having them write a report, make a blog post, or create a podcast to show their findings from the research on life cycles.

Now you have provided some negotiated choices, all of which you approve. This is like offering a toddler the choice between two outfits. You didn't ask whether they want to get dressed or not. Whether it's sweatpants or the jeans they choose, they get dressed! Make sure you're comfortable with any of the choices students may make.

Once you have started incorporating more choice and it feels more comfortable, build on it. Review the options you're including.

- **Do choices include varied entry points for different skill levels, interests, work styles, and background knowledge?**
- **Do all the choices help students to address the overall skill?**
- **Can you loosen the reins a bit more here and there and add even more choice?**

Yes? Now you have a choice of patting yourself on the back or doing a little dance to celebrate.

- **Engagement is low.**
- **Students complain about the work.**
- **There is a lot of off-task behavior during work time.**
- **You find assessing work tedious.**
- **Students are not particularly interested in their classmates' work.**
- **Homework is not getting done.**

**How do I know if this idea is working?**

- Engagement is high.

- Students are excited to get started.

- Grading is less painful because student work is varied.

- There is excitement around sharing work, because each student's topic or presentation is varied.

- Students do not complain (or complain less) about the assignments.

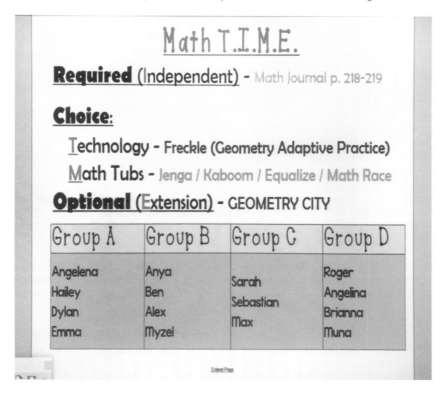

**Adapt for K–5**

- Young students will be overwhelmed with too many choices. Keep options limited in scope.

- Allow time to teach into the choices and show students why certain options might work better for some than others. Students may need support making choices that are right for *them* rather than choosing the same thing as a friend.

- Reflect with them after a time when you gave choice—on where to sit, for instance: "What helped you as learners? What made learning more difficult? What will you choose next time?"

- Expect and allow for poor choices, especially at the beginning of the year. Younger students have so much of their lives dictated for them. Empowering them to make decisions, even if they don't always choose what we'd choose for them, is important learning in itself.

- If one element of the day doesn't include choice, see if you can add it to something directly afterward to up engagement. For example, after they finish their assigned math problems (no choice), they can choose what math game to play with their partner.

- Older students crave autonomy, and granting it is an essential step toward upping their engagement and interest. Don't deny them (or yourself) this easy method because in real life they don't always have a choice. Rest assured there are many, many things dictated to them, and they are well versed in this life lesson.

- You can provide two options and then allow that students might have another idea, but they need to approve it through you first. This gives them some wiggle room to surprise you with unknown interests or preferences, but you still get to have final approval.

- Older students also benefit from hearing you walk them through the benefits and drawbacks of various choices, as well as have the opportunity to reflect on what choice in the end did or didn't work for them.

- Following what one's friend chooses is often a deciding factor. You might acknowledge when someone makes the choice to strike out on their own or discuss why choosing to part from the crowd is brave in classwork and in life.

- Bring a copy of an upcoming lesson or assignment to share with others. Trade or share out, and offer suggestions to one another where choice could be incorporated.

- Select one choice lens at a time to focus on with a colleague: process, product, or content. Plan an upcoming unit with that lens in mind. When you're ready, add another lens for choice, then another.

- Reflect together on a unit that incorporated choice, and think about when and how it helped up engagement and skills and when it wasn't as relevant.

*Want to know more about this strategy and others like it?*

**Check out:** Tomlinson, Carol Ann. 2016. *The Differentiated Classroom: Responding to the Needs of All Learners.*

Tunstall, Tricia. 2009. *Note by Note: A Celebration of the Piano Lesson.*

# 7.4　Learn Pop Culture

**Try This**

Find out what music, athletes, memes, TV shows, video games, movies, or viral trends on social media platforms your students are into right now. Don't just find out from one group of students—ask a lot of them. Make sure you get your information from actual kids.

Go watch, listen to, play, or follow one of those popular things. Make it the one you know the least about, or the one that a student you connect with the least mentioned. Watch it without judgment. Be on the lookout for anything admirable, creative, or interesting. Take note of any image or clip you could use in your instruction.

Reference that new knowledge however you can, but do not try to *be* one of your students when you do so. You risk looking desperate or out of touch if you get it wrong, if it's already out of date, or if you feign real knowledge. Mention it with a wink that you know you're no expert, but you're trying!

Use a popular (and appropriate) song video for theme analysis, analyze an athlete's torque to understand a law in physics, add coins from a video game in math, or sound out the syllables in the shark song. Be judicious in pop culture references, using them when you are teaching predictably challenging or dry material. Use what's popular in their world to engage and motivate when the content may not. And, as always, work to be culturally sensitive and aware of your biases as you choose references, particularly if the reference is from a culture not your own.

**How do I know if this idea will help?**

- You can't name the current top video game, TV show, movie, or song.
- You look up the current top video game, TV show, movie, or song, and you're not sure what it is.
- Your digital playlist is all songs from more than twenty years ago. Or, you just thought, "digital playlist?"
- When students reference their favorite YouTube star or laugh over a meme reference, it takes a lot of self-control to not roll your eyes.
- You sense there are a lot of inside jokes going on that you do not understand.

**How do I know if this idea is working?**

- You are newly aware of references that previously went right over your head.
- You smile knowingly when students talk about what they watched, played, or listened to the night before.
- You have a new TikTok account or whatever is now the latest social media trend.
- You entered a video game store for the first time.
- You no longer roll your eyes at what students watch, listen to, or play. Some of it actually isn't that bad, you think.

**Adapt for K–5**

- Students' exposure to pop culture may vary widely at this age, as some students may have lots of restrictions on what they access online or watch on TV, and some very few. Err on the side of extremely G rated.

- Talk to kids during snack time or on the walk to specials to build your understanding of their pop culture references. Make sure you ask the quiet students, too, so their interests are honored as much as the more confident sharers.

- Use cues like characters on T-shirts, favorite toys at share time, and more to tap into their interests.

**Adapt for 6–12**

- If you're on social media, make a point of following some younger people. See what younger popular celebrities are posting and what YouTube stars are sharing, and take note.

- Interest surveys are a great way to tap into what your students are into and care about. Include questions about music, TV, video games, and movies to get ideas of what to read, watch, and listen to.

- Be careful of devaluing pop culture that isn't to your taste or is unfamiliar to you. Be as open as you can to all students' preferences, whether it's anime, the newest sneaker launch, video game, reality TV, or K-pop that they love. To them, this is important. Judging their taste will feel like you're judging them.

**How to try this with others**

- Make a thorough list of categories of the pop culture your students know. Divide it up among yourselves, committing to researching that particular subculture. Share out your findings at a future date.

- Attend a popular movie or concert with a friend or colleague. If you don't have time, play a video game together or decide together who you'll both follow on social media.

*Want to know more about this strategy and others like it?*

**Check out:** Milner, H. Richard. 2012. *Start Where You Are, But Don't Stay There: Understanding Diversity, Opportunity Gaps, and Teaching in Today's Classrooms.*

Cruz, M. Colleen. 2015. *The Unstoppable Writing Teacher: Real Strategies for the Real Classroom.*

# 7.5  Plan for Breaks

**Try This**

We often feel so pressed for time that taking a short break can feel nonsensical. But planning for intermittent pauses will actually help with productivity in the long run. Think about when and where you can squeeze in even a minute or two as a short mental break, and then see what happens.

In East Asia, students often have ten-minute breaks after every forty minutes of instruction. In Finland, fifteen-minute breaks happen after every forty-five minutes of instruction. The breaks are unstructured, often outside, and consistent. It's unlikely you'll feel like you can grant such seemingly luxurious lulls, so for now, plan what you can.

- Plan for chunks of learning time followed by short "recesses" or free time.
- Write out and plan for the break time just as you would any other part of the lesson.
- Let students know the break is coming so they can pace themselves.
- Make the break as unstructured as possible. The benefits of the break are in direct proportion to the amount of freedom the students have in using it.
- Protect the time as you would any other part of the lesson.
- Enjoy the break yourself! Notice how your own energy dips and surges with the addition of breaks.

**How do I know if this idea will help?**

- Students are dragging—they are sluggish, resistant, or acting out during class.
- Attention spans feel short.
- You or students can feel close to a breaking point or arrive at breaking points.

**How do I know if this idea is working?**

- Students come back after the break with a bounce in their step.
- Students pay better attention before the break, knowing it's coming.
- Students smile more and get frustrated less.

Mr. Ahmed
Period 4 Math
October 17

**Learning Objective: To be able to rename fractions with denominators in the power of 10 into decimal form with ease.**

| Time | Activity |
|------|----------|
| 10:00–10:15 | Choice activities—math tubs, Jenga, math race |
| 10:15–10:25 | Lesson on fractions and decimals—teacher models work and does three checks for understanding while students quickly try it themselves |
| 10:25–10:28 | Break—stretches—Khalid leads |
| 10:28–10:40 | Independent practice—teacher meets with small group to review moving decimal points, confers with Alex and Rashad |
| 10:40–10:45 | Break—ball toss with multiplication game—two groups |
| 10:45–10:55 | Return to independent practice—one small group and two more conferences—Nate and Maria |
| 10:55–11:00 | Closing—share out of favorite mistake at tables |

This teacher builds break times into the lesson to ensure they don't get skipped due to time. He knows breaks are as important as the other lesson components to keep kids alert and engaged.

**Adapt for K–5**

- Find out if the gym or recess space is available. Get students moving if you can.

- If you have a free-choice space or play space already, this is the time to use it. If not, consider creating one by asking for games, toys, Lego, Magna-Tiles, or art supplies from the parent-teacher organization and creating options.

- Students can also use the classroom library to read at this time if they choose.

- Use the same protocols for respectful noise levels and use of time as students follow during free-choice time.

- You already feel stretched to cram everything into (forty-five, fifty, or fifty-five-minute) periods, and now a break, too? I get it, but try it knowing that there are plenty of moments during that forty-five minutes when learning isn't happening because students' attention spans are shot. Start small with one three-minute break and see if it helps. If learning increases during the other times, you will feel more entitled to grow the break time.

- Or, start with at least two days a week instead of all five, and use the break during days of new material being presented or other more intense instruction. Keep track of how attention surges (or not) on those days. Use that to build up to more time.

- Remind yourself students (6–8) have likely come from a school day just a year or two ago with built-in play time, and now, often, there is none. Or, remind yourself that high schoolers lives are jam-packed with very little unstructured time without a device into their hand. Unearth and share the abundant research behind movement and play at all ages if administrators or caregivers question this use of time.

- Set parameters for acceptable use of break time. No devices, perhaps. And provide alternatives to just "hanging out" as some students may feel ill at ease socially. They can draw, doodle, or read, but you can also offer decks of cards, Mad Libs, adult coloring books, and so on.

- Middle and high school is not too old to get outside. If your room has easy access to outdoor space, use it. Provide a few balls, hackysack, Frisbees. Watch your students become playful. See them in a new light.

- Decide a signal for how to pull everyone back together. Practice it together.

- Play *with* them. Don't use it as a time to grade papers, tempting as it may be. The rewards reaped when students see you play UNO, listen to a song they like, do a few stretches, or shoot hoops with them are too great.

# 7.6 Part 1: Begin with End Goals in Mind

**Try This**

Rather than starting your unit plan with "day one activities," start at the end. First think about what you want students to know, understand, and be able to do when the unit is finished. These learning goals are different from the topic or content (what many textbooks and curricula specify) or the standards, although both of those can inform your end goals.

By planning around the *desired learning* and not your content and actions, you are focusing on what matters most. Planning with the end learning goals in mind will also help eliminate two easy planning pitfalls: covering content and delivering fun but empty activities. Both can look like well-planned lessons, but they fail to get to authentic learning.

To form the unit's learning goal, try answering the following:

- **What real-world understanding do you hope students are able to gain through this unit?**
- **What new insights or thinking do you hope students leave with at the end of the unit?**
- **What big ideas and questions do you hope students explore, wrestle with, and ultimately answer for themselves by the end of the unit?**

Be careful not to just name content or topic. For example, "Learning the stages in the water cycle" is naming a topic, not the long-term skills and learning. If students understand this content, what can they see and do differently? "Understanding how the water cycle works to value this important process that is essential to our planet and all living organisms" is a long-term skill.

**How do I know if this idea will help?**

- You plan day by day.
- You plan fun activities that line up to the content, but you can't clearly articulate what students will understand and be able to do after completing them.
- Students are unable to answer the questions "What are you learning? Why?"

**How do I know if this idea is working?**

- You begin planning any unit by starting with the end goals in mind.
- The end-of-unit understandings and learning goals inform everything else in a unit.
- Students can answer the question: "What are you learning to do, and why?"
- You feel confident planning units and there is less guesswork. You know where you want students to end up and that informs everything.

**How to try this with others**

- Planning with others will help you develop end goals that align with your standards and your students. If you teach the same units, it makes sense to work together to create end goals together. Even if you aren't planning the same unit, however, you can work with a colleague to look over each of your end goals and provide feedback.

## Sample end goals for science unit, grade 2

- Students will understand that sound makes materials vibrate and that vibrating materials make sound.

- Students will be able to record information after exploring with vibrating materials in their notebooks.

- Students will know that we depend on technologies that use sound and vibration in our everyday lives, such as bells, car horns, whistles, tea kettles, and radios.

## Sample end goals for narrative writing unit, grade 4

- Students will know multiple ways to generate ideas for small moment stories and be able to choose from them the ones they like best.

- Students will be able to generate more writing in a sitting and across a unit than they did in the previous unit.

- Students will understand the writing process from brainstorming to rehearsing to drafting to revising to publishing.

## Sample end goals for world language unit, grade 7

- Students will know basic vocabulary for describing one's background and introducing oneself.

- Students will be able to conduct a brief conversation with several unscripted exchanges in which they introduce themselves and ask a partner about themselves.

## Sample end goals for art history unit, high school

- Students will be able to identify ways that works of art from popular culture reflect the past.

- Students will understand and be able to explain color hue, tint, shade, value shading, and pattern repetition.

- Students will know how to discuss and write about preferences for certain works of art by referring to artist's techniques and personal aesthetic preferences.

*Want to know more about this strategy and others like it?*

**Check out:** Wiggins, Grant, and Jay McTighe. 2011. *The Understanding by Design Guide to Creating High-Quality Units.*

# 7.7 Part 2: What Evidence Shows If Students Met the Learning Goal?

**Try This**

Determine how students will show their understanding, skills, and knowledge at the end of the unit. Keep in mind that you want students to *make meaning* of the content, not just recall it. Work toward designing assessments that ask students to transfer their learning of big concepts and understandings in new ways. This isn't to say students won't master content, but that they should also be asked to show genuine understanding by applying the content in new ways.

Then, see whether this assessment is in true alignment with learning goals by asking two questions:

1. Can students do well on this assessment without having mastered or understood the content?

2. Can students do poorly on this assessment while still having mastered or understood the content?

If yes, go back and revise the assessment so that it requires students to have truly understood the content in order to do well.

**How do I know if this idea will help?**

- Assessments are planned toward the end of the unit.
- You pull assessments from the textbook or online resources without making them your own.
- Students express confusion when doing the final assessment. It wasn't what they expected or studied for.
- Students perform poorly on the final assessment, even though you know they worked hard in the unit.
- Students perform well on the final assessment, even though you know they did not work hard in the unit.

**How do I know if this idea is working?**

- You design the assessments before you plan the day to day.
- Students know what the end product will look like even when the unit begins.
- The rubric for your final assessment clearly reflects the learning goals.
- You sit down to plan the final assessment with the learning goals out and ready. The goals inform the planning process.
- Students who work hard throughout the unit do well on the final assessment.
- Students do not express any confusion or surprise when working on the final assessment.

### Sample assessment that aligns to a learning goal for science unit, grade 2

- Students will use tools such as flashlights, tuning forks, kazoos, or whistles to design or build a device that uses light or sound to solve the problem of communicating commands such as "Come here" or "Move away" over a distance.

### Sample assessments for narrative writing unit, grade 4

- Student notebook showing evidence of multiple strategies for generating ideas.

- Story topic will be chosen from many ideas generated in notebook.

- Final published story will have gone through all stages of the writing process from notebook to separate paper to the published draft for author's celebration.

### Sample assessment for world language unit, grade 7

- Students will record an improvised conversation with a student from the other class section in which they ask and answer questions about themselves.

- Students will listen to a conversation between two native speakers and be able to generate a follow-up question that builds on their conversation.

### Sample assessment for art history unit, grade 10

- Students will choose a favorite pop culture artifact and explain in a presentation format of their choosing (Google Slides, podcast, or "live" artifacts) how it connects to at least two works from previous centuries, both in artists' use of color and tint and in terms of symbolic images.

*Want to know more about this strategy and others like it?*

**Check out:** Wiggins, Grant, and Jay McTighe. 2011. *The Understanding by Design Guide to Creating High-Quality Units.*

**How to try this with others**

- Planning with others will help you develop authentic assessments that clearly align with your learning goals. If you teach the same units, you'll be better able to work together. Even if you aren't planning the same unit, however, you can work with a colleague to look over the final assessments and provide feedback. Where is there authentic alignment? Where does it fall short?

# 7.8 Part 3: Plan the Day to Day

**Try This**

Now that you have established end goals and how students will show whether they've met those goals, it's time to plan the day to day.

What are the learning events or lessons that will help students succeed in meeting the end goals?

Sketch out your instruction and what kids will do each day, making sure you are not just covering content or filling in fun activities, but setting students up to achieve learning goals.

Check alignment.

1. Can students do the day-to-day activities without doing the end-of-unit assessment well?

2. Can students not complete the activities and learning events but still do well on the assessment?

If so, go back and reflect where things are not in alignment. Revise the day-to-day activities so each one sets up students to be successful on the final assessments.

**How do I know if this idea will help?**

- Students do not perform well on the final assessments, or only a select few do so.
- If you were to ask students what they're learning to do as a result of this activity, they don't have an answer that lines up with the goal.
- Class is busy and students may be having fun, but they aren't performing well on end-of-unit assessments.
- You plan day by day.

**How do I know if this idea is working?**

- You plan the final part of the unit first. You can clearly state what you want students to know and be able to do by the end of the unit. Then you go back to fill in the day to day.
- Daily activities clearly line up to the learning goals. You can easily trace any day's lesson to those final understandings.
- Students can tell you why they are doing any daily activity. They know what they are working toward.
- Class is busy and students are having fun, and they are doing well on end-of-unit assessments.

| Daily Activities: Small Moment Writing Unit, Grade 4 | | | | |
|---|---|---|---|---|
| *The Writing Strategies Book* | | | | |
| **Brainstorming ideas** by listing important people and moments with those people<br><br>Writing in notebooks<br>Small groups<br>Conferences | **Brainstorming ideas** by charting strong feelings and then moments when you had those feelings<br><br>Writing in notebooks<br>Small groups<br>Conferences | **Brainstorming ideas** by making a heart map and drawing the most important items in center, then fill heart<br><br>Writing in notebooks<br>Pair share<br>Small groups<br>Conferences | **Brainstorming ideas** by making a map of an important place and all the moments that happened there<br><br>Writing in notebooks<br>Small groups<br>Conferences | **Read through ideas and focus/choose**<br>Write about a pebble, not a mountain<br><br>Writing in notebooks<br>Writing partners<br>Small groups<br>Conferences |
| **Thinking Through and Organizing Your Idea**<br>Organize in Sequence<br><br>Writing in notebooks<br>Writing partners<br>Small groups<br>Conferences | **Developing that Idea**<br>Start with a Plan in Mind<br><br>Writing in notebooks<br>Small groups<br>Conferences | **Rehearsing the Idea**<br>Take Notes from an Illustration or Photo<br><br>Writing in notebooks<br>Small groups<br>Conferences | **Drafting**<br>Write the "Inside Story"<br><br>Writing on loose-leaf paper<br>Writing partners<br>Small groups<br>Conferences | **Revising**<br>Exploring Options for Setting<br><br>Loose-leaf paper<br>Small groups<br>Conferences |
| **Revising**<br>Slow down important moments and the heart of the story<br><br>Loose-leaf paper<br>Small groups<br>Conferences | **Choose another idea** from your notebook<br>Find a theme from your collection<br><br>Notebook reading<br>Writing partners<br>Small groups<br>Conferences | **Develop that Idea**<br>Sketch it out in a storyboard each time there is a new character or setting<br><br>Loose-leaf paper<br>Small groups<br>Conferences | **Develop that Idea**<br>Clarify the problem and then name the solution<br><br>Writing on loose-leaf paper<br>Writing partners<br>Small groups<br>Conferences | **Draft It!**<br>Show don't tell using senses to describe places<br><br>Loose-leaf paper<br>Small groups<br>Conferences |
| **Revise the Story**<br>Show don't tell the emotions of the characters | **Editing**<br>Look at mentor texts for punctuating dialogue | **Editing**<br>Decide where to paragraph with new people, scenes, and anyone new speaking | **Publishing**<br>Add a title to your story and have it ready for gallery walk tomorrow | **Celebration**<br>Gallery walk with other fourth-grade class—cafeteria |

Adapted from *The Writing Strategies Book: Your Everything Guide to Developing Skilled Writers* by Jennifer Serravallo. Copyright © 2017 by Jennifer Serravallo. Published by Heinemann, Portsmouth, NH. Reprinted by permission of the publisher. All rights reserved.

**How to try this with others**

- Planning with others will help you align your activities with your end goals. Look through your day-by-day plans with a colleague, and think carefully about what students are doing and how it sets them up to succeed in meeting the overall learning goals. Anytime an activity or plan veers a bit more toward "filler" or perhaps a fun task that isn't quite aligned, consider how it can be tweaked. Picture someone asking your students each day: "What are you learning to do today, and what is it building toward?" If they would have a hard time answering, that day's lesson is probably worth a second look.

*Want to know more about this strategy and others like it?*

**Check out:** Wiggins, Grant, and Jay McTighe. 2011. *The Understanding by Design Guide to Creating High-Quality Units.*

## 7.9 Plan for a Balance of Whole Group, Small Group, and One-on-One

**Try This**

To meet students' varying needs, you need differing types of instruction. Plan for a balance of whole-group, small-group, and individual learning. There are benefits to all for each kind of instruction, so intentionally vary them for every student across your week.

- *Whole-group instruction:* Use this for introducing new concepts or procedures that everyone needs to know. This is usually when you're addressing the standard-based curriculum goals or your daily teaching point. It brings everyone together, keeps you all on the same page, and establishes important routines and community building. Any need-to-know learning that applies to more than about 60 percent of your class should happen in whole-group instruction. This typically happens toward the beginning of class, and it shouldn't last more than about ten minutes. Any more than that and you risk losing students' attention or shortchanging the necessary differentiation offered in smaller groupings.

- *Small-group instruction:* Address the needs of groups of students when there is more than one student who will benefit from the same instruction, but it doesn't apply to the whole class. You will save time by not repeating the same instruction individually, and you will also pull together students with a shared goal and feedback, which can help develop relationships and group skills.

- *Individual instruction:* This is an important time for students to safely share and hear feedback that is personalized to them, to develop a relationship with you, and to grow new understandings without the distraction or pressure of peers. Use this when students have particular needs that differ from those around them, and sometimes to simply preserve this important one-on-one dialogue.

Look across your week as well as your data on your students' individual strengths and needs to plan for a balance of these varying structures. Think about who you can group together who will all benefit from the same instruction, who needs one-on-one, and what concepts you will teach to the whole class. Make a note of who and what kinds of grouping so you can make sure that students get a mix of both.

**How do I know if this idea will help?**

- Some students are showing progress on skills, and others are not.
- You tend to focus your instruction on what you say to the whole class.
- You meet with groups or individuals, but you don't keep track of those meetings.
- You see certain students a lot in groups or one-on-one, and others not at all.

- You don't have to guess how each of your students is doing on any skill. You know because you see them regularly in groups and individually.

- You have a record of who you see across the week, and it shows a balance of small-group instruction, whole-class instruction, and individual time with each student.

- You plan for whole-class instruction and smaller groupings equally. Both matter.

- Students expect to see you regularly in different configurations. They are ready with questions and successes.

Math: Understanding Place Value and Decimals

|  | Whole Class | Small Groups | 1 to 1 |
|---|---|---|---|
| Monday | Understand that digits in #s represents 1/10 of what they represent one place to left | Krishav Maddie / Saige Camille Maya S. | Ben T. Nayan |
| Tuesday | Compare values of digits in numbers | Anand Riya Nathan / Avi Hazel Nico | Audrey Ben C. Mahmood |
| Wednesday | Solve problems using place value understanding | Hazel Maya B. / ← leave open | Rashad Emory Maya S. |
| Thursday | Understanding that when place value extends to thousandths structure does not change | Ben T. Audry Mahmood / Rashad Ben C. | Anand Nathan |
| Friday | Writing decimal numbers in expanded notation | Maya S. Camille | Krishav Maddie Riya |

- It's likely you use a variety of group structures already, for centers, guided reading, or strategy lessons. If so, keep notes so that you know you are not only seeing some students in groups or one-on-one. Both have important benefits and every kid deserves some of each.

- Aim to see each student at least twice across the week, either one-on-one or in small groups.

| | |
|---|---|
| **Adapt for 6–12** | • Your classes likely feel jam-packed, which is even greater reason to keep track of your time working with students. It will be tempting (and efficient) to meet most students in small groups as opposed to one-on-one. Try to protect the individual instruction, however, as teens will speak and learn quite differently when they are on their own versus with peers. |
| | • Assuming you see about 80–100 students across your week, aim to see each student in a group one week and one-on-one the next. If this proves impossible for now, shift to every two weeks. |
| **How to try this with others** | • Share your methods for note-taking and planning your week. If someone is able to get to the goal of seeing their students two times a week, or once a week, visit their class and find out how they do it. |

*Want to know more about this strategy and others like it?*

**Check out:** Serravallo, Jennifer. 2014. *The Literacy Teacher's Playbook, Grades 3–6: Four Steps for Turning Assessment Data into Goal-Directed Instruction.*

# 7.10 Mini-Inquiries That Connect to Curriculum

**Try This**

Think of an upcoming unit that you fear may be boring or disconnected from students' lives. For example, Harvey "Smokey" Daniels talks about the predictably dry social studies units on state history (as opposed to say, units on immigration or war). One chemistry teacher easily named the hardest-sell unit from his curriculum: significant figures.

Now, search for the single most interesting thing in the unit, even if you have to skip ahead toward the end. This chemistry teacher knew it was that if you confuse significant figures even slightly when prescribing or giving medicine, you could potentially poison someone.

If you can't find anything, try an internet search using concepts from the unit or the unit name along with the words *weird* or *unusual*. See what comes up that is appropriate and interesting to your students. Daniels (2017), for example, was able to find odd laws about Texas state history such as a not being able to shoot buffalo from the second story of a hotel and that it's still a "hanging offense" to steal cattle.

Now turn that interesting tidbit into a question that could be answered over the course of the unit. For example, "How does my doctor make sure she doesn't poison me?" Or "What are the craziest laws in our state?"

After you share your questions, help students generate their own. They can do this after you've addressed a chunk of required content, or early on. They can adapt their questions and share findings throughout. Save some class time to let students read about and investigate their topics. Keep questions posted to spark wondering and remind students of authentic and relevant content that connects to what might otherwise have been a boring or forgettable unit.

**How do I know if this idea will help?**

- Students don't ask many questions in class. You are the only one posing questions.
- You may like the idea, but you don't feel like you have time to get to inquiry projects.
- Students don't display much interest or curiosity in the learning at hand. They're going through the motions, or you have to cajole them to take part.
- You want to incorporate more fun, play, flow, and passion in your classroom.

**How do I know if this idea is working?**

- Students are surprising you and themselves with their questions and self-discovered answers.
- You see risk-taking and trial and error in students' inquiries. They are trying things out in a safe space for inquiry.
- Students are pursuing their inquiries outside of class. They are hooked.
- You are having fun watching students in this discovery process.

| **Adapt for K-5** |
|---|

- Keep a running list of "wonders" in the room, a place where students can generate mini-inquiry ideas. Save them for the inquiry project or encourage students to take these on as a side project independently or with a friend.
- Make sure you model the entire inquiry process with your own authentic question. Ideally, your question is age appropriate for your students and one they can connect to: "How do light-up sneakers work?" not "Why are cell phones so addictive?" The more fun you have with yours, the more contagious the spirit of inquiry will be!
- The younger your students, the more you should scaffold their research by finding texts in the school or classroom library, printing out or bookmarking articles online that are reading level and age appropriate, or suggesting people in the building for informal interviews.

| **Adapt for 6-12** |
|---|

- As we are always crunched for time and this may feel harder to "fit in," consider the following as possible times to try out mini-inquiries:
  - At the start of the unit to prime the pump with the content, spend 1–2 days asking and answering questions.
  - Take advantage of days when there are assemblies or late starts and the schedule is already abbreviated.
  - When it isn't practical to start the next unit right away due to an upcoming break or weekend.
  - Anytime students finish work early and are ready for something else. This is their time! Their inquiries can serve as a trial run of sorts, as well as models for upcoming whole-class projects.
- Again, make sure to model the entire inquiry process with your own authentic question. The more fun you have with yours, the more contagious the spirit of the inquiry will be!

| **How to try this with others** |
|---|

- Conduct an inquiry with colleagues. In Daniels' book, *The Curious Classroom* (2017) a group of teachers pondered why so many faculty and students got sick with the flu, despite getting the vaccine. Each person took on various aspects of this question and set off to research.

## Want to know more about this strategy and others like it?

**Check out:** Daniels, Harvey. 2017. *The Curious Classroom: 10 Structures for Teaching with Student-Directed Inquiry.*

## Tech Integration Tip

**VIRTUAL FIELD TRIPS**

Although in-person field trips are wonderful, virtual field trips can provide easy, immediate access to the world. Consider what virtual tour would make learning come alive. Check out sites listed here, and also use search engines with search terms including your content and *virtual field trip*, *virtual tour*, and *cybertrip*, to find more.

Most virtual field trips consist of text and images, but some will include audio and video as well as hyperlinks to additional resources. You can also check out webcams with constant streaming of animal habitats and more. Think about your students' attention spans and interests when choosing. Go through all the tour's links and resources before students explore. Use the Smart Board to do a class tour together, or provide links so students can access the tour on one-to-one devices. Provide a listening task or set of "look-fors" so students have a purpose in exploring and a way to report back their findings.

After some experience with participating in virtual tours, you might ask students to *create* virtual field trips as a way to share information, using Wix or other platforms. Or, if you take a "live" field trip, consider collecting images, video, resources, and artifacts so that students can produce a virtual field trip. Let them be the expert tour guides and share their knowledge with others!

### Virtual Field Trips

ClassFlow

Google Expeditions

Google Earth

Nearpod

Google Street View

360Cities

Flipgrid GridPals

**Museums**

American Museum of Natural History
www.amnh.org/exhibitions/

Colonial Williamsburg
www.history.org/history/museums/online_exhibits.cfm

National Women's History Museum
www.womenshistory.org/

The Field Museum
www.fieldmuseum.org/science/research

# 8 Teacher-Led Instruction

## What you have in place, and what you're ready for next

You might be thinking, we're two-thirds of the way into this book about expert teaching and we're just now getting to the teaching part? Seems counterintuitive, I know.

This goal appears here because what we do and say can't count for much unless all those other things are in place (structures, relationships, plans based on what students need and know, etc.). And even then, our actual lessons may not be as pivotal as our egos may believe. In Hollywood movies, a teacher's moving speech can have students rapt—minds are moved in immediate and profound ways. In real life, without foundational elements in place, our "speech" might sound more like the garbled nonsense of the teacher on *Peanuts*—white noise for kids to get through until the real stuff starts. But by doing the hard work of creating highly responsive environments and planning lessons that set students up for success, you are ready to make your instruction count.

At this point, you have set up child-centered classrooms where students thrive. You have planned smart lessons and units that set you up to teach what really matters and what students need. Now it's time to think about how to maximize the impact of your instruction without inflating your voice so that it overshadows students.

This chapter will help you deliver content and concepts in ways that engage students and leave them energized to take on the learning. Instruction matters a great deal but only when it's used to empower students.

## Why is teacher-led instruction important?

This is our (brief) time onstage, typically toward the start of the lesson or class. We have to pack a big punch—so we address standards, teach the concepts kids need, and then get off the stage in time for students to practice transferring what we've taught to their independent work. When our teaching is lackluster or convoluted, we risk losing students before their real work has even begun. When it sings, however, we set them up to shine.

Teacher-led instruction has the power to spur new thinking, clarify big ideas, model concrete strategies for growth, and help students feel that taking risks is doable and important. You don't need a Hollywood monologue, just a practical set of strategies that will help students engage.

## What does the research say?

John Hattie's research (2012) on what impacts student learning the most makes clear that what we say and do is pivotal. Teacher credibility, scaffolding, and clarity of instruction are all things that Hattie shows significantly affect student growth. What we do and say matters. A lot.

All of these aspects—credibility, scaffolding, and clarity—are important elements of direct instruction—and having a good handle on them stands to move students toward a year and a half of learning in one year. The single most important factor in student growth, however, Hattie found, is "collective teacher efficacy." This refers to teachers' belief that they can affect students in positive ways (Hattie 2012). This core belief that you stand to make a difference, and a profound one, for each and every student that walks in your door is of singular importance. And the way we talk to and teach our students will make that belief either completely transparent or muddled and filled with doubt.

So above all else, what you do and say must carry with it a belief that all students can learn and that you are here to help make it happen. And now, let's get started!

## Is this the goal for me?

- Do you answer "yes" and "sometimes" for all statements? Consider moving to the next chapter. You've got this!

- Do you have a mix of "yes," "sometimes," and "not yet" answers? This might be the goal for you.

- Do you answer "not yet" for most of these statements? Go back and try the checklists from the previous chapters. You're likely to enjoy greater success and see quicker results by focusing there.

## What do you notice?

| | Yes | Sometimes | Not yet |
|---|---|---|---|
| My whole-class instruction is typically ten minutes or less per lesson. | ☐ | ☐ | ☐ |
| My instruction is layered so each student has something to grasp onto. | ☐ | ☐ | ☐ |
| My daily instruction leads up to explicit end-of-unit understandings and goals. | ☐ | ☐ | ☐ |
| Students can say what they are learning to do and why for any given class. | ☐ | ☐ | ☐ |

# 8.1 If It's Important, Teach It. Don't Remind, Correct, Fix, or Tell

Teaching requires the ability to multitask. We must cover a full curriculum in a short time and meet the simultaneous needs of a room full of human beings, along with managing countless other initiatives, assessments, and distractions.

As we work to balance it all, we may miss authentic teaching opportunities and instead:

- Remind: "Don't forget to put the $x$ in the equation."

- Correct: "Don't put the $x$ there; put it here."

- Fix: "Here's where you put the $x$ in the equation."

- Tell: "Put the $x$ in the equation here."

Instead, it's when we feel stressed that it's most important to slow down the moment, to show what we mean, to break down the skill. When we want students to genuinely understand, it's crucial that we take time to *teach* versus reminding, correcting, fixing, or telling.

First, watch for moments when you remind, correct, fix, or tell. You might even let students know you're trying to avoid these rushed attempts so they can help you be aware. Show them the previously mentioned examples so they know what you mean. You might even put a sticky note with similar reminders of what to avoid on your lesson plan, book, or wherever you look most frequently.

Remember that change is hard and that it takes a hyperconscious effort to catch these habits. When you do, celebrate—it's an achievement! Then say something like, "Oops! I was rushing that. Let's slow it down and I'll show you what I'm talking about."

Then, teach it.

- **Show students** what you mean. "Watch me as I go through solving this equation. I'll narrate what I'm thinking as I do. Pay attention to where I put $x$ and why."

- **Give them an example** and walk through it. "You have some authentic dialogue in your story, but it's hard for me to tell who is talking when. Let's look at your independent reading book and pay close attention to how that author punctuated dialogue. What do you notice? Great, let's try that."

- **Have a student explain and teach** while you listen in, offering feedback and clarifying as needed. "Sam, can you show Naomi how you structured your lab report conclusion? Make sure to explain your decisions in what information you included and what you left out."

| | |
|---|---|
| **How do I know if this idea will help?** | • You find yourself rushing. |
| | • You're under a lot of pressure to fit in a great deal of content, as well as other initiatives, in a short amount of time. |
| | • You often remind, correct, fix, or tell. |
| | • Students are not able to do the things you're teaching independently. |
| | • You feel like you've covered skills in the curriculum, but you're not seeing those skills in student's work. |
| **How do I know if this idea is working?** | • You're catching yourself when you remind, correct, fix, or tell. |
| | • You are slowing down your instruction, taking time to really explain and model even what might feel like basic or obvious concepts. |
| | • Student work reflects the skills you are teaching. |
| | • Students are able to independently apply the concepts in your lessons. |
| **How to try this with others** | • Invite a colleague to come to your class to help you keep an eye out for moments of correcting or fixing versus teaching. It is hard to stay objective when we're in the throes of teaching. |
| | • Try this for your own professional learning. If a staff meeting or professional learning community (PLC) is designed around a learning opportunity, make a conscious effort to make that a true teaching moment, devoid of reminding, correcting, fixing, or telling. Adults benefit from this same kind of instruction! |

## Want to know more about this strategy and others like it?

**Check out:** Keene, Ellin Oliver, and Matt Glover. 2015. *The Teacher You Want to Be: Essays About Children, Learning, and Teaching.*

## *Tech Integration Tip*

### TEACH STUDENTS HOW TO READ, DIGITALLY

Just as we teach students how to read math problems, books, articles, and scientific equations on paper, we need to teach them how to read all of these genres and more in a digital format.

Reading on a screen presents a host of new challenges, and we can give students quick and easy strategies for managing the screen and reading like digital experts.

1. **Preview the text.** The most important step when reading a digital text is to look it over to get a sense of what it's about and where it's going. Model how to look at the entire text, scan sections and headings, and check whether there are videos, images, or sidebars included.

2. **If there's a video,** teach students to watch it first before reading the text. Often the video will activate schema and provide important background knowledge. If students skip it, they run the risk of being confused and missing important information.

3. **Keep the ads.** If we always delete ads for students, they won't learn how to navigate distracting pop-ups and other advertisements. Show them how to turn off ads and how to ignore ads if they can't delete them.

4. **Show students how to use hyperlinks.** Click on some hyperlinks and question aloud if the linked article is worth reading or not. If the linked article is outdated or irrelevant, show students how to close it and move back to the original text. Model that you typically skip hyperlinks during the first read.

5. **Point out hashtags and other tags to social media.** Teach students how to use these and what they mean.

6. **Look at the author, source, and publication date.** Show students how you use these to consider whose voice is being heard, whose voice is not being heard, what audience this text may be intended for, and how credible the source is.

7. **Teach students to reread digital texts,** just as you would any other text, to clarify, dig deeper, question, and understand.

*Want to know more about this tech tip and others like it?*

**Check out:** Cruz, Colleen. 2018. *Writers Read Better: 50+ Paired Lessons That Turn Writing Craft Work into Powerful Genre Writing.*

Muhtaris, Katie, and Kristin Ziemke. 2015. *Amplify: Digital Teaching and Learning in the K–6 Classroom.*

# 8.2 On Your Good Days, Show It. On Your Bad Days, Channel Your Inner Actor

Try This

Because students feed off of our attitude, make your attitude and behaviors ones you want to spread like wildfire. Treat every student and every class as though you are happy to see them and happy to be there.

Our behavior makes a difference for students. It's not going to help you or your students to broadcast when you're less than happy to be at work. When you are exhausted or going through a tough time, don't go for authenticity. Those are the days you'll have to be an actor, as hard as it might feel to muster enthusiasm.

First, imagine someone in your building who always looks happy and seems to enjoy their job. How do they stand? What do they say? What does their body do? Their face? And how do you feel when you see them?

Or, imagine an event organizer, a party promoter, a cheerleader, or anyone whose job is to generate energy and enthusiasm. Be a researcher, studying them for mannerisms and behaviors you can adopt on your next rough day.

Those feel-good behaviors will project a positive attitude, which will create a positive tone in your room, which will up the likelihood that students want to learn, which will circle back and help you feel better. Faking it till you make it is a win-win.

Here's a list of some ways to convey enthusiasm for your job and for your students, even when you secretly long for someone (likely you) to be absent:

- Greet everyone at the door with a smile: "You're here!" "I'm so glad to see you!" "Happy you're here!"

- Move toward them. As much as you want to retreat behind your desk or busy yourself with something that avoids interaction, physically align yourself *with* your students, not apart.

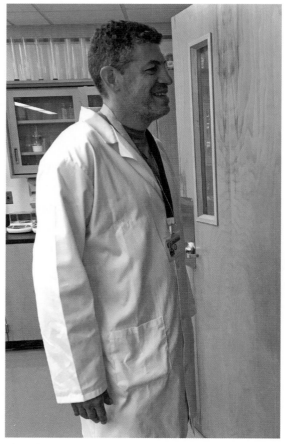

This chemistry teacher greets his students at the door with a welcoming smile.

- Use exclamations: "Welcome!" "Let's get started!" "I've got something great for us today!" Can this feel cheesy? Yup. Do it anyway. Important people (your students) are watching you. They might roll their eyes, but they prefer a rah-rah attitude to monotone.

- Ask questions. Enthusiasm can be conveyed by curiosity in others and about new topics. "How is this going to work?" "I wonder what you all will come up with when answering this problem." "I'm so curious to see what happens when . . . What do you all think will happen?" And of course, "How are you?" Then really listen for the answer.

- Pick up the volume to help put some pep to your step. Or, conversely, channel some quiet zen in your tone to calm kids and pull their attention. Either way, play with your voice as a creative tool.

- Make your face match your desired emotion. Smile. Open your eyes wide. Drop your jaw in professed awe when someone makes a comment. Does it feel exaggerated and somewhat ridiculous? Good. You're probably doing it right.

- Mentally book a time when you can fall apart, call a friend, or close your eyes, such as going to your car at lunch or heading home when the kids do after school. Knowing that reprieve is coming will help you channel your inner actor for now.

**How do I know if this idea will help?**

- Assessing one's attitude and behaviors is hard to do. We often inflate our ability to have a poker face when we're feeling down or frustrated. For this reason, you might even ask a colleague or your students how they perceive your attitude. Do you project a sense of pleasure with your job and students? If that feels too uncomfortable, take a hard look at what you say when students walk in:

  - Do you regularly walk to the door and smile at all of your students?

  - Do you physically locate yourself at your desk when students are in the room?

  - Is your voice usually quiet and/or monotone?

- You are having a hard time with a certain class, or struggling with something at work or in your personal life that sometimes impacts your mood in the classroom.

- Students look unenthusiastic coming into class.

**How do I know if this idea is working?**

- You catch yourself on bad days and make a conscious effort to turn up the volume in your attitude and behaviors.

- Your students come into class with more energy and happy expressions when they see you.

- Your students comment that you seem to love them and your job, because you seem so happy to see them each and every day. They may even tease you a bit for your relentless positivity.

# 8.3 Keep Teaching Short and Sweet So Kids Can Do More

**Try This**

Limit your teacher-led instructional time to eight to ten minutes or, when teaching very young children, to the age of your students.

Try these steps to keep instructions short and sweet, thereby protecting essential work time for your students:

- Look at the clock when you begin your instruction and announce the time you will end.

- Let students know that to keep your time, you will not answer questions or call on students until after you're done. They can stay at the rug (K–5) or ask questions (6–12) after everyone else has moved into independent work, but you won't keep the entire class there.

- Have students turn and talk or quickly, try something out during your instruction, or recap what you heard or saw them do. Again, don't call on them—too much of a time suck!

- If you need to, ask one student who is able to multitask to remind you when the clock gets to your stopping time.

- When time is up, stop talking. Move students into independent work, even if you did not finish what you planned. In all of my times of doing this, I've never once had a student say, "Oh please, keep talking."

- If students could use support with transitioning to independent work or have questions, try this:

  - Let them stay with you while you send others off to get started. Sometimes the lack of an audience minimizes unnecessary questions. Other times, it provides a safer space in which to ask them.

  - Ask them to try *something*, even if it isn't exactly the assigned task. Helping them get the pencils moving, so to speak, sometimes is enough to counteract their internal censor or doubts. Let them know you'll check with them in a bit, but you want to see something when you get there.

- If students are reluctant to get started and want more of you and your guidance, try to resist rescuing them. Work toward their independence. You can:

  - Repeat the lesson with a small group.

  - Keep them with you to answer quick questions, but send the rest of the class off to get started.

  - Tell them that you will come to them to answer questions only after they have tried or done something.

- Make sure you are occupied directly after instruction to physically reinforce the point that they need to get to work. You are unavailable right then.

- Schedule conferences or small groups and let them know you need to protect everyone's time with you by starting with those scheduled students. If there's time after, you will check in on them.

- Create a chart with options of what to do when they're stuck. Make sure waiting for you is not one of the options.

Many educators remind us that whoever is doing the most is learning the most. Shift the balance so that students are working harder than you. Turn it over to them.

**How do I know if this idea will help?**

- Your instruction regularly goes longer than expected.
- Students get restless during your lesson/instruction/explanation.
- Students often have less than thirty minutes to work independently.
- You suspect you are working harder than the students.

**How do I know if this idea is working?**

- Teacher-led instruction is consistently ten minutes or under.
- Independent work time is protected, and students regularly have twenty minutes and longer to practice the skill or do other independent work.

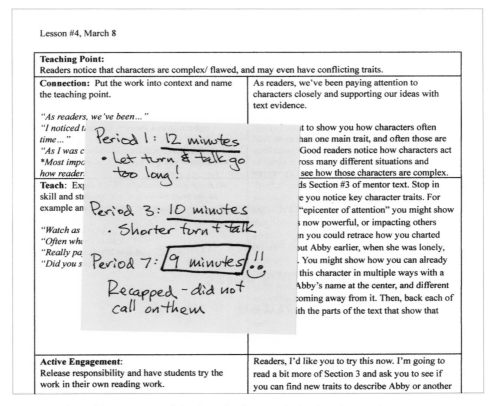

Try to track and keep notes of the length of your whole-class instruction.

- Even with reminders that you won't call on students, they may call out or keep hands raised. Let them know that they can stay at the rug (or wherever you are teaching) after everyone has set off to work if they still need to ask their question or share their comment. Once the class audience has dispersed, it's often less satisfying and they don't bother. Or, they will feel reassured they still get to make their comment.

- A good rule of thumb is no more than a minute of direct instruction per age (e.g., five minutes for five-year-olds, twelve minutes for twelve-year-olds). If you are working with first graders, try to limit your instruction to six or seven minutes. If it can't all fit, then save some teaching points for after they've had the opportunity to practice a bit. Call them back for that additional information or guidance, or let it go. Save it for the next day.

- Middle and high school students do a tremendous amount of sitting still and listening across their day. Work to combat that by getting off the stage sooner rather than later. Aim to have students doing, not listening, for the bulk of the class. For a one-period class, that means you're talking in front of the class for perhaps fifteen minutes total. Students are actively "doing" during the other thirty minutes.

- Visit a colleague's class and time them from start to finish when they are doing any direct instruction. Have them do the same for you. Often our perceived times are very different from reality. Help each other decide where to streamline and cut back. Was there too much information for one day? Did your colleague call on students and let focus go off track?

- If you're both feeling brave, record the teaching to watch and reflect on later.

**What to do When You Feel STUCK in Math:**

* Draw a picture or graph 🍎🍎🍎
* Read the problem aloud (If there are...)
* Make a number sentence 2 × 5 = 10
* Make tally marks IIII II
* Ask a friend
* Use fingers
* Look at the anchor chart
* Think of a similar problem

# 8.4 Teach a Gifted Class. No Matter What

Try This

Countless studies show the strong correlation between teacher expectations and student achievement (Hattie 2012). There are strategies embedded throughout this book about conveying high expectations for each and every student. Take it a step farther, and really believe that each one of your students *is* gifted and talented. Our educational and social system makes many students feel "less than"—they might start to believe they are, and so, unconsciously, might we. We might devalue (even out of misguided compassion) certain students because they are English language learners (ELLs), have a disability, have a parent struggling with addiction, live in poverty, or any other marker that our world has taught us limits a person's potential. When you talk to your students, treat them *all* as gifted and talented—they are.

Do your best to watch yourself from a distance. Or better yet, have a colleague observe and take notes for you:

- **How did you talk to them?**
- **What questions did you pose?**
- **Where did you stand in relation to them?**
- **What did your face look like?**
- **How much time do you give them to think things through?**
- **What was your tone of voice?**
- **What language did you use?**

Then, what did the students do differently?

- **When and how did they participate?**
- **What was their expression? Body language?**
- **What did they do or not do that was a change from the usual?**

Jot notes either during class or right after. What did you do to show students, "I believe you can do this?" How did it impact their behavior? It can take time to see change if students are not used to being seen as capable, ambitious, and high achieving. And you may have unintentionally sent signals that you don't expect some students to be as capable. That can't be undone in a day. But it is absolutely worth trying again tomorrow.

**How do I know if this idea will help?**

- You feel sorry for some of your students because of challenges you know they face. This well-intended compassion can often lead to lower expectations. Treat this as a possible indicator.

- You hear of certain students performing better or differently in other classes or with other adults.

- Some of your students haven't shown growth in their learning or behaviors.

- You have chalked up failure or lack of growth to students' circumstances.

- Student grades and performance are consistent no matter the content or skill.

**How do I know if this idea is working?**

- Students participate more, take more risks, or have more engaged body language.

- Your high-performing students take a bit more of a backseat.

- It becomes harder to predict who will do well and who will need more support with new concepts.

- You tie lack of progress from any student to something *you* can do differently, not to outside circumstances beyond anyone's control.

- You may empathize with students' circumstances, but you know they all have equally valuable strengths and abilities.

**How to try this with others**

- Invite a colleague in to take notes when you try this. Let them know the students in particular that you are working to treat with higher expectations. Reflect together—were there noticeable shifts? How did it feel? Set a goal for what you will keep doing, based on any language or moves that produced results.

*Want to know more about this strategy and others like it?*

**Check out:** Hammond, Zaretta. 2015. *Culturally Responsive Teaching & the Brain: Promoting Authentic Engagement and Rigor Among Culturally and Linguistically Diverse Students.*

# 8.5 Make Opting In the Default

**Try This**

Rather than only calling on students who raise their hand, make it the default that everyone participates and contributes. Guaranteed turns help reluctant or shy students, ELLs, and others.

The next time you're looking for student participation, don't call out a question and wait for raised hands. Instead, pose the question and then let students know that you don't want immediate answers. One teacher I know says with a smile, "Put your hands down! I'm looking for the kinds of thoughts that take time to generate!" Show that you value every student's voice.

Tell students that they will all take a moment or two to stop and jot down some thinking (or to turn and talk to a partner to do the same) to generate their answers. Explain you will be using an all-in approach to participation.

You might sweep around the room in a predictable order such as seating chart, letting students know you want to hear their thinking in just a sentence or two (to protect time and attention spans). Or, you could have every student share out their answers at tables or in groups. Then ask each table to share out one comment, or you circulate and listen in and recap what you observed. Or, you could assign students numbers and ask for all odds or evens to share out. For the next question, flip it. Regardless, you are creating a scenario in which every student's voice is valued and heard.

Emphasize that the default is hearing from everyone. This doesn't have to feel punitive or forced—you can allow students to opt out, or you can circle back to someone who wants another minute to formulate an answer. Explain that you operate on the premise that all students are opting in unless they choose otherwise. This shows that we value every student's voice. Opting in also increases the likelihood of 100 percent participation. Just as we are more likely to pay bills on auto-pay, see a friend if we have a standing weekly date, or visit the dentist with recurring six-month appointments, students are more likely to join in when it is automatically expected they will do so.

Giving students time to formulate their thinking before contributing particularly helps our ELL students and those with disabilities. You might even consider giving students who need even more support a sort of script, in advance. I used to meet one student, an ELL who didn't initially speak at all in class, in the hallway with an index card that had an upcoming question and an appropriate answer jotted down in advance. For some months, he used that script to participate. After a while, his comfort level was such that he would wave away the card. He had a voice and wasn't afraid to use it.

- You hear the same voices over and over in class.
- Those who participate are the students with high scores, who are privileged in terms of race, gender, sexuality, language, and more. ELL students, students with disabilities, or any other marginalized group participate less.
- You have a hard time getting students to participate.
- If you call on someone, they don't have an answer or try to avoid answering.

- A high percentage of students participate each time.
- There are a wide variety of voices in class, including ELL students, students with disabilities, and less academically successful students.
- You don't need to call on students—when it's time to participate, they follow known protocols such as circling around the room in a predictable order.

*Want to know more about this strategy and others like it?*

**Check out:** Newkirk, Thomas. 2017. *Embarrassment: And the Emotional Underlife of Learning.*

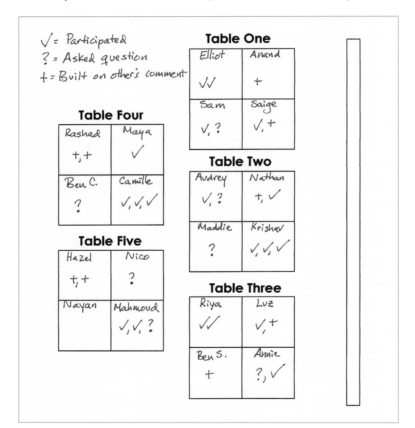

- This strategy works wonders in staff meetings or PLCs. Think of a meeting when a few voices dominated, frustrating and leading to disengagement from anyone not talking. Ask the group leader to try the opting-in approach and see what happens. It's likely that the shy new teacher, the guy in the back doing the crossword, and others had interesting insights. Who knew? Now you all do.

# 8.6 Celebrate Mistakes

**Try This**

Learning to do anything means embracing mistakes! Think of how you learned to ride a bike, swim, cook dinner, kiss, build a friendship . . . none of us were good at it right away. Good teaching can embrace and celebrate mistakes so students see them as an expected part of learning.

I used to share my writing models without showing the many drafts I created beforehand, the times I asked my husband if a sentence sounded OK, the Google searches I completed to cross-reference other examples. This likely intimidated more than inspired.

**When teaching:** As part of your modeling process, make it a point to show where you got stuck and where you got unstuck. Don't just show your beautiful end product—show all the goofs it took to get there. Exaggerate if necessary, but the more authentic the better.

**When showing student work:** Celebrate errors and note how those mistakes were an essential and inevitable part of learning. Encourage students to find their favorite mistakes, and publicly praise them. Anytime you notice a student make a mistake, ask if you or they can share it out, especially if this student typically performs at a high level. If students are reluctant to do so, go back and find more ways to model it yourself. Do this until the classroom culture naturally celebrates mistakes as a part of the learning process.

**How do I know if this idea will help?**

- You see a lot of erasing or deleting going on before much work is generated.
- Students are reluctant to share work with one another, especially in its early stages.
- You hear a lot of, "Is this right/OK?" while students are working.

**How do I know if this idea is working?**

- Students volunteer their favorite mistake to share.
- Work is posted on the walls that includes mistakes.
- Your models include errors and mistakes on a regular basis.

**How to try this with others**

- Try modeling mistake making with one another. This might actually feel more challenging than with students if you feel pressure to have it all together in front of colleagues. Ask everyone (or try it with one colleague first) to share a process that includes errors and fails. Debrief how that helped you as a learner.

- Each teacher plans out an upcoming lesson as you sit together, purposefully incorporating mistakes and learning curves. Share these out. Reflect on the mistakes that feel authentic and the parts of the process that seem overly smooth or finessed. How could real learning, full of false starts and missteps, be reflected in the process?

- Share out teaching mistakes. If you do this as a group, ask veteran teachers, administrators, or "rock star" teachers to start. Make it routine to embrace errors, sharing how we all get stuck and then, more importantly, unstuck.

*Want to know more about this strategy and others like it?*

**Check out:** Fisher, Douglas, Nancy Frey, and Russell J. Quaglia. 2018. *Engagement by Design: Creating Learning Environments Where Students Thrive.*

# 8.7 The Think-Aloud

**Try This**

Work through the task/problem/reading/writing in front of your class, and narrate your thought process. You might think aloud as you determine a theme in a text, serve a volleyball, organize the blocks, develop a hypothesis for a lab, estimate the length of a pencil, or evaluate the contributing factors of an event. Let students spy on you and see how you navigate the steps in the process.

**Planning:** First, determine what skill you want to teach and what steps you'll use. Remember, *naming* a skill is not the same as showing the steps for getting there. There are typically many different ways, sets of steps, or strategies for achieving any skill. As you plan out the concrete steps, write them out like a script so you remember each move.

Rehearse the think-aloud in advance, even though you'll want it to sound spontaneous in class.

**In class:** Let students know in advance that you won't call on them during the think-aloud, and that their job is to listen and pay attention to your thought process. As you think aloud, make sure you put yourself in the role of a student doing the work. Take time to model pitfalls and to troubleshoot in front of them. Try to ask yourself and answer questions as you go, note mistakes and talk through how you deal with them, and reflect and make corrections. Explicitly name the steps in the strategy you are using, and repeat those steps for emphasis.

Have a written display of the steps in the strategy, such as an anchor chart or handout. This will help students transfer the same expert thinking on their own.

After the think-aloud, give students time to practice the technique or strategy, and offer feedback.

When appropriate, ask students to do a think-aloud as they try the work. You can listen in on their thinking to find out what steps they are using or forgetting. You can also ask students to think aloud with one another, sharing their thought processes as a way to teach one another new ways of approaching the work.

**How do I know if this idea will help?**

- **You send students off to try a strategy, and they are hesitant or confused.**
- **You have to answer a lot of questions before students can confidently take on the work at hand.**
- **You typically go over what to do without showing students the process of what that looks like.**
- **Students may arrive at the correct answers, but they aren't sure how they got there.**
- **Students can't articulate strategies that will help them do the work.**

| How do I know if this idea is working? |
|---|

- Students are able to articulate specific steps in a strategy for getting to the skill.
- Students refer to the visual reminders as they work.
- Students see the skill as a result of concrete and specific steps, not luck or hidden talent.

| How to try this with others |
|---|

- Practice and rehearse your think-aloud with colleagues, especially if you are all going to teach the same strategy. Take turns narrating your thought processes, pitfalls and troubleshooting, and steps as you go.
- Record a think-aloud. Watch it with a colleague. Provide feedback about where it best reveals the hidden thinking behind a concept, as well as where it might skip over essential steps or thinking.

*Want to know more about this strategy and others like it?*

**Check out:** Wilhelm, Jeffrey D. 2012. *Improving Comprehension with Think-Aloud Strategies: Modeling What Good Readers Do.*

# 8.8  Ask Authentic Questions

**Try This**

There's nothing wrong with checking understanding by asking questions when we know the answer. But don't stay there. The bulk of our questions should invite true inquiry. Authentic questions treat students as creators of big ideas, not just recall experts.

You might start with questions that check for students' basic understanding. These are factual and literal questions like, "How many sides to a hexagon?" Then, when you know students have a basic understanding, move on to authentic questions that invite true inquiry. Of course, you could start with inquiry and find out students' understandings that way, too. Regardless, base authentic questions around the most important parts of the material. This way you emphasize concepts and ideas over details.

Here are five questions you can apply to any lesson that will get students thinking big and that won't set students up to guess the "right" answer:

- **"What do you think?"**
- **"Why do you think that?"**
- **"How do you know this?"**
- **"Can you tell me more?"**
- **"What questions do you still have?"**

Pose the question(s) and let students turn and talk or stop and jot so you don't just reward the fast, confident thinkers. In fact, if they immediately put up their hands, you might say, "Oh, it's really hard to come up with big ideas that quickly. Put your hands down and give yourself a little more time to think it over."

Let students share thinking with one another rather than calling on them to speak. When we call on students, they often "answer" us as opposed to building thinking with their classmates. When students share answers with one another, they are less inclined to see you as the evaluator of their thinking.

Use the following question stems to help you formulate authentic questions. Aim for as many authentic, open-ended questions as recall questions for any given class. If students have a hard time formulating answers, give them time, let them turn and talk with partners, and model your own thinking process as much as needed. If students need it, let them rely on your model. Don't worry—they'll move past it as you praise their original answers and invite new lines of thinking.

- "What are possible solutions to . . . ?"
- "Do you think . . . is a good thing or a bad thing?"
- "What is the problem with . . . ?"
- "How is . . . similar to/different than . . . ?"
- "Do you know of another instance where . . . ?"
- "What would happen if . . . ?"
- "How would you improve . . . ?"
- "What alternatives would you suggest for . . . ?"
- "Rank the importance of . . . Explain why you ordered them that way."
- "What is the most important . . . ? Explain why."
- "What is your favorite . . . ? Explain why."
- "What is your opinion of . . . ? Explain why."
- "What are the pros and cons of . . . ?"
- "What other examples of . . . can you think of?"
- "Why does . . . work?"
- "What are some of the causes that led to . . . ?"
- "What do you notice?"
- "What is the big idea or concept in . . . ?"
- "How does X relate to X?"
- "How would X person view this differently?"
- "What patterns do you notice in . . . ?"
- "How could you create or design a new . . . ? Explain."
- "What other information do you need about . . . ?"

Start with just a few of these and get in the habit of asking them again and again. Hearing them repeatedly will increase students' comfort level with the kinds of questions we aim to always ask when reading, discussing, thinking.

Encourage students to use these questions when working with partners or groups. Celebrate when you overhear a student posing such a question to themselves or to a classmate!

| | |
|---|---|
| **How do I know if this idea will help?** | • Students look to you to see if their answers are right.<br><br>• You hear from the same voices over and over.<br><br>• For the majority of your questions, you have a specific answer in mind.<br><br>• Students don't seem very interested in each other's answers. |
| **How do I know if this idea is working?** | • Students take time to answer questions.<br><br>• Answers to the same question are varied.<br><br>• Students are curious to hear how others answered questions.<br><br>• Participation in answering is higher because there is less fear of getting it wrong. |
| **How to try this with others** | • Create a set of authentic questions together for an upcoming lesson or unit. Test them out by seeing how you would answer them. What made answering these questions inviting or daunting? How will you help students accordingly?<br><br>• Use authentic questions to drive your learning with colleagues. Brainstorm authentic questions you want to answer: "How can I get my students to review their progress through checklists?" "What's getting in the way of my students making progress in X area?" |

*Want to know more about this strategy and others like it?*

**Check out:** Keene, Ellin Oliver, and Matt Glover. 2015. *The Teacher You Want to Be: Essays About Children, Learning, and Teaching.*

# 8.9 Interactive Modeling

**Try This**

Interactive modeling is especially effective when you teach procedures, routines, or protocols such as a discussion model. However, you can also use it when you teach academic skills such as solving a chemical equation or adding end points to sentences.

Interactive modeling is a way to show students explicitly what we expect. Say goodbye to the ineffective practice of leaving students to guess how to be successful in our classroom. Be totally transparent in saying, "Here's what it looks like to enter the room (or add two fractions or participate in a discussion). Let me show you and give you lots of opportunities to practice before I hold you accountable." Show students the skill or routine or procedure, step by step, and then let them try it while you provide feedback.

**How do I know if this idea will help?**

- Students are not using certain skills or routines that you assume they should know.
- You have taught a skill, but students are not able to do it consistently on their own.
- You may model skills and concepts, but students don't always have the opportunity to practice it and receive your immediate feedback.

**How do I know if this idea is working?**

- You can simply name or mention the skills previously taught with interactive modeling, and students execute them. Few or no reminders needed. They've got this down!
- You save time for students to practice the skill with your feedback, and these on-the-spot suggestions make all the difference.
- Students are willing to practice procedures and moves with you—they know this isn't going to be torturous. It's helpful and even fun.

**Adapt for 6–12**

- Although interactive modeling is not limited to teaching foundational procedures, it is a good way to get to any of the basic skills your older students may not be displaying, such as talking to a partner, taking turns, putting things back where they belong, or entering the room. If they aren't doing these things, teach them what they look like, without a punitive or sarcastic tone. Do your best to maintain a tone of kindness and a sense of playfulness so they feel comfortable trying it out.

**How to try this with others**

- Visit a colleague's room when they are ready for feedback on their interactive modeling. A kind move is to be the student when the interactive modeling is happening. This will also help you notice what helped and what may have been missed or rushed.
- Interactive modeling isn't just for kids! The next time professional learning is happening, see if the leader can practice this strategy. This is especially helpful when learning new technology applications.

| What to do | Example |
|---|---|
| 1. Clearly state what you are teaching students to do. Name it. | "I'm going through my draft and showing you how I take this big block of writing and separate it into paragraphs whenever there's a new idea, time, place, or someone different is talking." |
| 2. Give students a rationale for why you are teaching them this. We know why this skill is important, but until we let students in on that reason, we are only halfway transparent. Don't run the risk of students thinking this important skill is to fill time. | "Paragraphs are important for our reader to understand and make sense of our writing. They also allow us to affect the pacing of our story or essay. Short paragraphs tend to speed things up. Long paragraphs slow down our writing." |
| 3. Show students step by step how to do this. Do it one more time if necessary so they can jot down or keep track of details they may have missed the first time. | "Watch me as I read my writing aloud, and I insert a paragraph symbol each time I think I have a new idea, place, or someone new is talking." |
| 4. Have students share out what they noticed. You can chart these steps or qualities. Keep asking them, "What else did you notice?" until you get most of the steps or qualities. Then add in more tips or steps as needed. | "What did you notice about the places I chose to put paragraphs?" |
| 5. Have a student try the steps while others watch. Give reminders as needed—this isn't intended to catch them doing it wrong! | "Take out your draft. Read it quietly to yourself, and think about anytime you get to a new idea, place, time, or someone new is talking. You might even think about places to speed up or slow down the action with the length of your paragraphs." |
| 6. Recap again by asking, "What did you notice?" Refine steps and clarify as needed. | "Great! I noticed you . . ." "What did you notice?" |
| 7. Send everyone to practice. Observe and offer feedback, noting what students are doing that aligns to your modeling and offering suggestions for when they miss something or need support. | "So today we're going to keep working on adding purposeful paragraphs throughout our drafts. If you get stuck, you can look up here at my model and the chart of suggestions. I'll also be walking around to help you." |
| 8. Circle back to recap one last time. Does anyone have any suggestions, questions, or concerns? Praise them for what they did that aligned to the model. Ask them to make a mental plan (or jot it down) for how they will follow this model the next time. | "Your stories were transformed in beautiful ways today! What a difference paragraphs make for your reader. Let me put a few of your writings up on the document camera. You might get another idea for a paragraph in your own writing." |

*Want to know more about this strategy and others like it?*

**Check out:** Anderson, Mike. 2015. *The First Six Weeks of School.*

# 8.10 Incorporate Storytelling

Try This

Our brains are hardwired to learn through stories. Stories are a way to reach all of our students—many diverse cultures tell stories to connect communities and as a vehicle for teaching important lessons. Storytelling can be one aspect of culturally responsive teaching. Research about brain science shows that brains become stimulated and engaged when hearing stories. The most viewed TED Talks use story as the primary mode of persuasion (Gallo 2014). Stories are incredibly effective in getting us to listen, to engage, to believe, and to remember information. Think of powerful advertisements and how often they tell a story. Storytelling is used effectively in everything from Supreme Court cases to business pitches. So although we work hard to plan lessons that teach data, information, and skills, we can wrap those things in anecdotes to help our students connect to the information and engage.

## Tips

- Rehearse it. Although the telling of the story may feel spontaneous, the best stories are thought through and you've practiced them in advance.

- At the very least, know the ending. And make the ending one that cements the reason you told this story.

- Try writing your story in one sentence before telling it. Make sure you include the beginning, middle, and end. If you're unable to do this, it might be a sign that the story is overly complicated or that the gist will be lost to your audience.

- Simple is better. Keep it to the point. Use conversational language. Omit any detours, side stories, or minor characters that will confuse or keep your students from the primary learning point. Boil it down to the essence. If they have questions, they can always follow up later.

- Match their age level whenever possible. If you tell stories to a group of first graders about forgetting to pay your cell phone bill to illustrate responsibility, they are likely to tune out. Tell them about forgetting to feed your goldfish and the ugly results when you were six, and you'll have their attention.

- Don't be preachy. Stories shouldn't always deliver a moral, and avoid lecturing students about how you did something better than they did or "the importance of . . ." Tell stories of fallibility, of realistic and flawed experiences. Don't be afraid to be human.

A word of caution: this is a powerful strategy, but one we can overdo if the lead role in all of our stories is us, or if storytelling comes at the expense of succinctly delivered lessons. Here are some ways to prevent us from being blinded by the ego-stroking reward of a rapt audience and instead keep storytelling as a high-impact and inclusive teaching strategy:

- Have students create and tell their own stories, as opposed to just listening to others'. Help them to be the storytellers whenever possible. Encourage students to use this effective method of delivery in their work, presentations, and discussions.
- Look over the stories you have and plan to use: Are you always the central figure? If so, look to beef up stories where people in your content area play the starring role, or where your students do.

**How do I know if this idea will help?**

- Your upcoming lesson is dry or challenging. A story will up engagement.
- Students are tuning out or not connecting to the lesson.
- Students seem to get content for the day, but it isn't "sticking" or memorable.

**How do I know if this idea is working?**

- Students are tuning into your lesson and the content more.
- Students refer to the learning long after that day's lesson by remembering the story as well as the content.

**Adapt for K–5**

- Kids can get so easily engaged and then so easily distracted by storytelling. Keep in mind that after you tell your story, you may want to give them an opportunity to turn and share with a partner or put a thumbs up if they experienced something similar. Otherwise even the best stories derail some students' focus.

**How to try this with others**

- Take a week's worth of lessons and help each other designate the lessons that risk being the most challenging in terms of engaging students. Brainstorm stories together that will pull in students and make the material come alive.
- Try this in your own learning. Start off your next PLC or staff meeting by telling a story that introduces that day's topic. See how it impacts engagement and interest.

*Want to know more about this strategy and others like it?*

**Check out:** Gallo, Carmine. 2017. *Talk Like TED: The 9 Public Speaking Secrets of the World's Top Minds.*

Newkirk, Thomas. 2014. *Minds Made for Stories: How We Really Read and Write Informational and Persuasive Texts.*

## *Tech Integration Tip*

### WIDEN THEIR WORLD WITH VIDEO CONFERRING

Teacher-led instruction doesn't always have to mean you are the one teaching! Here's how to bring the outside world in and introduce a fresh teaching viewpoint.

**What to put in place first**

1. Have a device with a webcam and microphone, as well as an internet connection.
2. Create an account and profile through Skype in the Classroom (or another classroom-safe video conferring service).
3. Consider whether you want to explore virtual field trips, collaborating with other classrooms, guest speakers, or activities and lessons—all of which are available through Skype.
4. Make sure your collaborating classroom or other outside participant adds you as a contact, and vice versa.
5. Do a test call before the actual event.
6. Go over what the video session will involve with your students in advance. Let them know what to expect as well as your expectations of them. Have them prepare questions in advance for guest speakers.
7. Dive into some of the possibilities that follow.

**Ways to widen the world of your classroom with video conferring**

- Invite caregivers to participate in performances, events, presentations, activities, and more by setting up a Skype session. Save a few minutes at the end for Q and A.
- Interview an expert, or invite a guest speaker. Whatever content you are learning, see if someone who works in that area would connect with your class.
- Establish pen pals with another classroom, and periodically check in face-to-face via video conferring. Check out ePals, where classrooms across the globe post if they are interested in connecting with others.
- Take a virtual field trip. Many museums offer Skype sessions so students can "visit" virtually.
- Have authors talk to your students, answer questions, and/or do a reading of their book. Many authors will Skype with your students for free for about fifteen minutes, which is just about the right amount of time for attention spans anyway! A quick search will lead you to online lists of authors who are willing to do this. Or, reach out to authors on their websites and ask.

- Try Mystery Skype, where two classrooms can connect and guess one another's location through Q and A.
- Use video conferring to practice speaking other languages with students in other countries.
- Conduct interviews with experts, professionals, or other students and classrooms for another mode of research.
- Compete with another classroom community and announce the contest winner on live video.
- "Attend" civic meetings such as town hall meetings via video conferring.
- Try the Around the World with 80 Schools challenge on Skype, connecting with other classrooms in different countries across the year and learning about one another's cultures and languages.
- Work with musicians in different areas to create collaborative music by playing, practicing, and even performing together via video conferring.
- Connect with students remotely. Invite students who can't attend due to illness, create office hours, conduct parent-teacher conferences with those who can't come in person, or even touch base when you have to be absent.

# Student Talk and Collaboration

## What you have in place, and what you're ready for next

My dreamland classroom is one in which there is a palpable buzz of students working together, talking excitedly about the work at hand and generating new thinking. This is hard to get to, however, until we feel competent and confident in setting up that collaborative talk through planning and our teacher-led instruction. Now is the time to move students from talk about last night's game or what's for lunch to talk that grows ideas, stays on topic, and discusses the work at hand with passion and energy!

## Why are talk and collaboration important?

Gone are the days when talk is something teachers do while students listen. Fisher, Frey, and Quaglia (2018) remind us that talk "helps children focus their thinking, make their understandings known, and learn from others." If talk can do all that, we need to make it happen—consistently. And we need to help all ages learn how to do it well.

All state standards include a speaking and listening component. Talk is no longer an afterthought or an optional add-on feature of classrooms. It's an essential skill and component of classroom instruction.

The first way most of us learn is through talking and listening. Our brains are hardwired to learn through hearing speech and expressing speech. But often, classroom talk is heavily skewed toward teacher talk.

Getting better at anything requires repeated practice. These strategies are designed to help you intentionally incorporate student talk and collaboration in meaningful ways.

## What does the research say?

Research has shown that most of class talk is done by teachers, whose voices fill the room 50–80 percent of class time (Nunan 2003). We need to shift the balance so students' voices are the ones that dominate our classrooms. But we shouldn't stop there. After all, kids can be talking a lot, but it's not necessarily talk that grows new thinking. As it stands, 90 percent of student talk tends to involve rote talk, recitation, and regurtitation (West n.d.). Let's start infusing talk that is idea generating, not just recap.

Talk is also an antidote to this age of screen worship. Any of us teaching teens have likely feared that devices are replacing one-to-one conversation, and we want our teens to head out into the world ready to communicate personally. The solution, Sherry Turkle says in her book *Reclaiming Conversation*, is to have them talk more (2016).

Research shows that talk is a prerequisite to the development of thinking and understanding. For learning to happen, and for it to happen within a rich community of thinkers, we need strategies that foster talk (Alexander 2018).

## Is this the goal for me?

- Do you answer "yes" and "sometimes" for all statements? Consider moving to the next chapter. You've got this!

- Do you have a mix of "yes," "sometimes," and "not yet" answers? This might be the goal for you.

- Do you answer "not yet" for most of these statements? Go back and try the checklists from the previous chapters. You're likely to enjoy greater success and see quicker results by focusing there.

## What do you notice?

| | Yes | Sometimes | Not yet |
|---|---|---|---|
| Students talk to one another to build understandings and to help and learn from one another. | ☐ | ☐ | ☐ |
| When it's time to discuss, students speak freely and stay on topic. | ☐ | ☐ | ☐ |
| I don't have an answer in mind when I pose questions to students. | ☐ | ☐ | ☐ |
| The work and thinking students produce together is better than what they do on their own. | ☐ | ☐ | ☐ |

# 9.1 Catch Good Conversations on Camera

**Try This**

Show students what good discussion looks like by sharing a conversation you've recorded. Record a short video of your students in a strong discussion, or model it yourself with colleagues. Emphasize "look-fors" such as:

- making eye contact
- inviting others to participate
- building off of one another's comments
- looking in the text for evidence
- staying on one topic for a long time.

Show the video to the class for the first time without sound, and have students jot down what they notice people doing—they'll focus on body language, eye contact, and how much everyone talks. Show it again with volume on so students can pick up on verbal talk moves.

When students share out what they notice, list those qualities on chart paper or on the board. Then, make sure students have an opportunity right away to practice a conversation while paying attention to their use of those "good" conversational moves. Students can use the chart as a checklist to self-assess and reflect after their own discussion. They might also set goals and next steps for an upcoming conversation, deciding what qualities they want to work on when they talk again.

**How do I know if this idea will help?**

In pairs, small-group, or whole-class discussion, students are:

- slow to get talk going
- quick to say "We're done"
- not all contributing
- not referencing the text
- avoiding eye contact
- allowing one member to take over
- changing topics quickly without getting to big ideas.

**How do I know if this idea is working?**

- Students need less coaching or reminders during discussion.
- You are able to walk around and listen closely to each group because other groups are conducting discussions independently.
- Student talk reflects the "look-fors" you have generated together.
- Students are able to set specific goals for how to get better at discussion.

| | |
|---|---|
| **Adapt for K–5** | • Make sure your video captures clear and obvious talk moves. Make sure it's not hard for students to determine what's a strong conversational move and what's not. What will probably be easiest is to role-play a strong conversation with a colleague, channeling your inner actor and exaggerating eye contact, nodding, using phrases such as, "I think what you're saying is . . . ," "I agree because . . . ," and inviting your partner to take a turn talking. For younger students, it will also help them focus on the talk, not what is being said, if you discuss a familiar text. They'll pay close attention to the conversational moves when the conversation is familiar. |
| **Adapt for 6–12** | • We may assume that older students know how to talk to one another in productive, polite, and meaningful ways, but in fact they often benefit from having those skills taught explicitly. Don't be alarmed, in other words, that you need to devote instructional time to these essential talk skills.<br><br>• Then, you might find, too, that role-playing a video with a colleague to model the conversational moves you're looking for will be easier than finding one among students. If you go this route, you might even capture a "what-not-to-do" version, hamming up some less-than-thoughtful actions such as looking away, not having the text to refer to, being "done" after everyone talks once, and so on. |
| **How to try this with others** | • Brainstorm a list of strong conversation moves. Try working on those moves during your own meeting. At the end, reflect on what was hard and what went well. How can you help students get to those successes and avoid the pitfalls? What explicit instruction can you provide so they replicate the strong moves?<br><br>• Film a group of students during discussion and share it with colleagues. Ask them what they notice and how it might go one step further the next time.<br><br>• Visit one another's classes during pair, small-group, or whole-class discussion. Be another set of eyes for what is working and how it can build even further. |

*Want to know more about this strategy and others like it?*

**Check out:** Pranikoff, Kara. 2017. *Teaching Talk: A Practical Guide to Fostering Thinking and Conversation.*

# 9.2 Active and Focused Listening

Try This

Before good talk can happen, good listening must be in place. Don't assume students have mastered the art of listening—teach what it looks like and how to do it. Active listening is an act of kindness and respect. It deserves its own lesson.

First ask a student (or colleague) in advance to model active listening with you in front of the class. Practice it beforehand. The talk can be about anything, even non–content related. Make sure you model the following:

- nonverbal gestures such as nodding
- facing the speaker
- leaning in
- eye contact.

Record it in advance if that's easier. Keep the sound off when you play it the first time so students can better focus on the body language: nodding, facing the speaker, leaning in, and eye contact. If you don't record it, perform it two times so students have the opportunity to pick up on new things.

Let students practice with a set of questions to start off the conversation. Share out what was hard, what worked, and what to work on next time.

Then, add a layer of focused listening. Model live (or on video) an extra layer beyond silently listening attentively. For example, model what it looks and sounds like to recap what the speaker said, ask clarifying questions, and build onto what was said instead of just adding a separate thought or unrelated idea.

Send students off to practice again. Again, share out what was hard, what worked, and what to work on next time. Refer back to these qualities of active and focused listening as needed whenever students are discussing and collaborating.

**How do I know if this idea will help?**

- Conversation ends quickly.
- Students don't face one another when talking.
- Students listen only to wait for their partner to stop talking and then say their own point.

**How do I know if this idea is working?**

- Students look at one another and use appropriate body language.
- Conversation builds on one idea.
- Formerly reluctant speakers' voices are heard.
- Chairs/heads/bodies actually move when it's time to turn and talk.

## What is Active Listening in Mr. B's 7th grade?

- You are facing your body and head toward the speaker
- Your eyes are looking at the speaker or occasionally at your paper if you're jotting quick notes
- You respond by nodding and/or smiling
- You follow up w/ questions and comments to build on what they said
  - I agree with you because...
  - I was thinking... but now I think
  - Can you tell me more about..?

**Adapt for K-5**

- Students enjoy modeling an example of what not to do and then revising their actions to show what active listening looks like.
- A chart with photos of students engaged in active listening is a helpful support. This could also be duplicated in smaller form as a visual checklist.
- Listening can be harder than talking, especially at this age. Give students plenty of opportunities to practice, as well as specific praise for what you notice going well.
- Silliness may dominate at the beginning, but try to let it go unless it persists.
- At first, assign partners so that quick and confident speakers are together, and so are kids who like taking a little more time to formulate their thinking. Both will be forced out of their comfort zone by listening and responding to like-mannered partners.
- You can assign a peer coach to partnerships, who can whisper or point out reminders as they watch others engage in conversation.

**Adapt for 6-12**

- Don't assume older students know how to listen, but also don't say you're doing this because they are lousy at it. Emphasize how much you value everyone's voice in the room, so today is a chance to practice truly listening and hearing every voice.

- Eye contact and physical proximity can be awkward at this age. Work up to these for students who feel uncomfortable.

- At first, assign partners so that quick and confident speakers are together, and so are students who like taking a little more time to formulate their thinking. Both will be forced out of their comfort zone by listening and responding to like-mannered partners.

- You can assign a peer coach to partnerships, who can whisper or point out reminders as they watch others engage in conversation.

- For high school students, remind them how essential this skill is for job or college interviews. Practice will help everyone get over the awkwardness.

**How to try this with others**

- Create model videos for active and focused listening with a colleague.

- Try active and focused listening with one another in a meeting or small group. What came easily? What was hard? Now that you've tried it, what challenges can you anticipate for students?

- With a colleague, commit to improving active and focused listening in your personal and professional conversations across the next day or week. Reflect on what you noticed. How did it lift the level of conversation? What did you notice shifting for you and for your conversational partner?

# 9.3 Carousel Charts to Prime Student Thinking and Get Kids Talking

Try This

Gather four or five big pieces of paper or chart paper and number them. Post a different open-ended question related to that day's content at the top of each paper. Tape them on different walls in your classroom where students can see and reach them.

As students enter the room, count them off in as many groups as there are pieces of paper. Have them stand by their numbered paper. Give a different-color marker to each group. As soon as groups are gathered, ask them to start writing words and phrases that answer the question on their paper. Usually one person scribes for the group as the others share ideas. After a few minutes of this, have each group rotate to the next chart.

When students get to the next chart, a previous group will already have written on it. Groups can add their own ideas, and they can also respond to the previous group's ideas with some pre-chosen symbols, such as 😊 😮 or stars and question marks.

Have the groups rotate until everyone has visited every chart. As rotations go on, there will be more time spent reading previous responses and adding symbols than generating new ideas. This will allow everyone's thinking to build on the day's topic/content.

Provide additional time for each group to rotate among the charts and reread the entire class's contributions.

## Options for follow-up

- Move into paired, small-group, or whole-class discussion on the topic now that students have had the opportunity to do some prethinking together. You might start with one of the chart's questions and post it on the board where everyone can see as a starting point. Or, you might move onto an entirely new question if it feels like they have exhausted that topic.

- Have each group take down one of the chart papers to recreate in a synthesized, coherent version on a fresh piece of paper. Eliminate repetitions, remove symbols, and combine comments when needed. These charts can serve as discussion starters, evidence of thinking, or representations of prior knowledge as the unit progresses.
  - If the questions are content based and determining prior knowledge, the teacher can distribute the correct information for students to compare against the synthesized response.

- Ask students to write a personal reflection after the activity. Have them record their initial thinking and explain how it was pushed or changed, how it compared to the distributed information, and how the process felt.

- Conversations start and stay at a surface level of thinking.
- A few voices dominate discussions.
- There is little opportunity for movement in the class.
- It is hard to get talk going—students aren't sure where or how to start.

- Students fill up the papers with comments.
- There is a general "buzz" in the room as students discuss the questions and generate ideas.
- Students respond to one another's comments.
- Talk in groups or as a class starts off more readily and with more sophisticated thinking.
- Students build off of one another's comments more often.
- You hear more voices in small-group and whole-class discussions.

- Allow younger students to use drawings and symbols to show their thinking.

- Aim for about three students per chart for easier management. This may mean creating more than five charts.

- If students are getting off task, it may be that you are giving too much time.

- Decide in advance if they carry the marker with them or leave it at the station. Having different-color markers per chart or per group, however, will help them see layers of thinking.

**How to try this
with others**

- Plan a round of carousel charts together. After trying it in your classrooms, come back and debrief. What were the successes? What did you notice students doing or not doing? What were the challenges? How will you try it again?

- Use carousel charts in a staff or department meeting. Afterward, debrief. What did you notice? How will you use that experience to inform your own instruction when you try it with students?

*Want to know more about this strategy and others like it?*

**Check out:** Edwards, Susan. 2014. *Getting Them to Talk: A Guide to Leading Discussions in Middle Grades Classrooms.*

# 9.4 Sorting Items to Structure Purposeful, Inquiry-Based Group Talk

**Try This**

Think about how social gatherings can often be less awkward when we have an activity or game to pull us together and frame our interactions. Student groups also benefit from having a tangible set of artifacts, as well as a defined task in how to sort and handle those artifacts (in this case, a specific goal of choosing which artifacts go with which and in what order). A concrete goal with "live" objects gives structure and purpose to student talk—there's no way to do this silently! And, it often feels more authentic and accessible for students than discussing an abstract idea or a two-dimensional text.

Provide groups of 2–4 students an assortment of artifacts, manipulatives, images, dates, scenarios, texts, musical scores (you see just how many directions this could go). Task students with organizing the items according to a factor or quality that you have determined in advance. Students might sort, rank, or label the items.

Give a time frame for the group work to provide a sense of urgency. Remind students they need a rationale behind their sorting method that they can explain to you and/or the class at the end.

As groups are sorting their items, circulate among them. You are there to offer feedback but not to steer their decisions. The level of thinking and engagement will be higher as students come up with their own methods.

After the set time, ask groups to share how they sorted/ranked/categorized/labeled the items and why.

Some examples of ranking and sorting exercises across grade bands and content areas:

**Science, grade 1:** Students receive 10–20 labeled images of animals. They have five minutes to sort them into mammals, reptiles, and amphibians. This could be done as an introduction to a unit on animals to assess what students already know or as a culminating activity after studying the characteristics of each group to reinforce and assess student learning.

**Music, grade 3:** Give each group of students four different recordings and have them rank them in terms of tempo. Which is the slowest and which is the fastest? Or, give them four different written notes (whole note, half note, quarter note, eighth note) and have them rank them in terms of length.

**Language arts, grade 6:** Provide four relevant themes to the class novel (by sixth grade, there are numerous themes to a novel). Students rank them from most to least important theme in the text, backing up those rankings with their thinking and with evidence from the text. Alternatively, provide four to five pieces of text evidence to support an already established theme in the text. Ask students to rank the evidence from most to least relevant to the theme. Discuss as a class what makes a theme or text evidence more or less relevant or important.

The rules of masculinity can make growing up harder than it needs to be.

It's important to take the risk of opening up to others.

Bullying can be emotional violence, not just physical violence.

When people are abandoned at an early age, it can be hard to trust others.

*Want to know more about this strategy and others like it?*

**Check out:** Wilhelm, Jeffrey D., Rachel Bear, and Adam Fachler. 2019. *Planning Powerful Instruction, Grades 6–12: 7 Must-Make Moves to Transform How We Teach— and How Students Learn.*

**Geometry, grade 9:** Each group receives shape properties along with a list of shapes. Students label each property according to the appropriate shape (rhombus, trapezoid, circle, etc.). For additional challenge, they can label properties that align to more than one shape.

**History, grade 12**: Each group receives 15–20 factors that led up to and helped end the Cold War. Students label them according to leading up to or ending the war, and then rank them in terms of how much they impacted or contributed to the beginning or end of the war.

**How do I know if this idea will help?**

- Students are not in the habit of actively working in groups with information they receive.
- Students are quick to decide one right answer as opposed to sharing and building thinking in groups.
- Students are quiet or not on task when they work in groups.

**How do I know if this idea is working?**

- Students are talking and sorting, and grouping and labeling as they do.
- Students have made decisions and can back up those decisions with reasons at the end.
- You see higher participation levels during group or paired work.

**How to try this with others**

- When planning a unit, try to generate several activities across the unit that ask students to sort, label, or rank items. Delegate this among yourselves so everyone generates one day's activity. Then, regroup at the end of the unit to reflect: Which sorting tasks both invite and require students to dig in with debatable ideas, make decisions that could go one way or another, and come up with an arrangement or grouping that shows you they understood a concept? Can you try it out yourselves and see if you were nudged into conversation, or were you able to quickly sort and be done? Go for the former and watch conversation and thinking grow!

# 9.5 Remove Obstacles for One and All: Tools to Help Everyone Collaborate

**Try This**

As discussed in Strategies 2.6 and 5.8, protecting kids with disabilities or who are learning English benefits all of our students. Think through design changes in how talk and collaboration are structured, so that everyone has the tools to succeed. Encourage students to see such tools as resources for everyone. If a discussion tool is student created, have everyone create the tool. Provide access to these tools and allow students to choose what works for them.

## Tools to support talk and collaboration

- **Personal portfolios** for students to introduce themselves to new classmates, teachers, and groups:
    - Portfolio can be in paper, audio, or video format.
    - Have students share images, artifacts, work samples, notes from family/friends/previous teachers, accomplishments, favorite music/books/games.
    - Include helpful information the student wants others to know such as any sensory issues, allergies, how to pronounce their names correctly, and so on.

    - Search online for "all about me" printables that come ready-made with categories for students to fill out about themselves, their preferences, their hobbies, and more.
- **Question jar** filled with questions that students can ask one another during class discussion or group talk:
    - Any subject: What is the most interesting part of today's lesson? What is a tip you have for others? What is another way of explaining this?
    - Math example: Can you share a real-world example?
    - Language arts example: Which character is most interesting and why? What was the moment of truth in this book?
- **Small groups of four or less.** Any larger will limit the ability of hearing-impaired students to track conversations, and the smaller size will help increase everyone's comfort level (and accountability) in taking part.
- **Write key points for all to see.** This will help hearing-impaired students to pick up on any missed discussion points, and it will help everyone follow changes in topic.

- **Talking sticks** are preprinted conversation starters.
  - Use tongue depressors or sticks from the craft store and write questions that are appropriate for your students' age group and environment. You can even involve your students and ask them questions that range from silly and fun to thought-provoking.
    - » "What's your favorite breakfast?"
    - » "If your friend is sad, what do you do to make them feel better?"
    - » "What's your idea of a perfect playground?"
    - » "What makes you laugh the most?"
    - » "What's your favorite show/game/movie?"
    - » "What do you like most about yourself?"
    - » "Who is a celebrity you admire?"
    - » "If you had $100, what would you spend it on?"

- **Give them supportive content.** If your goal for a student is to help them talk, then give them content that they can add on to. This can sometimes be the needed step to speaking up.
  - Hand the student a card or sticky note with the question and supportive content in advance so they feel comfortable chiming in. Later when they're comfortable, you can remove the scaffold. For the whole class to try this, give everyone talking points in advance and let them practice the art of participating and listening without needing to worry about content.

- **Peer tutoring**—Provide the steps and script so they can easily work with a partner.
  - Write out the lines that a peer tutor will say and practice it with them before they try it with a partner. For example, if peer tutors are working on math with flash cards:
    - » Show the first flashcard.
    - » "What is the answer?"
    - » If they get it, say, "You got it right!"
    - » If they don't have the answer say, "Do you want to try again?"
    - » If they still don't get it, show them the answer. Then say, "Try it again."
    - » Put all the right answers in a pile.
    - » At the end, count the right answers and let your partner know the number.

| How do I know if this idea will help? |
| --- |

- Some students appear to need support in conversation and discussion. They let others take over.

- Some students are reluctant to talk because they aren't sure what to say.

- You spend time coaxing students to participate in class or group discussion.

- You have students with individualized education plans who need accommodations for speech.

**How do I know if this idea is working?**

- A greater percentage of students readily participate in paired, group, and class discussion.
- You see students with individualized education plans as well as other students using the tools.
- You don't need to coax students to talk—they are doing so on their own.

**How to try this with others**

- When your students hear that their teachers have tried these tools and rated them as "helpful," they will be much more willing to give them a go. Choose a few to try together and decide the ones that will be most helpful and inviting for your students. Let students know that this is preapproved, and that other tools are to come!

*Want to know more about this strategy and others like it?*

**Check out:** Kluth, Paula, and Sheila Danaher. 2010. *From Tutor Scripts to Talking Sticks: 100 Ways to Differentiate Instruction in K–12 Inclusive Classrooms.*

# 9.6 W Board

**Try This**
Designate a wall or board space in the room for *W* (who, what, where, why, why, how) questions about the topic(s) you are teaching, such as the earth's structure, the Civil War, fractions, painting self-portraits, or the periodic table. Provide index cards and pencils. When introducing the *W* board, model the first few questions and provide sentence starters as support. See examples per grade level on page 244.

Explain when and how students can post questions, and where the materials are. As soon as questions are posed, do a short inquiry with students about how they might find answers.

Encourage students to seek answers to one another's questions. Provide time for them to share their findings, then celebrate those discoveries. Celebrate answers by expressing interest (fascination if you can muster it!) as students share. If you know an answer to be incorrect, let that emerge by encouraging more inquiry about the question.

If time is tight, allow the questions and answers to exist as their own dialogue on the board or on a Padlet, Flipgrid, or other digital forum. Don't expect this to take off, however, unless you devote your own time to participate in the forum and talk it up in class.

Use these questions to start off discussion. Refer to them frequently. Express wonderment for potential answers.

**How do I know if this idea will help?**

- Discussion around content always puts you in the role of facilitating talk. You may feel like it's pulling teeth to get students to participate in discussion.
- Students look to you for answers, not their fellow classmates.
- The spirit of inquiry is flatlining. You hear a lot of "Is this graded?" when it's time to discuss.

**How do I know if this idea is working?**

- Students are excited by inquiry and are proud of the answers they discover.
- Talk is fostered and built upon by classmates with less dependence on you for direction and "answers."
- *W* questions and student answers reflect new resources not used in the classroom, whether adult experts in the community, websites, print resources, or local institutions.

| Adapt for K-5 | • Give time in class to research answers. |
|---|---|

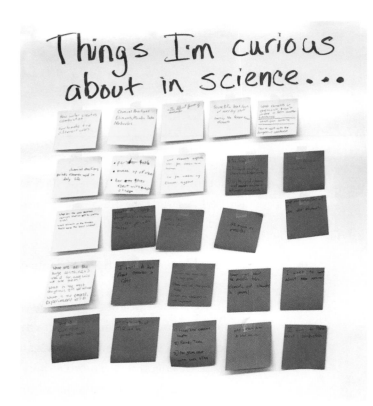

- • Provide text sets of books from the classroom library or school library that may afford answers.

**Want to know more about this strategy and others like it?**

**Check out:** Emdin, Christopher. 2016. *For White Folks Who Teach in the Hood—and the Rest of Y'all Too: Reality Pedagogy and Urban Education.*

- • At the start of the year, have a student bring in a picture, stuffed animal, or trinket that will stay in the classroom for the week. Throughout the week, the kids come up with questions that they have about that item. They can jot them down or have the teacher jot them down on a sticky note. This will help kids to learn how to ask questions about a particular topic and stay on that topic without sharing stories. This will also help students to learn the difference between questions and comments.

- • Encourage students to ask other adults in the building for information. You can also suggest names of students (in your class or in others) who have expertise in these areas. Encourage students to see peers as resources.

| Adapt for 6–12 | • You might hear "Is this graded?" If you value collaboration, inquiry, and student-fostered thinking and debate, then give credit for participating. Extra credit works well. Assess participation, not whether answers are correct. Thoroughness of answers, quality of open-ended questions, and time spent researching could mean more or less points. |
|---|---|

- • At the start of the year, ask rotating students to bring in an image or an actual artifact (skateboard, artwork, album cover, baseball cap, snapshot of a favorite place) to post on the board. Throughout the week, have the class come up with questions that they have about that image. They can jot them on a sticky note. This will engage them in questioning, help them learn how to ask focused questions, and build community.

| How to try this with others | • Visit one another's *W* boards. What do you notice? Which are the best questions? Can you take a picture or jot them down to share with your class as models? |
|---|---|

- • Open up your classes to visit each other's *W* boards (could be done digitally if too hard to physically visit) and answer those questions.

# 9.7 What's the Pattern?

**Try This**

Write three examples of a pattern, each of which demonstrate the concept you want to teach. For instance, create three sentences with appositives, three words that have the digraph *ck*, three vertex equations, three proper nouns, three irregular Spanish verb conjugations, three named binary molecular compounds, or three states of matter that follow a set of rules you want students to know and use.

Have groups of three or four students determine what the examples have in common and the unwritten rules for using them correctly. Before teaching it yourself, ask students to each replicate that pattern creating three of their own examples. Students then need to check each other's work to make sure each group member's examples follow the pattern and rules correctly.

Circulate after students have the opportunity to check one another's work. Choose one group member's examples to check for accuracy. Because they had time to help one another, everyone's examples should reflect the group's determined rules.

Now you can teach the whole class the name of the concept and the official rules. If you have a document camera, show students' examples that correctly show the concept. Walk everyone through the patterns and rules, using those as an example. Students can then go back and revise their examples as needed.

## Tips

- Students do not need to use academic language when they're discussing. You can tell them at the end that these are called appositives or vertex equations. At first, you want them to genuinely understand the patterns and rules of that concept in their own language.

- Give them a short time frame to do this. Five minutes to determine the rules as a group and another five minutes to create and cross-check their three examples is plenty. Create a sense of urgency!

- Use this as an entry activity for a new concept. Celebrate any risks they take or rules they determine. But no points off for getting it wrong.

- If this concept is a review or familiar to students, you could assess it. But don't collect these and create more grading for yourself. Instead, announce that you'll be visiting each group and randomly selecting one to spot check. If that one person's examples are done correctly, the entire group gets a point. This spurs the entire group to help each other out and reinforce their learning.

**How do I know if this idea will help?**

- Groups tend to allocate the work to one member.

- The energy and urgency in group tasks can easily die out.

- Your students can relay information, but they don't always understand the concept behind it.

- Group members take part in the work equally.
- There is an energy to completing the work quickly.
- Students are able to explain the concept in their own words.

---

7th-grade English

What is the pattern? What do these sentences have in common?

- Karen, a ninth grader, was the star of the basketball team.
- The puppy, a golden retriever, refused to sit when told.
- That group over there, the ones wearing red shirts, is here on a field trip.

---

Want to know more about this strategy and others like it?

**Check out:** Gallagher, Kelly. 2011. *Write Like This: Teaching Real-World Writing Through Modeling & Mentor Texts.*

Grade 4 Math

What is the pattern? What do these decimals as words have in common?

- 0.03 = three hundredths
- .47 = forty-seven hundredths
- .7 = seven tenths

---

Spanish III

What is the pattern? What do these irregular verbs in the yo form have in common?

- hacer = hago
- traer = traigo
- poner = pongo

---

- Develop the examples of "threes" together, or delegate a few topics across a unit so you all have a few to use. Bring student work back and reflect on what concepts work well with this strategy and where you will build on it in future lessons.

## *Tech Integration Tip*

### CREATE A BACK CHANNEL FOR STUDENT DISCUSSION

Expand your students' opportunities to talk, ask and answer questions, and grow thinking with a back channel. A back channel is an online classroom tool that allows groups to share thinking in real time using tablets or computers, often alongside the live event, lesson, or activity. Back channels are informal, secure (no ads or personal information is collected), and typically high interest.

Before you balk at students typing away while a lesson or event is happening, think of an event you've attended recently when phones were allowed. How many people at that concert or workshop had fingers to screens, tweeting or note-taking about what they were seeing and hearing?

As Sara Ahmed writes, giving students a way to pose questions and comments actually ups engagement and understanding as opposed to diluting it (Harvey and Ahmed 2015). Rather than risk losing the students who are confused and check out, why not let them deepen understanding in a chat? As opposed to shushing the kid who shouts out comments, why not give her a way to shout out that thinking in an appropriate manner? And instead of wondering what students are thinking and understanding (or not), why not get a transcript that shows just that?

*Want to know more about this tech tip and others like it?*

**Check out:** Daniels, Harvey, and Sara K. Ahmed. 2015. *Upstanders: How to Engage Middle School Hearts and Minds with Inquiry.*

A few back channel options to check out (free as of publication):

- Google Classroom (a Google Doc or the stream)
- Backchannel Chat
- GoSoapBox
- Mentimeter
- Tozzl
- Edmodo
- AnswerGarden

# 9.8 Written Conversation

**Try This**

As a precursor to talk in groups or as a class, have students engage in a note-passing activity. Let them generate thinking together on paper first, and watch the level of talk jump once they move from written conversation to spoken conversation.

Ask students to form groups of three or four, and have everyone get out an 8.5 × 11-inch piece of blank paper. Have them write their names on the top left corner and address the note/letter with "Dear friends," or by the names of their group members.

Explain the three rules:

1. Use your best handwriting so friends can read what you wrote.
2. No talking.
3. Write the whole time.

Start off the writing exercise by having everyone choose from three to four prompts or sentence frames. Display those questions or sentence frames on the board. Design the questions to get students thinking about the content they are going to discuss. (See the examples that follow.)

Rotate around the room and look over their shoulders. Provide reminders as needed regarding the three rules. Have students stop writing once most of them have about a quarter to a third of a page written. Ask them to rotate their papers once to the left.

Explain they will read what their classmate has written and respond to it right below. Students can agree, respectfully disagree, ask questions, or move to a new topic—the idea is to simply keep the conversation going. This time when they write, remove the prompts and questions—students are no longer answering those prompts but responding to their classmate. Again, send them off to write until everyone has written approximately a quarter to a third of a page.

Have them rotate once more. This time allow slightly more time as students are reading two classmates' thinking. Remind them again to keep that conversation going. Have writers trade once more, and then have them return the letters to the original author.

Allow time for each student to read over the conversation they started. Ask them to underline the single most interesting thing someone else wrote. As a group, ask them to choose one of those lines as the starting point for their group discussion. Encourage groups to stay on that topic for as long as possible before moving onto another comment.

Celebrate the volume of writing produced. Most papers will show (cumulatively) at least a page of writing in about ten minutes. Now you know they are capable of writing about a page in ten minutes. Hold them to that volume in other writings as well!

- Talk often stalls after each member has contributed.
- Time is spent clarifying the content in discussion versus thought-provoking conversation.
- Students need support to generate a decent volume of writing.
- Students do not listen or respond to one another in discussion.

- Students collectively compose over a page.
- Everyone is writing.
- The level of talk jumps as students clarify misunderstandings and build on one another's thinking first in writing.
- You see a higher percentage of participants in discussion.
- Students refer to one another's comments when sharing their thinking.

To start your own written conversation choose one of the following:

- What did this TED talk make you think about?
- The big ideas I came away with were...
- When I hear "Identity" I think about...

The first round of letter writing was prompted by the questions. Then students kept the conversation going by responding to the letter.

Michelle

Dear Friends,

This TED talk makes me think about the books I've been reading this year in this class and in my other classes. It makes me wonder if I'm really reading stories that give me different viewpoints or if I'm getting similar viewpoints over and over. I can think of a few times that an essay gave me a different viewpoint like when we read about why would we celebrate Columbus Day? But it also got me thinking that I don't like it when someone or lots of people look at me in just one way. Cause I'm not.

I know what you mean because even in my own family people say I'm the smart one and my brother is good at sports. The TED talk made me think that sometimes we don't bother getting to know people past this one big identity. Like what they're known for might not be their only thing. Or what they post or like isn't necessarily the only story about them.

| **Adapt for K–2** | • Give students enough time to write just a thought or two. Pass two times to keep energy up. |
|---|---|
| | • *If they can't yet read one another's writing, you might wait on this strategy.* |
| | • A variation of "talking" is to write letters or notes to one another, or to the whole class, using mailboxes in the classroom. Students can pose questions and answer one another during writing time, or by writing at home and using the mailbox when they come to school. |

| **Adapt for 3–5** | • Students may need a bit of time to get to a third of a page, so you can adapt as needed. Either provide additional time or have them change papers after a fifth or quarter of a page is completed. Prioritize maintaining energy around the assignment. |
|---|---|
| | • Remind them to underline something someone else wrote. Younger students are often compelled to choose what they said. Or, let them choose one of each. |

| **Adapt for 6–8** | • If students are wholly resistant to writing, you may initially see one or two students not take part. Let it go and let them pass that blank page. Most often, they will start writing by the second pass. |
|---|---|
| | • If students prefer to use keyboards, they could do this same work on a Google Doc. For this to work, everyone in the group needs to compose online. |

| **How to try this with others** | • Do this as a team of teachers to practice. Make it authentic, reflecting on a recent professional development course, text, or topic before discussing as a group. |
|---|---|
| | ○ Consider what worked, what modifications you might make for your students, and how it felt for various members. |
| | ○ Be ready to share out your own experience with students. |

*Want to know more about this strategy and others like it?*

**Check out:** Daniels, Harvey, and Elaine Daniels. 2013. *The Best-Kept Teaching Secret: How Written Conversations Engage Kids, Activate Learning, Grow Fluent Writers, K–12.*

# 9.9 Circle Structures for Talk

**Try This**

Circular talk structures allow everyone to see one another, build community, and can adapt to fit discussion goals.

**Sequential circles.** Talk travels around the circle, student by student. Students talk when it is their turn in the circle. This prevents a back-and-forth, strengthens patience skills, supports a respectful tone of listening and turn taking, and allows quieter voices a predictable opportunity to speak without interruption.

**Nonsequential circles.** There is no fixed order in a nonsequential circle. Students may participate when and if they choose. It can help to have a leader or facilitator (who may or may not be the teacher). If needed, students can hold a designated object (anything from a stuffed animal to a ball to a brightly colored ruler) to signify it is their turn to talk and to pass on to the next speaker.

**Fishbowls.** A smaller group (3–5) of students form a smaller circle in front of the class or within the larger circle of their classmates who observe. The fishbowl participants conduct the conversation, attempt to solve the problem, debate the issue (or whatever topic or skill is being addressed) while others watch. This can be used to model or reflect on conversation or problem-solving skills. One variation is keeping an extra chair in the fishbowl for outer circle observers to jump in when they wish to add something.

**Inside/outside circles.** Two concentric circles with the inner circle chairs facing the outer circle. Students pair with the student across from them. Provide a question or statement for students to think about. Have the inner circle start by sharing their thinking with their partner. After a short time, have talk switch to the outside circle. Then, have one of the circles rotate one to the left or right and discuss the same topic or question with their new partner. Or, assign a new topic or question.

**How do I know if this idea will help?**

- Students are accustomed to turn and talk and other paired structures. They're ready for more.
- Students will benefit from hearing from the entire class, not just a partner or small group.

- You can put students into various circle structures without needing to spend a lot of time on the directions. They know what to do.

- Students participate in circular structures just as they would in paired talk, meaning they listen, speak, and push one another's thinking.

- Try out a circular structure or two at a staff meeting. Reflect on which one felt most helpful and engaging. Start with that one in class.

## Want to know more about this strategy and others like it?

**Check out:** Emdin, Christopher. 2016. *For White Folks Who Teach in the Hood—and the Rest of Y'all Too: Reality Pedagogy and Urban Education.*

# 9.10 Take Turns Questioning the Text

**Try This**

This strategy fits best in literacy classrooms, but almost every class will involve reading at some point. Questioning the text as we read is a useful skill for checking understanding and for going a bit deeper with our thinking. High-level questions help readers dive into meaning, craft, bias, purpose, and connections among texts.

One way to get to both surface-level (basic comprehension) and deeper-level questioning is to alternate the roles of posing and answering questions by teacher and students. First, the teacher reads a segment of the text and poses questions to the students. These questions can check comprehension by asking students to recap the basics. Then, the teacher can pose questions that extend to deeper thinking.

For the next chunk of text, switch roles. Now students pose questions to the teacher. The teacher answers. Keep trading roles for segments of the text, posing and answering questions as you go.

Students benefit by collectively answering questions with classmates, by clarifying misunderstandings through group discussion, and finally, by using the teacher's questions and answers as models. Student questions tend to elevate throughout the process, going deeper and considering big topics beyond surface-level comprehension.

Eventually, you may turn over the questioning process to students in pairs as you circulate among them.

*Want to know more about this strategy and others like it?*

**Check out:** Fisher, Douglas, and Nancy Frey. 2014. *Checking for Understanding: Formative Assessment Techniques for Your Classroom.*

**How do I know if this idea will help?**

- Reading any text tends to be done independently or by the teacher.
- You want the students to do more with the texts beyond simply understanding them.
- Students wait for you to explain what a text means or how to read it.
- You have students who need support to read the texts used in class.

- Students begin using some of the questioning moves you model.
- Students are more actively engaged during this shared reading—you don't have to coax them to take part.
- Students are displaying more critical thinking when reading—they don't just recap the basics.
- You're having more fun during the reading and questioning process—students' questions keep you on your toes!

**Adapt for K-5**

- Keep the questioning focus narrow—one thing at a time. For example, one day you might model asking and answering questions that get kids thinking about the text features and the purpose they serve.
- Provide a visual reminder for the kinds of questions you model and want students to try.

**How to try this with others**

- Try out the questioning and answering process with a colleague or two on your own first to get a more authentic sense of what your students will respond to and need. Take turns and reflect afterward on what scaffolding and support will benefit your students. Mark up the text with possible places to switch, and add your notes of what "moves" applied to what sections of text.

## *Tech Integration Tip*

### BUILD A RECORDING BOOTH IN TWENTY MINUTES

Giving students a way to show their thinking through talking and recording versus writing often ups engagement and builds digital skills. If your students are creating podcasts, video recordings, tutorials, video newsletters, or any other sort of recordings, they will benefit from a designated space that allows them to create high-quality sound recordings. Plus, they will feel more official!

Create a space to record thinking where others won't be disrupted. A recording booth can be as simple

as a cardboard box with foam padding inserted on each wall, flipped on its side. The box needs to be big enough for students to put their smartphone, iPad, tablet, or computer inside it. This will improve sound quality immensely. Recording booths or studios can stay in one designated space, or students can transport them to their desks or other areas as needed. If you want to be fancy, look for acoustic foam already precut into 12 × 12 squares, and adhere battery-powered lights to the top for improved visuals.

Then, add a chart or set of instructions near the booth to serve as a reminder of what you've taught students to do when using the booth. Include steps for starting, recording, and stopping the camera.

Providing a handheld headphone/microphone will also reduce distractions and improve sound quality.

### Some ways students might record their thinking and learning

- Summarize learning at the end of a unit as a strengths-based assessment.
- Provide feedback for one another's work.
- Bring in math manipulatives and explain and demonstrate how to solve problems.
- Record book club discussions.
- Record themselves practicing another language.
- Play a musical instrument.
- Read aloud for fluency and expression.
- Create podcasts.
- Interview a classmate or other school members.
- Record presentations or voiceovers.

*Want to know more about this tech tip and others like it?*

**Check out:** Muhtaris, Katie, and Kristin Ziemke. 2015. *Amplify: Digital Teaching and Learning in the K–6 Classroom.*

# Summative Assessment and Grading

## What is summative assessment, and why is it important?

Say the words *summative assessment*, and most of us hear *grading*. I've been known to pull every dead leaf off my houseplants before sitting down to grade. Then I'll grade one essay and count the stack again as if the number magically reduced to single digits. Then I'll shuffle one paper to the bottom of the pile because I'm just not ready for that one yet. But there is a different way. We can see summative assessment as drudgery—or, we can see it as a way for teachers and students to celebrate growth and figure out what's next.

Both grading and marking progress are inevitable and essential parts of teaching. In my dream world, we'd have just the latter. But almost all of us contend with both. And now we're ready to look at how to make summative assessment work for us and for students.

## What does the research say?

Early in our students' academic lives, grades start to shape their school mind-set, and rarely for the better, in terms of increasing curiosity and self-worth (Kohn 2018). Even kindergartners can respond to seemingly benign evaluations and come away with the sense either that they belong in school or that they aren't really cutting it.

Although we may all have some painful memories associated with grades, hopefully we all can also remember the feeling of a final assessment that lifted us and bathed us in a golden light of "I'm good at this! I can really do this hard thing!" Maybe there were times we got so lost in working on a project that everything else got put on a back burner. Or we were so proud of our work that we didn't even care about the grade. Kohn and others remind us that our students need more of those moments (Kohn 2018).

Not to mention, all too often grading reinforces the inequities of our society at large—good grades aligning disproportionately to already privileged groups and lower grades being overallocated to those who are already at risk (Feldman 2019). The system of grading is set up to privilege a certain kind of competency, while leaving out or devaluing others. How do we create equitable grading structures that encourage growth, not stunt it?

## What we're ready to tackle

How we assess and evaluate and how we share this information with students have a profound impact on students' sense of self, their desire to keep trying, and their identities as students. This all adds up to whether they show up ready to learn in the short term, and long term, whether they just show up. Talk to any high school dropout and listen to when they "found out" that they weren't good at school. Talk to any college professor, too, and listen to their common refrains that inflated grades have their own wreaked havoc. Both the punitive and the inaccurately glowing assessments can leave damaging long-term ripple effects.

Assessments that are fair and engaging and that set up students to shine are not always easy to create, but they make all the difference. And then of course, there's that small matter of creating assessments that don't require that we hunker down for hours of grading.

There are ways to hold our students accountable, measure their strengths and challenges, engage them in meaningful work, and help them thrive. And there are ways to evaluate these works and still sleep eight hours. Here's how.

## Is this the goal for me?

- Do you answer "yes" and "sometimes" for all statements? Consider moving to the next chapter. You've got this!

- Do you have a mix of "yes," "sometimes," and "not yet" answers? This might be the goal for you.

- Do you answer "not yet" for most of these statements? Go back and try the checklists from the previous chapters. You're likely to enjoy greater success and see quicker results by focusing there.

## What do you notice?

| | Yes | Sometimes | Not yet |
|---|---|---|---|
| I spend more time checking for understanding and responding accordingly than grading final work. | ☐ | ☐ | ☐ |
| Students accurately predict how they will perform on assessments. I know this because they assess their work before I do. | ☐ | ☐ | ☐ |
| Assessments reflect what I have taught and what I most value. | ☐ | ☐ | ☐ |
| Assessments allow for multiple ways for students to show understandings. | ☐ | ☐ | ☐ |

# 10.1 Publish to a Wider Audience Than Yourself

**Try This**

No matter how much students love you (and they do love you), sharing final work with a wider audience lifts both engagement and work quality. When students know their work will be shared with classmates, students in other grades, the school community, members of the local community, or a whole other audience in the world at large, the stakes for creating beautiful and high-level work become that much higher.

It's not that students don't want to impress you, but you are a very comfortable audience. Think about what you wear around the house (for me, the faded pajama pants at the end of my bed that are reworn a half dozen times without a second thought) versus what we wear when we go out in the world. We just aren't that worried about impressing our family compared with the world at large.

"Publishing" means students take the time to make their final work polished and viewer friendly, and then they put that work out into the world. Taking the time for this step for any major assignment shows that your students' work is valued, relevant, and worthy. Protect this publishing step and watch the payoff in the form of quality work that students are proud of.

For your next summative assessment or major assignment, broaden the scope of who will see that work. Consider the following options:

- Invite another class to see the work by setting up a gallery walk (post student work around the room like an exhibit so others can view it and leave sticky note compliments) or have them come in for a reading or share. This can be particularly interesting to do with grade teams that are addressing similar concepts, skills, or content at different levels. Think about having the sixth-grade students share their time lines on the revolutionary war with the fourth-grade students who completed time lines for the solar system. Save time for questions and comments.

- Use that super fancy technology of stamps and envelopes. Decide who might benefit from seeing this work, and show students how to mail it to them. Bonus if they get a response!

- Have a laminating machine? Have students put their work onto a colorful, one-page spread. This can work for anything from times tables to comic panels to graphs to musical scores. Laminate the one-pagers and have students bring them home as celebratory placemats that can be viewed again and again with their families.

- Digital publishing! The possibilities are endless, and rest assured that digital publishing is often free and that you don't have to be a tech wizard to use it. Check out:
  - Flipsnack
  - Canva
  - Joomag
  - Lucidpress
  - Classroom Authors.

Kindergarten students left short comments on each other's stories after sharing them aloud in a publishing party.

| Develop that idea | Draft it! |
|---|---|
| Clarify the problem and then name the solution<br><br>Writing on loose leaf paper<br>Writing Partners<br>Small groups,<br>Conferences | Show don't tell using senses to describe places<br>Loose leaf paper<br>Small groups,<br>Conferences |
| **Publishing** | **Celebration** |
| Add a title to your story and have it ready for gallery walk tomorrow. | Gallery walk with other 4th grade class. All work will be on walls with sticky notes for readers to leave specific compliments. Caregivers and administration invited! |

**How do I know if this idea will help?**

- Students run out of steam toward the end of a unit.
- Students don't take care with final projects.
- Students are concerned about their grades, but they are not so concerned with their audience.
- Students don't know or appreciate what others are doing/writing/creating.

**How do I know if this idea is working?**

- Students create work with an audience in mind—they're mindful of what a viewer will see and work accordingly.
- Students are motivated and inspired by what others are doing, and they know what that looks like because they see it on shared platforms.

| **Adapt for K–5** | • An audience will make the work engaging and meaningful, and it will help build community inside the class and with caregivers. That said, be reasonable about the amount of revision you hope for from this age. The celebration of what they've worked on is key. |
| --- | --- |
| | • Have students create a few different versions of the same kind of work—multiple songs, drawings, or stories. Then they can choose the one they like best to share. |
| **Adapt for 6–12** | • Don't be fooled that older students are too big or "cool" to like sharing their work with each other, the outside world, and caregivers. Look at the tech tips throughout this book and check out more opportunities too for podcasts, audio recordings, online collages, comic panels, infographics, narrated slideshows, screencasts, and more. |
| **How to try this with others** | • Get students sharing across classrooms—whether you do a joint publication across classes, a gallery walk of one another's rooms, or a presentation to one another's classes, interest and community will both increase. Even if you don't involve students yet in trying this across classrooms, you can take the time to visit and ooh and aah over other class' publications. Be the appreciative audience for others teachers—we all benefit from this acknowledgment! |

*Want to know more about this strategy and others like it?*

**Check out:** Serravallo, Jennifer. 2017. *The Writing Strategies Book: Your Everything Guide to Developing Skilled Writers.* (See the Appendix.)

# 10.2 Highlight the Mistake and Leave Off the Grade, for Now

Try This

In the inspiring book *Upstanders* (Daniels and Ahmed 2015), Sara Ahmed shares a rationale for not talking about students' final work product or grades at all toward the beginning of a unit. This goes against the notion that we should raise the stakes early on by emphasizing where our units are headed. In her classroom, Ahmed shares her rubrics and discusses final products much later on—letting imagination, wonder, sharing, and the process itself drive the work at first.

This philosophy is echoed, too, in intentionally letting students' work exist without a grade for some time. By holding off on giving students a number grade after you've looked at (and assessed) their work, there is a greater opportunity for learning to take place. Students can see your feedback and review their work with the objective lens of a few days' separation, taking the time now to look at any mistakes as well as strengths and learn from them both. Eventually you let them access their grade either by giving it to them on a sticky note or putting it on PowerSchool or other online grading database. Providing this space first, however, to consider what worked and what they will work toward apart from the grade benefits everyone.

If we believe in learning from mistakes, then grading systems should reflect that belief. So, get out your highlighter the next time you grade a test or quiz. (This will work with a straightfor-ward assessment such as a test, but you can adapt it for a lab, project, or writing piece as well.) Highlight all incorrect responses. No need to add a comment or number. Leave off the grade on the actual test, but record it elsewhere in your grade book (just not on PowerSchool or another publicly shared system). Hand the assessment back to students at the beginning of class, or while there is still time for them to thoroughly look it over, note the highlighted areas, and think through what they might do to improve their responses. Resist answering questions about how much each problem is worth, and so on. Encourage students to reflect on what they did and why those answers could use more thought.

Allow students to resubmit with corrections. This will be a powerful message in showing students that we can learn from mistakes and keep trying. If you don't feel ready to take on that second round of grading, however, you can still use this strategy to boost learning. Giving the assessment back with time for students to reflect on what they did and how to improve (without the focus on the number/grade) is powerful all on its own. Adding in time for students to turn and talk to a partner or discuss as a class common mistakes and how to correct them will allow for truly learning from one's mistakes.

Provide the final grade on PowerSchool (or on a sticky note or other paper distribution) the following class.

**How do I know if this idea will help?**

- You stay up late grading, then find student work in desks, on the floor, in the trash after you return it. Students look at the grade and then they're done.

- You hear, "Is this right?" a lot when students are working. They're anxious about the grade.

- Students make the same mistakes in future assignments.

- You value learning from one's mistakes, but there isn't explicit time set aside to do so.

**How do I know if this idea is working?**

- Students get work back with highlighted areas and spend time reflecting and fixing.

- Students can articulate what they did well and what they need to work on after getting work back without the grade.

- Students take more intellectual risks in their work.

- You see skills developing more across assignments—students are learning from mistakes.

Students receive their work with mistakes highlighted but not corrected. Now they know what to improve.

---

### Spanish Conversation Script Oral Report- Violet and Madeleine
A= Student A or Violet, B= Student B or Madeleine

A= "¡Hola!" "¿Cómo estás?"
B= "¡Hola!" "¿Estoy bien, y usted?"
A= "Estoy bueno, gracias."
B= "¿Cómo te llamas?"
A= "Me llama Violet." "¿Y tú?"
B= "Me llama Madeleine."
B= "¿Donde vives?"
A= "Yo vivo en Maplewood, New Jersey." "¿Y tú?"
B= "¡Yo vivo en Maplewood, New Jersey, tambien!"

---

**Adapt for K-5**

- For the youngest grades it's likely you don't need grades, or not many. Wonderful! This strategy won't mean delaying the grade as much as delaying your judgment of "right" or "wrong." You're allowing them to join that assessment more fully.

- Many students will benefit from more scaffolding—rather than simply highlighting mistakes, model what corrections look like first. Do this as a whole-class lesson where you look at highlighted answers marked wrong, and then find out the right answer by looking at relevant anchor charts, asking a friend, checking classwork, going back to the textbook, and other such methods to make the correction. If a student has a lot of the same kind of answer wrong, you might correct one of the mistakes yourself so they see how to do so. They can make the rest of the corrections themselves, using your example.

- If you find you're highlighting more than a few things, stop and decide what your one focus area will be. Don't overwhelm them with noted mistakes.
- Simply affording lots of low-stakes practice before assessing their work or giving a grade will be an important step (and perhaps enough on its own).
- Let students redo the work as many times as they want, or as long as you have patience!
- Say, "Your mistakes are great!" They'll internalize this.

**Adapt for 6–12**

- Explain why you're leaving off the grade and let students know you believe in their abilities to learn from mistakes.
- Set students up for success by showing them what this looks like first.
- On traditional tests, you might be understandably concerned that students will look up the answers after the test and then be able to correct it for credit. To address this concern, you might decide that if the learning took place, it doesn't matter when. Or, you can give half credit for corrections and ask that students explain in writing why this new answer is better. Or, you could have them reapply these new understandings to a new version of the test.

**How to try this with others**

- Look at before and after work together with a colleague, ideally from each of your classes. Use it as the basis for your collaborative reflection. What new learning took place? How did students grow from mistakes or not? What will you do differently next time?

*Want to know more about this strategy and others like it?*

**Check out:** Edutopia. 2019. "Developing Confidence Through Delayed Grading."

# 10.3 Real-Life Assessments

**Try This**

By mid-elementary school, students are often asked to show their understanding by writing a five-paragraph essay. However, the five-paragraph essay is not a genre that exists outside the classroom. Not to mention, my students didn't enjoy writing them, and I certainly did not enjoy grading them.

This same need for authentic, real-world assessments applies to all of us. Think of multiple-choice tests, end-of-textbook/-chapter questions, grammar quizzes, and the like, and consider how to replace these nonauthentic assessments with real-world applications of learning.

Look over your assessments. Start with one that students perform poorly on or one that you dread grading. Ask yourself:

- **Is this a format or genre that exists in the world?**
- **Will students ever produce similar work outside of school?**

If not, consider whether you can provide a different structure, format, or genre for students to show their understanding. Do this by thinking of what professionals in this content area—scientists, mathematicians, artists, health practitioners, athletes, historians—do to show their thinking.

Think, too, of what genres you actually create and consume in real life: social media posts, texts, emails, Yelp reviews, podcasts, blogs, vlogs, interviews, hashtags, tweets, memes, infographics, iMovies, grant proposals, billboards, comics, movie scripts, web pages, résumés. Could your students choose from those authentic genres to show their skills and understandings?

Start small. Ditch the chapter quiz and ask students to write a tweet-sized chapter review or fill in the blanks on a comic panel to show a time line of events. Watch renewed interest and engagement. Notice you aren't quite as reluctant to face the deadly grading pile. Now think bigger!

**How do I know if this idea will help?**

- Your students' assessments follow similar written formats.
- You are spending a lot of time grading.
- You suspect students may plagiarize on assignments.

**How do I know if this idea is working?**

- It is impossible or unlikely for students to Google or cut and paste to complete the assignment.
- Students' work surprises you, in a good way. Results are unexpected and varied in terms of creativity and presentation.
- Assessments invite unexpected "stars"—students who emerge as successful videographers, screenwriters, diagrammers, coders, and so on.

- You find models and inspiration for assessments in noneducation-related resources (i.e., podcasts, infographics, advertisements, interviews).
- Grading is more enjoyable because students enjoyed completing the assignment.
- Student work is increasingly varied.

**Adapt for K–5**

- Ask students to help generate genres that interest them and that they consume. This could be a brainstorming session before they are asked to show their understanding in a unit.

**Adapt for 6–12**

- Invite guest speakers from your content area to talk about the formats of work they produce the most, as well as what production and creative skills they depend on. Use that information to develop upcoming assessments.
- Contact and poll former students now in careers and college about the work they're asked to produce. Invite them in, too!
- Embed related life skills in content whenever possible—math skills to budget, science to research eco-friendly products, writing to send professional emails, and so on.

**How to try this with others**

- Look over unit assessments in pairs or as a group. Flag the ones that are not real world or authentic. Brainstorm possible replacement formats.
- As you all create assessments to better reflect authentic work, put them in an online shared folder. Even if you can't use that exact assessment, they will serve as models for everyone to adapt and build off of in future units.

*Want to know more about this strategy and others like it?*

**Check out:** Rademacher, Tom, and Dave Eggers. 2017. *It Won't Be Easy: An Exceedingly Honest (and Slightly Unprofessional) Love Letter to Teaching.*

*Tech Integration Tip*

**DON'T JUST TAKE IT—MAKE IT!**

Do your students produce digital content as much as they consume it? Even out the balance by having students create iMovies and HyperDocs, tweet, curate sources, collaborate locally or globally with others on Google Hangouts or Skype, and more. Survey students to see what technology they regularly use and what they know how to create. Shore up the gaps by making opportunities to create materials similar to the texts or materials they already consume. Although our own comfort level with technology may be limited, we can still introduce new options and learn alongside our students. It's OK if we aren't experts as long as we've explored the apps enough to know whether they're appropriate and user-friendly.

# 10.4 Side-by-Side Grading

Try This

Stop taking home piles of notebooks, projects, and papers to comment on and grade. Move feedback and assessment into the classroom. When you grade in class with students, it:

- provides immediate and meaningful feedback
- shifts the focus from grades to learning
- helps put students in the driver's seat of their learning
- motivates students to listen to your feedback and apply it right away
- ensures students don't look at the number/grade and ignore your helpful suggestions
- saves you precious time and energy out of school
- makes assessment visible so students understand the grade
- drastically reduces/eliminates complaints and confusion around grades.

Set up class time for students to be doing work in stations, pairs, or independently. Meet with each student by sitting next to them and looking at their work together. Do this before students finalize their work and hand it in for a final grade.

Have a copy of the rubric with the skills, which students have already been introduced to and used while creating their work. Ask the student to think aloud as they assess their work and fill in the rubric. Guide them as needed. Provide feedback on the spot, and jot it down on the rubric (if the student keeps it) or on the work directly so students can hold onto it. If students are fourth grade or older, ask them to write notes for themselves, while you keep notes for your records. This process can be a helpful check for understanding—look at what they wrote down. Does it accurately reflect your feedback? If not, use this as an opportunity to immediately clarify and explain.

After students have had the opportunity to make changes to their work based on this feedback, meet with them again. This is a shorter meeting during which students show you how and where they made changes to their work, and again think aloud as they make any changes to how they've marked the rubric. Sign off on the rubric with them and put the grade into your grade book. Let them see you do this and confirm you are both agreeing to the grade.

Set a goal with them for what they want to work on in the next assignment, based on their successes and challenges this time. Both of you (fourth grade and above) write down that goal.

- You have taken a personal day to catch up with your grading.
- Students get your feedback long after submitting their work.
- Students express confusion or surprise when they see their grade.
- Your feedback doesn't seem to impact change—you see the same issues in the next assignments.

- You take home much less grading.
- Students are a part of the conversation so there are no upsets or surprises with final grades.
- You and students agree together on next steps—and you see the results in their work.

*Want to know more about this strategy and others like it?*

**Check out:** Tucker, Catlin. 2017. "Rethink Your Grading Practices."

- This process is ultimately about helping students to understand their strengths and areas for growth—you likely do much of this already in one-on-one conferences. If you don't, this is a good reason to start.

- Consider digital and collaborative writing tools to help with comments, such as Google Docs.
- Try group quizzes for math or any other subject. Give the group detailed feedback based on reading one group member's quiz. Spend the same amount of time as before grading, but the feedback will be of higher quality as will their response to it.

# 10.5 Adapted Tests for Equitable Grading

Try This

Most tests are designed for the at-grade-level student, meaning every student gets the same questions. We might, therefore, create thirty multiple-choice questions, anticipating that a few students will get them all right, some will get most right, and a few will get many wrong.

This static assessment can be ineffective, however, for both ends of the scoring band. The top scorers who get all of the questions right hit a ceiling, in a sense, and we can't assess where they may need to go next or how to challenge them. The lowest scorers are demoralized and are also unable to give us much information about what they need or how to help them. This is doubly damaging because these low scorers get the stigma of low performance and we don't get the information we need. Just how much of an intervention they need is unclear because we only see a vast gap or deficit.

Although there are CAT (computerized adaptive testing) programs available, such as FastTest, that allow you to create computerized tests adapted to students' first answers, they can be expensive and time-consuming. Check them out if you've got the time and energy. Or, try this easier method: Make your own adapted (paper or digital) tests by creating a wide band of questions and then asking students to answer a specified number. To prevent students who perform at higher levels from only answering the lower-level questions, you can indicate starting points for various students depending on their last performance level. Or, you can distribute slightly modified tests with those lowest or highest skill-level questions taken off completely.

Another option is to distribute the same test to all, ask students to complete as many as possible, and then select a specified number of questions they want you to grade. Allow for retakes, too, to more accurately assess students' knowledge and to promote authentic learning.

Consider if there are other adaptations that will make this assessment more user-friendly to certain students, or all students. For example:

- Provide a bank of answers for students with language or recall issues who have trouble remembering specific terms or domain-specific vocabulary.

- Space out the text if some students find a lot of print on the page visually overwhelming.

- Start with straightforward, easier questions and build up to more complex and challenging questions, such as putting algorithms at the start of a math assessment and word problems at the end. Otherwise you risk setting kids up for frustration or difficulty in pacing their work.

Finally, include this question to make every test an adapted test: "Is there anything else you learned that you didn't get to show on this test?"

- Students sometimes give up on tests or don't complete every section of tests.
- Some students perform poorly or inconsistently on assessments.
- You have a hard time seeing progress from all of your students.

- You have a clearer understanding of each student's learning zone.
- You see increased motivation and engagement on tests—students enjoy working within their knowledge base.
- Students don't answer or use the same questions as their neighbors.
- You are able to capture progress over time, especially for your students who perform at the highest and lowest levels.

---

Name:_____

5th Grade Social Studies Unit Test

*There are **20** questions on this test.
Answer as many as you like, and then circle **10** that you want graded.

1. All of the following are needs, except:
   a) shelter
   b) entertainment
   c) food
   d) water

2. The turning point of the Revolutionary War was the Battle of:
   a) Washington
   b) Lexington
   c) Saratoga
   d) New York

3. The colonists wanted to be free from British rule, so they wrote:
   a) The Declaration of Independence
   b) The Constitution
   c) The Magna Carta
   d) The Mayflower

---

- Design an upcoming assessment together, incorporating adaptations that will work for your students or groups of students. This can be done across content areas, too, as you discuss students' strengths and gaps and how your tests will adapt to their needs. Make sure to come back together after administering the test. Celebrate upped engagement and your increased understanding of their needs!

# 10.6 Set a Unit End Date and Stick to It

**Try This**

Before the year begins, decide how much time you will need to get to the final steps of long-term projects or units so that all units will fit within the year. Choose an appropriate date for finishing each unit and put it on the calendar. Ideally, choose dates that your grade team can all agree to.

Then the hard part: try not to waver from that date! Send it out to caregivers and/or administrators to help hold yourself accountable. Tell students that regardless of logistical hiccups or challenges with the coursework, they will finish their projects or unit-related work by that day. Whatever stage they are at will mean finished for them. When that date comes, celebrate the work in whatever way you choose. Begin the following unit the next day!

This will help keep the pace moving. Everyone's energy plummets when we linger too long in a unit. When we extend units because students aren't performing the way we expected, we can become overly invested in the final product as opposed to the process. Rest assured that they got something out of this unit, think about how you might improve the unit next time, and then, move on.

Of course, you may want to leave an asterisk on all end dates to allow for a well-reasoned extension, such as a still-high level of energy and momentum. Nothing should be so rigid that you can't respond to students and their needs. Use this strategy to relieve yourself of the need to perfect units, but keep your students at the forefront, always. Although you set your deadline and communicate it to the class, you'll hopefully not penalize lateness—see Strategy 10.9 on page 279.

**How do I know if this idea will help?**

- Units linger and students (or you) lose momentum or emotional attachment to their work.
- You're finding it hard to fit it all in.
- You're worrying about the product more than the students' overall growth.
- Celebrations or publishing is rushed or skipped due to time constraints.

**How do I know if this idea is working?**

- Students and/or caregivers discuss due dates as a known entity, not a maybe.
- There is time for celebrating and publishing student work at the end of units.
- You feel invested in the student learning more than the final product.
- You and your students see their work as a process.
- You and students see works in progress as deserving of celebration.

*Want to know more about this strategy and others like it?*

**Check out:** Moore, Beth. 2018. "Next Level Unit Planning: Beyond the Fundamentals of Writing Workshop." twowritingteachers.org.

| | |
|---|---|
| **Adapt for K–2** | • Younger students are experts at operating in the here and now. You may choose, therefore, to emphasize the end date of a unit when it is very close so that it will feel relevant to your students. Use end dates more to hold yourself accountable than to distract them with an out of sight, out of mind date far in the future.<br><br>• If the end date of a unit, project, or writing publication piece is important for students to know as a way to urge them to the finish line, however, expect to remind them frequently with visuals, spoken reminders, and through parent communication. |
| **Adapt for 6–8** | • Middle school students often forget to convey key information such as deadlines to caregivers. Increase accountability and communication by posting all deadlines on the class website, Remind app, ClassDojo, or whatever method you use to keep families in the loop.<br><br>• With the number of teachers and logistics middle school students manage, support their planning by posting reminders on the board and/or the Remind app in countdown form.<br><br>• Whenever possible, let students make up any work after the due date, even if you have moved on in the plan. The point is for them to take on the learning! If there are grade-based penalties for late work, make that policy consistent and clear in advance. |
| **Adapt for 9–12** | • Be mindful and check in with other big dates like SATs, school plays, midterms, and other subjects' deadlines.<br><br>• Whenever possible, avoid the end of marking period when so much else is assigned.<br><br>• Remember lots of low-stakes, high-volume assignments throughout a marking period versus only one high-stakes assignment will benefit your students in getting ready for college.<br><br>• Whenever possible, let students make up any work after the due date, even if you have moved on in the plan. The point is for them to take on the learning! If there are grade-based penalties for late work, make that policy consistent and clear in advance. |
| **How to try this with others** | • Meet with your grade team before the beginning of the year to set publishing dates together. Consider sending those dates to caregivers and administrators.<br><br>• Check in with colleagues to see how this feels. Do the dates feel manageable? What changes could be made this year or next to make it feel workable?<br><br>• Share publishing dates with colleagues in other departments and check that your dates don't conflict heavily with their big assignments.<br><br>• Review publishing dates with students before setting them in stone. Make sure there are not conflicts on their end that you hadn't anticipated (SATs, field trips, etc.).<br><br>• Leave some wiggle room for yourself and others to extend due to high energy or momentum or unforeseen circumstances. |

# 10.7 Design Rubrics with Students by Ranking Examples of Student Work

Try This

Showing students what their end product can and should look like is a great way to lift the level of their work! Now take another step. Have students reflect on and rank examples of work to create criteria together for what the end products should include and illustrate.

Collect three examples of student work that represent a range of the work you are assigning. These might be from your previous years' students, other teachers' classrooms, or something published in the "real world." Remove names and mask any identifying features. These work examples might be an exact match for what your students will create, or they might match the format only. For example, if your students will create a data graph showing their results of testing buoyancy of floating cylinders, you could show them data graphs measuring the viscosity of fluids in glass tubes.

Try to find three examples that are varied in terms of style and, to some degree, quality. It will be more clear to students how to rank them if not every piece of work is top-notch. But remember that these models will all imprint on students in terms of modeling just how their own products can look—creative and wide-ranging styles will inspire your students as well as help them differentiate between nuanced qualities of success.

Make copies for students.

First have students look them over individually and take notes on strengths. Then students should rank them 1, 2, and 3. Students should list reasons why they ranked the examples in that order. Then students should meet in small groups to compare their findings and try to come to consensus.

Finally, the whole class meets, sharing out their findings and coming up with three to five criteria that will go on the rubric. These are qualities that everyone agrees to try to meet in their final works.

**How do I know if this idea will help?**

- You grade student work on criteria that they may or may not be aware of.
- You use rubrics that you designed on your own or that you received from another teacher or source.
- Students are sometimes surprised or disappointed by their final grades.
- A small percentage of students receive top scores on summative assessments.

## VIOLET'S VALID, VIBRANT, VERSATILE, VICTORIOUS BLAB (BLOB LAB) REPORT

$H_2O$ = Water
$C_3H_8O$ = isopropyl alcohol

### INTRODUCTION

Water. $H_2O$. One of the most important substances on Earth. You will perish without it. Okay, okay, enough with the serious stuff. $H_2O$ is *cool*. It's 2.5 times more polar than $C_3H_8O$, which means it's more magnetic, or sticky than $C_3H_8O$. This may be kinda hard to believe, considering we usually use $H_2O$ to wash *off* sticky stuff. Well, it's not *that* kind of sticky. $H_2O$ is sticky because it has hydrogen bonding. Hydrogen bonding is when the negative poles in a liquid gently stick to the positive poles in a liquid. $H_2O$ has a positive pole that is the 2 hydrogen atoms. The negative pole has the oxygen atom. The negative pole and the positive pole stick to each other. $H_2O$ has a lot of hydrogen bonding, meaning it has more polarity than $C_3H_8O$.

We saw how the $H_2O$ stuck to itself because of hydrogen bonding firsthand during our Blob Lab, when the $H_2O$ formed a dome on top of the penny, without falling off! Well, eventually it did.

When you take gravity out of the equation, you can see firsthand how $H_2O$ sticks to itself. In our lab in class called Blob Lab, we experimented with

---

## Modeling Meiosis Lab
### Alexis Murray

**i. Introduction**

Meiosis involves two cell divisions, one after the other, that produce four haploid cells from one diploid parent cell. A haploid cell contains only a single set of chromosomes, and therefore a single set of genes. The gametes of sexually reproducing organisms are haploid. A diploid cell has two, or a full set of chromosomes. Thus, during meiosis, two cells divisions occur to create the four haploid cells from the diploid- Meiosis I, the first cell division, and Meiosis II, the second cell division, separates the sister chromatids of each duplicated chromosome in the two cells that were produced during Meiosis I, to create two more cells for a total of four haploid cells. In humans, these haploid cells that are produced are gametes known as sperm and eggs. When these two gametes meet during fertilization, they become a complete diploid set.

Throughout this lab, I worked in a group to model the steps of meiosis, while drawing out each demonstration and answering questions along the way to answer the final question/problem: How does meiosis increase genetic information? I learned how to model a type of cell division using pop beads, as well as working with a partner and drawing observations/knowledge from my models.

Hypothesis: Meiosis increases genetic variation due to chromosomes "crossing over", or the exchange of genetic material between 2 homologous chromosomes.

**ii. Materials**
- Sheet of paper
- Scissors
- Colored pens/pencils
- Pop beads(used to represent genes)
- Magnetic piece for pop beads(used to represent centromeres)

**iii. Procedure**

The diploid cell you will be creating should have two pairs of homologous chromosomes, with one pair longer than the other for clarity. The pop beads represent the genes, and the magnetic pieces for the centromeres. The sheet of paper should represent the cell.

    **Part A: Interphase**

    Before meiosis begins, the chromosomes are replicated.
- Use 10 beads and a centromere, both of the same color, to represent on long chromosome, or a 10-mer. Use another color of 10 beads and a centromere to represent the other long chromosome in the pair.
- Then repeat this process with only 5 beads, or a 5-mer.
- Replicate the pop-bead strands to model the replication of the chromosomes, attaching each copy to the original at the magnetic centromeres.

    **Part B: Meiosis I**

    In Meiosis I, the cell divides into two diploid daughter cells.

---

## ABO Blood Typing Lab
### Daniel Mackey

**I. Introduction**

To type blood is a process in which one classifies blood in relation to the presence or absence of specific proteins on the surface of red blood cells, known as erythrocytes. A certain blood type is an inherited characteristic and is imperative for medical uses, family relations, and more. Austrian physician Karl Landsteiner first discovered that human blood would clump, or agglutinate, in other animals in the late 1800s. He later discovered two distinct proteins that could be on the surface of an individual's blood cells, coining them A and B proteins. He later recognized four distinct blood types based on the combinations o resulting in blood types A, B, AB, and O. These proteins are anti creates a immune response. Therefore, a person with blood type respond when blood type B is added, and vice versa. Blood type blood type O has both anti-A and anti-B antibodies. Throughout to identify different blood types based on the reactions occuring how to recognize different blood types based on their appearance group.

Problem: How do you determine one's blood type?

Hypothesis: I can work with a group to determine different blood types A, B, AB, or O by analyzing which types react or agglutinates to the anti-A or anti-B serums.

**ii. Materials**
- Donor 1 simulated blood sample
- Donor 2 simulated blood sample
- Donor 3 simulated blood sample
- Donor 4 simulated blood sample
- Simulated anti-A serum
- Simulated anti-B serum
- Four blood typing trays

**iii. Procedure**

To determine the blood types of our substances, an anti-serum with antibodies in it was added to each carefully labeled blood type. The anti-serum's antibodies react against specific antigens on the surface of the red blood cells, causing the blood to clump, or agglutinate in the tray. If there is agglutination present in the anti-A serum, then the blood type is A. If there is agglutination with the anti-B serum, then the blood type is B. If there is no clumping in either

---

Ellie

**Problem:** How does exercise affect a person's heart rate, breathing rate, and perspiration level?

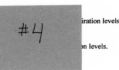

**Hypothesis:** If a person exercises, then their hear    iration levels will rise.

**Skills:** The ability to accurately measure heart rat    n levels.

**Materials:**
- Groups of three people
- A stopwatch

**Procedure:**

1.) Choose one person in your group to complete light exercise for 8 minutes.

2.) Take the test subjects heart rate, perspiration level and breathing rate before they begin to exercise. Take the subjects heart rate by placing your second and third fingers around their wrist and feel for a pulse. While this is happening, have another group member count how many breaths the subject is taking by watching their chest as the air moves into the lungs and out. Count both the heart rate and breathing rate for fifteen seconds and multiply the number by four to find the amount of beats and breaths per minute.

3.) Record the subject's perspiration level on a scale of 1-5. Add the data to the chart.

4.) Record the heart rate, breathing rate and perspiration level on the chart and begin exercise. Every two minutes, have the test subject stop and record their heart rate, breathing rate and perspiration level. Repeat until the subject has exercised for 8 minutes.

5.) After 8 minutes of exercise, have the test subject rest for 1 ½ minutes, then record their levels again.

---

Students looked at four examples of lab reports before ranking them and providing reasons for those rankings.

| | |
|---|---|
| **How do I know if this idea is working?** | • Students are fully aware of what high-level work should look like—you know this because they refer to the examples and the rubric with familiarity. |
| | • Students refer to the rubric as they work. |
| | • When work is returned to students, there are few surprises. They knew what top-level work looked like, and they could self-assess how theirs matched up. |
| | • More students receive high scores on summative assessments because there is little mystery of how to get there. They know what it looks like and can envision how to get there. |
| **Adapt for K–5** | • For your very youngest students, you may not be using many rubrics. Transferring abstract concepts to their work can be daunting. You may not want to do a lot of ranking work until after grade 2. |
| | • For upper elementary, consider making this process more user-friendly by modeling it first yourself in front of them. Narrate your thinking as you sort the examples, and don't be shy about praising all of it. Students can be quick to find fault even when we would not! |
| | • Consider simplifying this by limiting their focus to just one or two aspects, such as organization or visual appeal. |
| **How to try this with others** | • Help collect examples by looking at student work together. Work together to choose pieces that broaden students' understandings of the possibilities. |
| | • Try this together: look at student work and create a rubric based on the work, not on your standards or textbook or other resources. Talk about how it felt to generate criteria solely based on student work. |

*Want to know more about this strategy and others like it?*

**Check out:** Wilhelm, Jeffrey D., Rachel Bear, and Adam Fachler. 2019. *Planning Powerful Instruction, Grades 6–12: 7 Must-Make Moves to Transform How We Teach —and How Students Learn.*

# 10.8 Stop Grading Homework. Do This Instead

Try This

Grading homework assignments is a common practice, thought to instill good habits and reinforce learning. It turns out, though, this is not typically the case. Here's the reality of grading homework:

- It's a huge time suck for teachers. And homework doesn't always guarantee improved learning or engagement, especially for younger students (Cooper, Robinson, and Patall 2006).

- Homework doesn't help us assess understanding—a poorly done or incomplete assignment might have nothing to do with actual comprehension. (See later in this section on why homework reinforces inequalities.)

- Copying homework can be rampant and hard to control, giving us an inaccurate picture of student comprehension.

- Homework rewards kids for behavior and compliance, not necessarily learning.

- Homework grades reinforce inequalities.

  - Students from higher-income families are more likely to have educated caregivers with time and resources and who help children with homework, professional tutors, less time conflicts with after school jobs or taking care of siblings, and quiet spaces in which to concentrate and they are less likely to have the gas or lights turned off, evictions, or other complicated hardships.

  - We can't know why homework was not completed or done poorly—that time is out of our control. Punishing or rewarding doesn't help.

- Homework tends to diminish genuine inquiry and authentic learning.

- Homework conditions students to believe that anything worth learning or doing must be graded.

So, let's try other methods that reduce inequalities, boost ownership of learning, reduce cheating, foster inquiry more than compliance, and help us assess understanding:

- **In-class quizzes:** Check student understanding or review material right then and there. Frequent, low-stakes quizzes actually do increase learning.

- **Flipped classroom model:** Put content online to review outside of class, and move the homework or assignments to inside of class when you're there to offer support.

- **Homework planning forms:** Let students reflect on what they need to review by listing unit concepts and letting them plan adequate and personalized homework support.

| Homework and Outside Support Plan for Unit 4, Biomes | | |
|---|---|---|
| Concepts/skills I need to master for this unit | How well do I understand? (1-5) | What homework can I do, and what other support do I need to learn this concept? |
| ECOLOGICAL LEVELS IN BIOSPHERE | 5 | n/a |
| ABIOTIC AND BIOTIC FACTORS | 3 | Ch 6 unit review questions #6-22 |
| IDENTITY FACTORS THAT DETERMINE POPULATION GROWTH RATE | 2 | Worksheet 4 Afterschool help Thursday Review sessions |
| TERRESTRIAL BIOMES | 4 | n/a |
| AQUATIC BIOMES | 2 | Worksheet 7 review class notes Peer tutoring Tues. |

Students fill out a planning form to help them determine gaps in their learning and to make a plan for how they will learn those concepts.

- **Rotating lunch rooms for academic support and/or assignments:** This removes some of the iniquities of at-home assignments. You and grade team colleagues offer a rotating space in which students can work quietly. You'll be surprised how many students take advantage, get ahead on their work, and happily escape the cafeteria!

- **Student tutors:** Cross-age mentoring boosts community, raises achievement, and develops social and learning skills.

**How do I know if this idea will help?**

- You spend a lot of time grading homework.
- Homework completion varies. Some do it, and others do not.
- Some students' grades are brought down by their homework grade.

**How do I know if this idea is working?**

- Homework, if assigned at all, is completed by a greater percent of students.
- You spend time that used to be spent on homework doing other things like planning, getting to know kids, or providing meaningful feedback on in-class work.
- Students' final grades reflect what they do and know as evidenced in class, not outside of class.
- The teacher can suggest homework assignments that align to each concept, but the student is in charge of planning the assignments and supports they'll choose from to shore up their personal gaps. Homework, then, is not uniform but something students self-select to improve their skills as needed.

| | |
|---|---|
| **Adapt for K-5** | • There is little correlation between completing written homework in elementary school and academic gains, so make sure there is a solid reason if you are assigning it. For example, you might assign choice reading only. Or possibly you know students have hectic lives at home and very straightforward weekly review packets are helping them develop responsibility and planning skills they'll need later on. |
| | • If you do assign homework, make sure the directions are readable by the student, without adult help. If you're unsure if they can read it, go over it with them in advance. Remember you won't be there to remind them at home, so add a visual or modify it further to set them up for success. |
| **Adapt for 6-8** | • Weekly assignments rather than nightly ones allow students to plan their time with some flexibility and choice. |
| | • Make homework review only. If adult support or outside resources will be needed, then consider if it can be classwork instead. |
| **Adapt for 9-12** | • Use homework to help students take ownership of the learning process and to reflect on what they need to study. |
| | • Let students complete only homework questions that connect to what they didn't understand, as a way to improve on those gaps. |
| | • Provide ways for students to check their answers. Homework should be for them, so put them in the driver's seat! |
| | • Offer support sessions with student mentors in the library or other designated spaces, especially at exam time. Older students are a huge untapped resource in high schools. |
| **How to try this with others** | • The more homework policies are consistent across grade teams, classrooms, and the school at large, the more effective they will be. |

*Want to know more about this strategy and others like it?*

**Check out:** Dueck, Myron. 2014. *Grading Smarter, Not Harder: Assessment Strategies That Motivate Kids and Help Them Learn.*

# 10.9 Don't Penalize Late Work

**Try This**

Create and announce due dates for assignments. These planned dates help you and students stay organized, prevent grading from piling up at the end of the quarter, help students schedule their work, and maintain the flow of units. Announce these dates with plenty of advance notice, and talk to colleagues to ensure everyone is not assigning a lot of projects, tests, and papers at the same time.

If we value the learning, then we should value the work being completed. If the work happens on a later schedule for some, let it be. It's not worth your high blood pressure or students' failing, as long as they are willing to take on the work. Stop worrying that you are enabling poor habits, and start celebrating that you are enabling more students to learn. *Don't take off points if students hand in the work late.* This doesn't mean deadlines are unimportant. They certainly have a role in our pacing—for example, see Strategy 10.6 on page 271.

Before starting this policy, talk it over with administrators and grade team colleagues. Explain your rationale and why this policy rewards learning and effort. Share information about a growth mindset. If you can, make this the policy from the beginning of the year. Explain the thinking behind it to students (and caregivers). Also communicate up front that you may not be able to provide as much timely feedback, however, when work comes in late.

When students don't turn in work by the due date, mark it as missing. Remind students and families that the assignment is missing. Let them know that the work can still be completed, and explain how students can find the directions and assignment if necessary, such as on the class website. When students hand in the work, don't criticize, chide, or punish lateness. Thank the student for handing it in, and move on. Encourage those who are still not completing assignments on time by telling them about full-credit late work from others. Grade the late work when you have time (because you may now have a different time schedule for assessing it too!) and put the grade in your grade book just as you would have if it were turned in on time.

To support students' time management—and to maintain your own energy—you may use the end of the marking period as a final "due" date for any remaining work. Otherwise you may receive a deluge of rushed work at the end of the year—not ideal for anyone! Allow students to start each new marking period with a clean slate.

Then, watch engagement lift, mutual respect grow, and learning levels rise as students see that their learning is prioritized above all else.

> 7C Grading Policy for Late Work:
>
> 1. All work is graded for mastery. There will be a suggested due date for all work, but NO points will be deducted for late work. *
> 2. You will see an INC on PowerSchool indicating any missing assignments. That will change when work is handed in.
>
> Remember:
> - All assignments will be given at least a week in advance to help you plan.
> - If I miss hearing about big assignments due in other classes, let me know.
> - Work that is handed in on time is likely to get faster and more thorough feedback.
>
> *Occasionally work will need to be done within a certain time frame, such as the end of the unit or before I pass back other students' work. You will know this in advance.

This teacher's grading policy makes it transparent that mastery is prioritized over the due date and also gives the heads up that feedback may be impacted by timeliness.

**How do I know if this idea will help?**

- Students start to fall behind and then disengage.
- Students balance demanding schedules and many out-of-school demands.
- You spend a lot of time reminding students about due dates and following up for late and missing work.
- You have students who don't hand in assignments or ask to turn them in late.

**How do I know if this idea is working?**

- Students who previously missed work entirely are now completing it, either late or on time.
- Students are using the flexibility to better plan around their busy times.
- There are fewer and fewer missing assignments in your grade book.
- Your communication with caregivers includes this reminder.

**Adapt for K-4**

- Assuming homework is ungraded and there are no penalties for late work at this age, this strategy may apply more to classwork. If you are rushing certain students to get work "done," stop and reflect: What's getting in the way? Consider how appropriate pacing will look different depending on each student's skills in that area, and do your best to let go of a uniform completion time for all.

- Give instructional time (or work with those who need it) to teaching time-management skills, advance planning, and breaking down the work in smaller chunks.

- If you worry that you are not preparing students for the deadlines they'll need to meet in college or careers, be open with them about the fact that there will be less flexibility later on. Explain how due dates work in college and how deadlines function in the workplace. Teens can understand the difference between now and then, and they will adapt when they get there. Getting the work done in high school, even with flexible dates, actually ups the likelihood they will go to college and have the opportunity to manage college workloads. Concentrate on setting them up for success here and now.

- Another way to accommodate the upcoming reality of due dates in college and careers is to shift this policy by senior year, letting students in on the "why and how" well in advance. Devote instructional time to teaching time-management skills, advance planning, and how to break down the work in smaller chunks.

*Want to know more about this strategy and others like it?*

**Check out:** Dueck, Myron. 2014. *Grading Smarter, Not Harder: Assessment Strategies That Motivate Kids and Help Them Learn.*

# 10.10 No Zeros. Use Interventions and Incompletes Instead

Try This

A zero might feel like an appropriate grade when the student doesn't hand in anything. After all, how can you give credit for work that doesn't exist? Plus, the thinking goes, zeros teach students responsibility.

Let's consider an alternate view, however, that zeros are an inaccurate reflection of a student's knowledge and skills. Who has zero percent understanding or skill level? Sadly, zeros don't tend to teach much of a lesson other than, perhaps, "School is not a place for me."

The students we most want to encourage and rally into doing the work are unlikely to make a change due to the threat of a zero. Even if we don't hold their finished product in our hands, that student knows *something*. So how can a grade better reflect what *is* understood and help motivate students to stay in the game?

It's time to do something different.

Use interventions and incompletes instead of zeros. The beauty of entering an incomplete and then following up with interventions is that we are teaching life skills (get help, recover from setbacks, don't let failure stop you from trying again) and preventing the punitive and damaging impact of a zero.

Explain early on to your students that you will input an incomplete in the grade book anytime they don't hand in the work. Until the work is done, they will have an incomplete in your class. Students will also fill out an intervention form each time, letting you know why the work wasn't completed. This will necessitate a follow-up chat so you can problem solve together what to do next.

The upshot is that having the INC (incomplete) in the grade book typically results in the student doing *something* eventually. They will not want an INC for the class and they will have to produce work to avoid that mark on their report card. And doing *something* as opposed to nothing is a good lesson to learn. Also, the intervention form teaches the student to keep trying after a setback and that we can recover from a perceived failure. Students will have to stay in the game, recognizing what gets in the way of their work completion and then finding ways to target those problem areas.

Although this takes more time and effort on your part than entering a zero and moving on, you will see upped engagement and you will teach important life skills. That is time well spent.

If the class is long over and the student never completes the work, you will come up with your own system. Will you enter a grade similar to that of the lowest grade they received on other assessments? Do you give them a grade higher than a zero but lower than any other grades so that their final average is about the same as it would be without the missing assignment?

Let go of the fear that you are rewarding bad behavior or not holding students accountable. You did hold them accountable, and you taught them life lessons in responsibility. You also showed them that they have an adult in their life who does not give up on them.

I encourage you, too, to explore the thinking about how zeros foster inequity. Who among us hasn't had an illness, emergency, or other outside circumstance that prevented us from handing something in? Now imagine a student whose lights get turned off, who doesn't have food in the house, or whose life is complicated in ways we might never know about. Why give them a grade that is impossible to recover from?

**How do I know if this idea will help?**

- You currently give zeros.
- You don't know why work is unsubmitted.
- Students find it hard to recover from one bad grade.
- Student engagement drops after receiving a zero.

**How do I know if this idea is working?**

- You find out reasons for unsubmitted work that surprise you.
- Engagement does not drop after one assignment is missed.
- Students problem solve and keep trying after missing an assignment.
- Intervention forms are used.
- Most students eventually do something as opposed to nothing when they get an incomplete.

| Name: | Assignment: |
|---|---|
| Reason for work not handed in on time (check as many as apply) | ☐ Assignments in other classes<br>☐ Sick<br>☐ Outside-of-school commitments (job)<br>☐ School extracurriculars or an athletic event<br>☐ Didn't plan time well<br>☐ No interest<br>☐ Didn't understand the assignment |
| Intervention request | ☐ Meet the teacher after school<br>☐ Arrange for peer tutor (or ask the teacher to help)<br>☐ Adjust due date<br>☐ Visit with guidance counselor or coach for support<br>☐ Modify assignment<br>☐ Look at examples from other students or other models for clarification |
| Plan for next steps | I will get the assignment in on _____ by doing the following: |

**How to try this with others**

- The more teachers who take on this important practice, the better. Go to administration and help them consider this as a school-wide policy. If it's more comfortable for now, however, start with someone on your grade team. Collect data on how it's working and be ready to share it with others as a way to get them to try it, too.

*Want to know more about this strategy and others like it?*

**Check out:** Dueck, Myron. 2014. *Grading Smarter, Not Harder: Assessment Strategies That Motivate Kids and Help Them Learn.*

# Keep Growing and Giving Back

## (Coda)

Although we'll never be done growing and learning, you deserve tremendous cheers, champagne toasts, ticker-tape parades, and hugs for making it thus far. Perhaps a mental, if not actual, sabbatical is in order so you can bask in the glow of growing and learning across so many essential teaching skills. This is a good time to find a book to read for pleasure, catch up on shows you've missed, nap, or just take a look around your class and witness a thriving classroom of learners.

Oh, you're back already? Of course you are. Knowing most teachers, you got in half an episode or a cat nap, and now you're ready for more. That's what great teachers do—they keep learning and growing. And one of the best ways to sustain that growth is by paying it forward.

Here's a brief collection of ways to nurture your teaching self and give back to others who can benefit from your expertise. And I hope one of the ways you do that is by keeping me in the loop with your success stories and ideas at beritgordon.com. I'll keep paying it forward however I can.

You deserve to sustain your happiness as a teacher for the long haul. Celebrate yourself, your profession, and your students. I'd wish you luck, but you won't need it. You've got this.

## 1. Establish Yearlong Goals

Start each year deciding what you want to get better at. Prioritize one goal in particular. This will help you throughout the year as you make decisions around your professional reading, workshops to attend, committees to join, blogs to follow, and more. If it's your first year, you might focus on routines and rituals. Another year, it might be protecting students' independent work time. Another year, you might work on keeping notes and informal data. Choose a goal that is personal and meaningful—something you are curious about that will directly benefit you and your students.

285

Start by asking yourself:

- What is a question I want answered about teaching? How can I make that my goal?
- Why have I selected this goal?
- What books might I read on this topic?
- Whose classroom might I visit to see this in action?
- What ways will I see evidence of this growth/work in my instruction?
- How might I share what I have learned with colleagues?

Find one book to get you started, one blog and/or Twitter handle to follow, and one workshop to attend (either in person or virtually). Revisit your goal each month. Track your growth, celebrate progress, and adapt your goal to keep moving forward. Determine how you will share with others so they can learn with you. How might you share within your building? How might you share with the larger community of educators? Online? At a conference?

---

goals:
How do I help students find their voice?
How can I incorporate more play & fun?
What are more equitable grading practices?
How do I get all my paperwork organized?

Books I'll read:
Purposeful Play by Kristine Mraz and Alison Porcelli
Play: How it Shapes the Brain, Opens the Imagination, and Invigorates the Soul by Stuart Brown

Classrooms to visit:
Abigails' class
Try to visit Ms. Tinari's 2ⁿᵈ grade
Mr. Perry's gym class!

---

## 2. Get Involved in What's Going on Outside Your Classroom

Opening your classroom door to let others *in* to your practice is important, but it's also important get *out* there and join the school community beyond your classroom walls! What makes your school great, and how you can get involved? Is it the school play? The robotics team? Parent outreach? Outdoor learning? School garden? Think about what you can offer, or just let the leaders know you are there to help however you can. You might alternatively find a less known or celebrated program and find out what you could do to help turn it around. Feeling super ambitious? Brainstorm some ideas for a new activity or program and propose it to the powers that be. If it's not approved, ask what *would* help students that doesn't already exist. There is likely a long list!

## 3. Advocate with Students

Doing advocacy work to promote positive change is energizing and empowering. Extend good vibes and your change-making impact by involving kids.

- Gather students to discuss school, local, national, and even global issues that concern them. As a group, choose an issue everyone feels passionate about, and consider whether you will address it within your own group, schoolwide, locally, or beyond.

- Research the chosen issue with them, modeling yourself as a learner throughout.

- Let students share out their ideas and questions while you chart them for the group to reflect on at the end.

- Help students identify next steps and make an action plan. It will help to have a big vision for the long term and to break it down into immediate and small-term steps, along with possible time frames for each step.

- Decide who the audience will be for this advocacy work and how you will go public.

## 4. Study Your Biases and Then Read on to Challenge Them

No matter how well intentioned and thoughtful we are, it is impossible to avoid ingrained biases and stereotypes. Our society is built on a system of historical white, male, heteronormative, Christian, wealthy privilege. Even if we don't want to support that system, it has influenced all of us. Unraveling and replacing those biases cannot be done overnight. It takes conscious, deliberate effort. One way to begin is to read authors who push your thinking and challenge these biases.

Choose a text that will help you name, reflect on, and work to dissolve assumptions, stereotypes, preconceptions, and intolerance. A great place to start is to read about culturally sustaining pedagogies. Read about educating kids of color—especially if you are white. But don't stop there. Find books by authors and about students who are non-cisgender, disabled, from nontraditional families, adopted, immigrants, English language learners, Muslim, poverty-stricken backgrounds, and more—look for texts that represent the backgrounds and identities of all of your students. Think about how these new viewpoints will impact your instruction.

A beginning list of titles to check out:

*Why Are All the Black Kids Sitting Together in the Cafeteria?* by Beverly Daniel Tatum

*Pushout: The Criminalization of Black Girls in Schools* by Monique Morris

*The Guide for White Women Who Teach Black Boys* edited by Eddie Moore, Jr., Ali Michael, and Marguerite Penick-Parks

*White Fragility: Why It's Hard for White People to Talk About Racism* by Robin DiAngelo

*Between the World and Me* by Ta-Nehisi Coates

*Changing School Culture for Black Males* by Dr. Jawanza Kunjufu

*Biased: Uncovering the Hidden Prejudice That Shapes What We See, Think, and Do* by Jennifer L. Eberhardt

*Culturally Responsive Teaching & the Brain: Promoting Authentic Engagement and Rigor Among Culturally and Linguistically Diverse Students* by Zaretta Hamond

## 5. Teacher Research Doesn't Have to Be "Academic"

Be a researcher. But don't wait to start your professional research until summer or a professional development day. Start here and now, with micro-observations. Begin with a question you want answered—the basis of all good research. Maybe you want to know:

- How can I make my voice less prominent in my classroom?
- What helps students to really listen to one another and have their thinking pushed?
- What makes feedback effective?

Keep your question in mind as you observe relevant moments, or collect a few samples of student work as data. Start small. One or two observations or just a few pieces of student work can tell you a great deal. As you sit next to a child, watch a group discuss, eavesdrop on an inquiry project, or look over a drawing, simply pay attention to what you see happening. Try to spend more time on it than you think you have. What emerges may surprise you. Assess it. What do you notice that helps answer your question? Modify your instruction based on your discoveries.

No one has a better sense of your students than you—and no one has better access to everyday here and now data about what works best for your kids.

## 6. Write for Others

In her advice column "Dear Sugar," Cheryl Strayed suggests that in our troubled world, writing establishes a kinship that, "transcends every divide, across all time and place. . . . Connecting us is the thing writing most powerfully *does*" (2017). Indeed, sharing your writing—and reading others'—has the power to make teaching feel like a less lonely and arduous road for all of us. Decide how you will connect to and support others through writing.

Although a regular blog may be in your future, start with just one idea—submit a short piece to an academic journal, website, an educator's blog or a website like Edutopia or WeAreTeachers. Start with those forums that you already read and enjoy, and look up their submission guidelines. Some will be academic and research-oriented; others will want conversational styles or replicable ideas for teacher-readers. Remember that you do not need to "know it all" to publish and that, in fact, honest recountings of challenges and even failings are not just valuable but comforting to others. Stories, student examples, and images from your classroom can be powerful tools.

All online publications can serve as mentor texts—study them to see how pieces are structured and what works. Don't be discouraged if there are other pieces out there on your topic—your voice will add something new to the discussion!

## 7. Professional Book Study

1.  *Build a team (in person or via email invite).*
    - Form a group of interested colleagues who want to explore an issue, topic, or teaching goal. Two to five people is best, but larger groups can work, too.
    - Stick to your best friend if you wish, but consider extending the group to a wide range of colleagues for a richer range of voices, experience, grade level, content area, and professional strengths.
    - Designate a coordinator who is willing to spearhead the communication. They will collect contact information and handle reminders, dates and times, and logistics. This position should rotate with each book so no one feels burdened.

2.  *Choose a text (in person or via email or shared Google Doc).*
    - Start with a list of choices that address the shared goal or topic. Be picky and vet your choice well—read reviews, flip through a copy. If the topic or goal is something addressed in this book, you might look to the book references at the end of most strategies.
    - Clarify what you hope to learn from this book and discussion.
    - Choose the book far enough in advance that everyone can access a copy.

3.  *Make a plan (in person).*
    - You might meet once before starting the book to establish dates that work for everyone, where you will meet, page number goals, focus areas for each meeting, and any norms or discussion protocols.
    - Decide, too, how you will track your shared thinking. Will you use a discussion journal, a shared Google Doc, Evernote, individual notes, or some other method? It is important to have some kind of written documentation that records your thinking and how it grows together. This will be a useful resource for you all to refer back to later on, when the specific details in the book may be long forgotten.

| Book: *The Teacher You Want to Be* (Keene and Glover 2015) | | | |
| --- | --- | --- | --- |
| Focus: Celebrating our teaching successes and moving toward a more student-centered practice | | | |
| June 4 (Sonya's house) | June 30 (Glenny's house) | July 16 (Panera) | July 31st (Panera) |
| Chapters 1–4 What are our core teaching beliefs? How is this book pushing our thinking therein? | Chapters 5–8 How do we define the teacher we want to be? What are the qualities we already possess? What are the ones we want to strengthen? | Chapters 9–12 How do we already create democratic classrooms that foster independence? What new methods are we going to try? | Chapters 13–15 What does it mean to foster collaboration versus compliance? What are our big takeaways from this book? What will we each try in September? |

A sample schedule

## 8. Find a Younger Mentor

Mentoring helps both mentor and mentee to be better at their work—and it increases job retention. Finding a less traditional mentor in a younger colleague helps them feel valued, helps you to gain new expertise, helps you both to build relationships that make you want to stick around, and, finally, helps build a culture of honoring everyone in the room. If we want our students to value and appreciate all of their classmates and what they have to offer, isn't it important that we walk the talk in our own work, too?

Think about gaps in your teaching that might be shored up by learning from a younger colleague. Are you curious but unsure about digital publishing? Flexible seating? Flipped classrooms? Ask around and visit younger colleagues' classrooms to see what they can teach you in that area. Invite them to eat lunch together and discuss how they can support you.

Or build the mentoring around the person first and the learning second. Think of a younger colleague whom you want to know better and support. Let them know you're looking to learn from them. Ask to visit their class and talk to them about their practice. When you see something that interests you, find out how your colleague does it. Be the questioner and listener, then go try it out. Invite your new mentor to come watch and provide you with their expert feedback.

After you've met with your mentor, tried out their suggestions, and received their feedback, let others know. Announce your new learning at a staff meeting, send out an email with a public thank-you for their support, or fill in your administrators about what you two have learned together. Celebrate your colleague's expertise and help others get excited at the fresh mindsets all around them.

## 9. Make Sure Any Discussion Starts with "What Would Most Help Students?"

No one will challenge the notion that teaching is ridiculously hard. A sample list of pressing issues at any school might include scheduling, low test scores, bullying, excessive paperwork, prescribed curriculums . . . and that's just a start.

Almost any meeting among teachers, staff, administrators, and/or caregivers will be an attempt to work toward addressing the issues at hand. Here's a simple step that will help you keep the ball moving forward, solve problems authentically, and prioritize what's most important: start and end any discussion with, "What would most help students?"

Don't stop with a perfunctory answer. Bring in and look at student work whenever possible. Generate a list of multiple students of varying learning styles, cultures, socioeconomic groups, and more. Test out any hypothetical solution by considering each of those students within that scenario. Would they thrive? Finally, go out and talk to actual students. Poll them, interview them, include them in the conversation. Although teachers' needs are also essential, the fact is that what is best for students will *also* be best for the adults. When students thrive, so do we. Keep them at the forefront, always.

# WORKS CITED

Adichie, Chimamanda Ngozi. 2009. "The Danger of a Single Story." *TED: Ideas Worth Spreading* .www.ted.com/talks/chimamanda_ngozi_adichie_the_danger_of_a_single_story/up-next.

Alexander, Robin. 2018. *Towards Dialogic Teaching: Rethinking Classroom Talk*. New Orleans, LA: Dialogos.

Allison, Jay, and Dan Gediman. 2007. *This I Believe: The Personal Philosophies of Remarkable Men and Women*. New York: Holt.

Anderson, Mike. 2015. *The First Six Weeks of School*. Turners Falls, MA: Center for Responsive Schools.

Ashante the Artist. 2014. "I, Too, Am Harvard." March 3. www.youtube.com/watch?v=uAMTSPGZRiI.

Black, P. J., and Dylan Wiliam. 1998. "Assessment and Classroom Learning." *Assessment in Education: Principles, Policy & Practice* 5 (1): 7–74.

Bomer, Katherine. 2010. *Hidden Gems: Naming and Teaching from the Brilliance in Every Student's Writing*. Portsmouth, NH: Heinemann.

Brackett, Marc. 2019. *Permission to Feel: Unlocking the Power of Emotions to Help Our Kids, Ourselves, and Our Society Thrive*. New York: Celadon Books.

Calkins, Lucy, with Kelly Hohne and Audra Robb. 2015. *Writing Pathways: Performance Assessments and Learning Progressions, Grades K–8*. Portsmouth, NH: Heinemann.

CAST. 2019. "About Universal Design for Learning." April 23. www.cast.org/our-work/about-udl.html.

Cheryan, Sapna, Sianna Ziegler, Victoria Plaut, and Andrew Meltzoff. 2014. "Designing Classrooms to Maximize Student Achievement." http://ilabs.washington.edu/sites/default/files/14Cheryan _etal_Meltzoff_Designing%20Classrooms.pdf.

Cirillo, Franscesco. "Do More and Have Fun with Time Management." francescocirillo.com/pages /pomodoro-technique.

Clear, James. 2018. *Atomic Habits: An Easy & Proven Way to Build Good Habits & Break Bad Ones*. New York: Penguin Audio.

Coates, Ta-Nehisi. 2015. *Between the World and Me*. New York: Spiegel and Grau.

Cooper, Harris, Jorgianne Civey Robinson, and Erika Patall. 2006. "Does Homework Improve Academic Achievement? A Synthesis of Research, 1987–2003." *Review of Educational Research* 76 (1): 1–62.

Cruz, M. Colleen. 2015. *The Unstoppable Writing Teacher: Real Strategies for the Real Classroom*. Portsmouth, NH: Heinemann.

———. 2018. *Writers Read Better, 50+Paired Lessons That Turn Writing Craft Work Into Powerful Genre Reading*. Thousand Oaks, CA: Corwin.

DailyHealthPost. 2019. "How Complaining Physically Rewires Your Brain to Be Anxious and Depressed." https://dailyhealthpost.com/complaining-brain-negativity/2.

Daniels, Harvey. 2017. *The Curious Classroom: 10 Structures for Teaching with Student-Directed Inquiry*. Portsmouth, NH: Heinemann.

Daniels, Harvey, and Sara K. Ahmed. 2015. *Upstanders: How to Engage Middle School Hearts and Minds with Inquiry*. Portsmouth, NH: Heinemann.

Daniels, Harvey, and Elaine Daniels. 2013. *The Best-Kept Teaching Secret: How Written Conversations Engage Kids, Activate Learning, Grow Fluent Writers, K–12*. Thousand Oaks, CA: Corwin.

Danielson, Charlotte. 2007. *Enhancing Professional Practice: A Framework for Teaching*. Alexandria, VA: Association for Supervision and Curriculum Development.

Dewey, John. 1997. *Experience and Education*. New York. Touchstone. (Original work published 1938).

———. 2018. *Democracy and Education: An Introduction to the Philosophy of Education*. Gorham, ME: Myers Education Press.

DiAngelo, Robin. 2018. *White Fragility: Why It's Hard for White People to Talk About Racism*. Boston: Beacon Press.

Dillon, Robert W. 2016. *Redesigning Learning Spaces*. Thousand Oaks, CA: Corwin.

Ditchthattextbook.com. 2018. "20 Virtual Field Trip Ideas and Activities for Your Classroom." ditchthattextbook.com/2018/10/12/20-virtual-field-trip-ideas-and-activities-for-your-classroom/.

Doorley, Scott, and Scott Witthoft. 2012. *Make Space: How to Set the Stage for Creative Collaboration*, Hoboken, NJ: John Wiley and Sons.

Dueck, Myron. 2014. *Grading Smarter, Not Harder: Assessment Strategies That Motivate Kids and Help Them Learn*. Alexandria, VA: Association for Supervision & Curriculum Development.

Dweck, Carol S. 2016. *Mindset: The New Psychology of Success*. New York: Random House.

Earick, Mary E. 2009. *Racially Equitable Teaching: Beyond the Whiteness of Professional Development for Early Childhood Educators*. New York: Peter Lang.

Eberhardt, Jennifer L. 2019. *Biased: Uncovering the Hidden Prejudice That Shapes What We See, Think, and Do*. New York: Viking.

Educator Resources. 2017. "Classroom Library Questionnaire." www.leeandlow.com/uploads/loaded _document/408/Classroom-Library-Questionnaire_FINAL.pdf.

Edutopia. 2019. "Developing Confidence Through Delayed Grading." George Lucas Educational Foundation. February 28. www.edutopia.org/video/developing-confidence-through-delayed -grading.

Edwards, Susan. 2014. *Getting Them to Talk: A Guide to Leading Discussions in Middle Grades Classrooms*. Columbus, OH: Association for Middle Level Education.

Emdin, Christopher. 2016. *For White Folks Who Teach in the Hood . . . and the Rest of Y'all Too: Reality Pedagogy and Urban Education*. Boston: Beacon Press.

Erwin, Jonathan C. 2004. *Classroom of Choice: Giving Students What They Need and Getting What You Want*. Alexandria, VA: Association for Supervision & Curriculum Development.

Faber, Adele, and Elaine Mazlish. 1996. *How to Talk So Kids Can Learn at Home and in School*. New York, New York: Fireside.

———. 2017. *How to Talk So Kids Will Listen and Listen So Kids Will Talk*. London, UK: Piccadilly.

Feldman, Joe. 2019. *Grading for Equity: What It Is, Why It Matters*. Thousand Oaks, California: Corwin.

Finley, Todd. 2019. "A Look at Implicit Bias and Microaggressions." *Edutopia*, George Lucas Educational Foundation. March 25. www.edutopia.org/article/look-implicit-bias-and -microaggressions.

Fisher, Douglas, and Nancy Frey. 2014. *Checking for Understanding: Formative Assessment Techniques for Your Classroom*. Alexandria, VA: Association for Supervision & Curriculum Development.

Fisher, Douglas, Nancy Frey, and Russell J. Quaglia. 2018. *Engagement by Design: Creating Learning Environments Where Students Thrive*. Thousand Oaks, CA: Corwin.

Gallagher, Kelly. 2011. *Write Like This: Teaching Real-World Writing Through Modeling & Mentor Texts*. Portland, ME: Stenhouse.

Gallagher, Kelly and Penny Kittle. 2018. *180 Days: Two Teachers and the Quest to Engage and Empower Adolescents*. Portsmouth, NH: Heinemann.

Gallo, Carmine. 2014. *Talk Like TED: The 9 Public Speaking Secretes of the World's Top Minds*. New York: St. Martin's.

Gawande, Atul. 2014. *The Checklist Manifesto: How to Get Things Right*. New York: Penguin.

Goldsmith, Marshall, and Mark Reiter. 2010. *Mojo: How to Get It, How to Keep It, How to Get It Back When You Lose It*. London, UK: Profile.

Gonzalez, Jennifer. 2013. "Notebooks for Classroom Management, Part 1." *Cult of Pedagogy*. September 5. www.cultofpedagogy.com/notebooks-part-1/.

———. 2013. "Find Your Marigold: The One Essential Rule for New Teachers." *Cult of Pedagogy*. August 29. www.cultofpedagogy.com/marigolds/.

Hammond, Zaretta. 2015. *Culturally Responsive Teaching & the Brain: Promoting Authentic Engagement and Rigor Among Culturally and Linguistically Diverse Students*. Thousand Oaks, CA: Corwin.

Hare, Rebecca Louise, and Dr. Robert Dillon. 2016. *The Space: A Guide for Educators*. Irvine, CA: EdTechTeam.

Harper, Jennifer, and Kathryn O'Brien. 2015. *Classroom Routines for Real Learning: Daily Management Exercises That Empower and Engage Students*. Portland, ME: Stenhouse.

Harvey, Stephanie, and Harvey Daniels. 2009. *Comprehension and Collaboration: Inquiry Circles for Curiosity, Engagement, and Understanding*. Portsmouth, NH: Heinemann.

Hattie, John. 2009. *Visible Learning: A Synthesis of Over 800 Meta-Analyses Relating to Achievement*. New York: Routledge.

———. 2012. *Visible Learning for Teachers: Maximizing Impact on Learning*. New York: Routledge.

Herrera, Tim. 2019. "Do You Keep a Failure Résumé? Here's Why You Should Start." *The New York Times*. February 4. www.nytimes.com/2019/02/03/smarter-living/failure-resume.html.

Hertz, Christine, and Kristine Mraz. 2018. *Kids First from Day One: A Teacher's Guide to Today's Classroom*. Portsmouth, NH: Heinemann.

Hoffman, Stephen. 2012. "Zero Benefit: Estimating the Effect of Zero Tolerance Discipline Policies on Racial Disparities in School Discipline." *Educational Policy* 28 (1): 69–95.

Jensen, Linda. 2001. "Planning Lessons." In *Teaching English as a Second or Foreign Language*, edited by Marianne Celce-Murcia. Boston: Heinle & Heinle.

Johnston, Peter H. 2004. *Choice Words: How Our Language Affects Children's Learning*. Portland, ME: Stenhouse.

Karpov, Yuriy. 2014. *Vygotsky for Educators*. New York. Cambridge University Press.

Kay, Matthew R. 2018. *Not Light, But Fire: How to Lead Meaningful Race Conversations in the Classroom*. Portland, ME: Stenhouse.

Keene, Ellin Oliver, and Matt Glover. 2015. *The Teacher You Want to Be: Essays About Children, Learning, and Teaching*. Portsmouth, NH: Heinemann.

Kluth, Paula, and Sheila Danaher. 2010. *From Tutor Scripts to Talking Sticks: 100 Ways to Differentiate Instruction in K–12 Inclusive Classrooms*. Baltimore, MD: Brookes Publishing.

Kohn, Alfie. 2018. *Punished by Rewards: The Trouble with Gold Stars, Incentive Plans, A's, Praise, and Other Bribes*. Boston: Houghton Mifflin Harcourt.

Kondo Marie. 2016. *The Life-Changing Magic of Tidying Up: The Japanese Art of Decluttering and Organizing*. Scotts Valley, CA: CreateSpace Independent Publishing Platform.

Kunjufu, Jawanza. 2013. *Changing School Culture for Black Males*. Chicago, IL: African American Images.

"Language Supports for Number Talks." 2018. *Teaching Channel*. September 14. www.teachingchannel.org/video/sentence-frames-ousd.

Larmer, John, John Mergendoller, and Suzie Boss. 2015. *Setting the Standard for Project-Based Learning*. Alexandria, VA: Association for Supervision & Curriculum Development.

Lenz, Laura. 2016. "A Strength-Based Approach to Teaching English Learners." *Cult of Pedagogy*. www.cultofpedagogy.com/strength-based-teaching-esl/.

Lorain, Peter. n.d. "Brain Development in Young Adolescents." www.nea.org/tools/16653.htm.

Lucas, Lisa J. 2017. *Practicing Presence: Tools for the Overwhelmed Teacher*. Portland, ME: Stenhouse.

Malik, Rasheed. 2017. "New Data Reveal 250 Preschoolers Are Suspended or Expelled Every Day." www.americanprogress.org/issues/early-childhood/news/2017/11/06/442280/new-data-reveal-250-preschoolers-suspended-expelled-every-day/.

Martin-Kniep, Giselle O., and Joanne Picone-Zocchia. 2009. *Changing the Way You Teach, Improving the Way Students Learn*. Alexandria, VA: Association for Supervision & Curriculum Development.

Midemo. "Sentence Frames: Helping Students Become Writers." *Ldstrategies*. March 28. ldstrategies.wordpress.com/2012/03/28/sentence-frames-helping-students-become-writers/.

Milner, H. Richard. 2012. *Start Where You Are, But Don't Stay There: Understanding Diversity, Opportunity Gaps, and Teaching in Today's Classrooms*. Cambridge, MA: Harvard Education Press.

Mogel, Wendy. 2008. *The Blessing of a Skinned Knee: Using Timeless Teachings to Raise Self-Reliant Children*. New York: Scribner.

Montessori, Maria. 1995. *The Absorbent Mind: A Classic in Education and Child Development for Educators and Parents*. New York: Henry Holt and Company. (Original work published 1967).

Moore, Beth. 2018. "Next Level Unit Planning: Beyond the Fundamentals of Writing Workshop." February 5. twowritingteachers.org/2018/02/05/next-level-unit-planning-beyond-the -fundamentals-of-writing-workshop/.

Moore, Eddie, Ali Michael, and Marguerite Penick-Parks, eds. 2018. *The Guide for White Women Who Teach Black Boys: Understanding, Connecting, Respecting.* Thousand Oaks, CA: Corwin.

Morris, Monique. 2016. *Pushout: The Criminalization of Black Girls in Schools.* New York: The New Press.

Mraz, Kristine, and Christine Hertz. 2015. *A Mindset for Learning: Teaching the Traits of Joyful, Independent Growth.* Portsmouth, NH: Heinemann.

Mraz, Kristine, and Marjorie Martinelli. 2014. *Smarter Charts for Math, Science, and Social Studies: Making Learning Visible in the Content Areas K–2.* Portsmouth, NH: Heinemann.

Muhtaris, Katie, and Kristin Ziemke. 2015. *Amplify: Digital Teaching and Learning in the K–6 Classroom.* Portsmouth, NH: Heinemann.

Mulligan, Tammy, and Clare Landrigan. 2018. *It's All About the Books: How to Create Bookrooms and Classroom Libraries That Inspire Readers.* Portsmouth, NH: Heinemann.

Munson, Jen. 2018. *In the Moment: Conferring in the Elementary Math Classroom.* Portsmouth, NH: Heinemann.

Nakaya, Rion. "The Kid Should See This." thekidshouldseethis.com/.

NEA. 2005. "Research Spotlight on Recruitment and Retention." www.nea.org/tools/16977.htm.

Newkirk, Thomas. 2014. *Minds Made for Stories: How We Really Read and Write Informational and Persuasive Texts.* Portsmouth, NH: Heinemann.

———. 2017. *Embarrassment: And the Emotional Underlife of Learning.* Portsmouth, NH: Heinemann.

Niemann, Dr. Yolanda Flores, and Carla LynDale Carter. 2017. "Microaggressions in the Classroom." https://vimeo.com/204588115.

Nunan, David. 2003. *Practical English Language Teaching.* New York: McGraw-Hill.

Owocki, Gretchen, and Yetta M. Goodman. 2002. *Kidwatching: Documenting Children's Literacy Development.* Portsmouth, NH: Heinemann.

Pearson, P. David., and Margaret C. Gallagher. 1983. *The Instruction of Reading Comprehension.* Champaign, IL: University of Illinois at Urbana-Champaign.

Petty, Bethany J. 2018. *Illuminate: Technology Enhanced Learning.* San Diego, CA: Dave Burgess Consulting.

Pondiscio, Robert. 2016. "Failing by Design: How We Make Teaching Too Hard for Mere Mortals." https://fordhaminstitute.org/national/commentary/failing-design-how-we-make-teaching-too -hard-mere-mortals.

Pranikoff, Kara. 2017. *Teaching Talk: A Practical Guide to Fostering Thinking and Conversation.* Portsmouth, NH: Heinemann.

Rademacher, Tom. 2017. *It Won't Be Easy: An Exceedingly Honest (and Slightly Unprofessional) Love Letter to Teaching.* Minneapolis, MN: University of Minnesota Press.

Rami, Meenoo. 2014. *Thrive: 5 Ways to (Re)Invigorate Your Teaching.* Portsmouth, NH: Heinemann.

Rapp, Whitney H. 2014. *Universal Design for Learning in Action: 100 Ways to Teach All Learners*. Baltimore, MD: Paul H Brookes Publishing.

Reuell, Peter. 2019. "Lessons in Learning." https://news.harvard.edu/gazette/story/2019/09 /study-shows-that-students-learn-more-when-taking-part-in-classrooms-that-employ-active -learning-strategies/.

San Francisco Unified School District. 2013. "Restorative Practices Whole-School Implementation Guide." www.healthiersf.org/RestorativePractices/Resources/documents/SFUSD%20Whole%20 School%20Implementation%20Guide%20final.pdf.

Schott Foundation. 2014. "Restorative Practices: Fostering Healthy Relationships and Promoting Positive Discipline in Schools. A Guide for Educators." http://schottfoundation.org/sites/default /files/restorative-practices-guide.pdf.

Schwartz, Sarah. 2019. "Marie Kondo in the Classroom: How Teachers Are Tidying Up." *Education Week Teacher*. January 25. blogs.edweek.org/teachers/teaching_now/2019/01/ marie_kondo_in_the_classroom_how_teachers_are_tidying_up.html.

Seeger, Chris. 2017. "Improve Your Teaching by Asking for Student Feedback." *Teaching Tolerance*. www.tolerance.org/magazine/improve-your-teaching-by-asking-for-student-feedback.

Serravallo, Jennifer. 2014. *The Literacy Teacher's Playbook, Grades 3–6: Four Steps for Turning Assessment Data into Goal-Directed Instruction*. Portsmouth, NH: Heinemann.

———. 2015. *The Reading Strategies Book: Your Everything Guide to Developing Skilled Readers*. Portsmouth, NH: Heinemann.

———. 2017. *The Writing Strategies Book: Your Everything Guide to Developing Skilled Writers*. Portsmouth, NH: Heinemann.

———. 2019. *A Teacher's Guide to Reading Conferences*. Portsmouth, NH: Heinemann.

Shalaby, Carla. 2017. *Troublemakers: Lessons in Freedom from Young Children at School*. New York: New Press.

Singh, Sunil. 2019. *Math Recess: Playful Learning in an Age of Disruption*. San Diego, CA: Dave Burgess Consulting.

Smith, Dominique, Douglas Fisher, and Nancy Frey. 2015. *Better Than Carrots or Sticks: Restorative Practices for Positive Classroom Management*. Alexandria, VA: Association for Supervision & Curriculum Development.

Solomon, Andrew. 2012. *Far from the Tree: Parents, Children and the Search for Identity*. New York: Scribner.

Souto-Manning, Mariana, and Jessica Martell. 2016. *Reading, Writing, and Talk: Inclusive Teaching Strategies for Diverse Learners, K–2*. New York: Teachers College Press.

Spencer, John, and A. J. Juliani. 2017. *Empower: What Happens When Students Own Their Learning*. San Diego, CA: IMpress.

Spires, Ashley. 2014. *The Most Magnificent Thing*. Toronto, ON: Kids Can Press.

Strayed, Cheryl. 2017. "The Power of 'Me Too.'" May 16. https://onbeing.org/blog/cheryl-strayed -the-power-of-me-too/.

Sturtevant, James Alan. 2016. *Hacking Engagement: 50 Tips & Tools to Engage Teachers and Learners Daily*. Cleveland, OH: Times 10 Publications.

Tatum, Beverly Daniel. 2017. *Why Are All the Black Kids Sitting Together in the Cafeteria?* New York: Basic Books.

The Teacher Toolkit. n.d. "Inside/Outside Circles." www.theteachertoolkit.com/index.php/tool /inside-outside-circles.

———. n.d. "Stop and Jot." www.theteachertoolkit.com/index.php/tool/stop-and-jot.

Tomlinson, Carol Ann. 2016. *The Differentiated Classroom: Responding to the Needs of All Learners*. Alexandria, VA: Association for Supervision & Curriculum Development.

Tucker, Catlin. 2017. "Rethink Your Grading Practices." December 28. catlintucker.com/2017/12 /grading-practices/.

Tunstall, Tricia. 2009. *Note by Note: A Celebration of the Piano Lesson*. New York: Simon & Schuster.

Turkle, Sherry. 2016. *Reclaiming Conversation: The Power of Talk in a Digital Age*. New York: Penguin.

Wagner, James. 2019. "Need a Hug? Just Ask the Yankees' Cameron Maybin." *New York Times*. September 12. www.nytimes.com/2019/09/12/sports/baseball/cameron-maybin-yankees-hugs .html.

Walker, Tim. 2018. "How Many Teachers Are Highly Stressed? Maybe More than People Think." *neaToday*. May 11. http://neatoday.org/2018/05/11/study-high-teacher-stress-levels.

West, Lucy. n.d. "Types of Talk." *The Learning Exchange*. thelearningexchange.ca/videos/lucy-west -types-of-talk/.

Wiggins, Grant, and Jay McTighe. 2011. *The Understanding by Design Guide to Creating High-Quality Units*. Alexandria, VA: Association for Supervision & Curriculum Development.

Wilhelm, Jeffrey D. 2012. *Improving Comprehension with Think-Aloud Strategies: Modeling What Good Readers Do*. New York: Scholastic.

Wilhelm, Jeffrey D., Rachel Bear, and Adam Fachler. 2019. *Planning Powerful Instruction, Grades 6–12: 7 Must-Make Moves to Transform How We Teach—and How Students Learn*. Thousand Oaks, CA: Corwin.

Willis, Judy. 2014. "The Neuroscience Behind Stress and Learning." *Edutopia*. www.edutopia.org /blog/neuroscience-behind-stress-and-learning-judy-willis.

Yamada, Kobi. 2014. *What Do You Do with an Idea?* Seattle, Washington: Compendium Ink.